Ignite Author's Testimonials

"Since the beginning of time, women have gathered together to tell stories. Through these stories, they teach, empower and ignite change. What an honor to be a part of this historic ritual with this tribe of changemakers." Stacey Yates Sellar - United States

" 'JOY' pure joy, to have the opportunity to be part of this, to be able to collaborate, evolve, and grow in a supportive space with 34 other beautiful women! A powerful process expressing feeling, emotions popping... but knowing all the time it will help you, help others." Alex Jarvis - Australia

"I always had a book inside me. I bored people for years about how it would emerge and it did not until the juxtaposition of my life experiences and training in helping others allowed it. Then the feedback was amazing. It was total synchronicity. What I didn't expect was the level of love, care, professionalism and support that the team would put into it. It makes me love publishing. And being a woman. Thanks. xxx" Rosalyn Palmer - United Kingdom

"Yes, it was a new level of vulnerability! But I am very happy with the way it turned out. I hope to help and inspire others to take the really hard steps to heal." Shannon Silvermoon - Canada

"I'm so appreciative of you including me in this book, which is such an amazing idea. I feel really lucky to be part of it. I thought your editing was brilliant. You pushed me to uplevel my work and get in touch with my full range of emotion and have the courage to put it all out there. I learned so much from working with you and with the wonderful Rusti." Heather Kerr - Canada

"Writing my story has been a beautiful and enjoyable experience. As my story began to reveal itself, I found a flow and ease through the writing process which has left me feeling lighter and more fulfilled. I am most thankful and grateful for all the love and care that JB and Rusti have poured into creating this book." Vivien Hunt - England

Dedication

This book is dedicated to every woman. The ones that forever hug, help, nurture, laugh, give, encourage and support those around them. It transcends all barriers to connect with the very heart of a woman. Age does not matter. Nor does religion, color or creed, as this book speaks the very essence of the woman in each of us. It will impact and inspire. It is limitless in its potential to move the spirit of a woman, one woman at a time.

IGNITE

YOUR LIFE

FOR WOMEN

Thirty-five inspiring stories that will
create success in every area of your life.

FOREWARD BY

Lisa Nichols, Speaker, Author, and CEO of Movating the Masses.

PRESENTED BY

Alex Jarvis, Andrea Reindl, Angela Legh, Annie Lebrun, Astuti Martosudirdjo,
Carol Benson, Catherine Malli-Dawson, Cynthia Morgan, Deepanjali Sapkota,
Dr. Judy Gianni, Georgia Vanderville, Heather Kerr, Helle Brodie, Jade Green,
JB Owen, Jenni Walke, Jennifer Monaghan, Joanna Mercado Peters,
Karyn Kerr Pettigrew, Katarina Amadora, Lourdes Aldanondo, Marnie Tarzia,
Phyllis Roberto, Rosalyn Palmer, Rusti L Lehay, Shannon Silvermoon,
Shirley Whing Chow, Stacey Yates Sellar, Susanne Rodriguez, Suzanne Hall,
Taranum Khan, Trish Mrakawa, Valentine Owen, Virginia L Lehay, and Vivien Hunt.

Published and printed by JB Global Inc.

Publisher's Note:

We are delighted to offer the first compilation book in the IGNITE YOU series. Our mission is to produce inspiring, motivational and authentic real-life stories that will Ignite You in your life. Each book contains 35 unique stories told by 35 exceptional authors. They are of the highest caliber to offer engaging, profound and life-changing examples that will impact the reader. Our mandate is to build a conscious, positive and supportive community through our books, speaking events, writing workshops, ignite experiences, podcasts, immersions and a product marketplace. We welcome new authors onto our platform and new book ideas. Should you desire to be published and featured in an Ignite You book. Please apply at www.igniteyou.life/apply or reach out to us at suppport@igniteyou.life.

Ignite Your Life For Women

Copyright © 2019 JB Global Inc.

First Edition May, 2019

Published and printed by JBO Global INC.

5569-47th Street Red Deer, Alberta, Canada T4N 1S1 - 1 877-377-6115

ISBN# 978-1-7923-0664-8

Ordering Information: Quantity sales. Special discounts are available on quantity purchases by corporations, associations, and others. For details, contact the publisher at the address above. Programs, products or services provided by the authors are found by contacting them directly. Resources named in the book are found in the resources pages at the back of the book.

FOREWORD BY
LISA NICHOLS

I invite you to deep dive into these stories. Light a candle or dim the lights. Crawl under your favorite quilt or make yourself a comforting cup of tea. Now, you are ready to enter into the realm of 35 exceptional women, who have each found that 'Ignite' moment in their lives. Many of these women are just like you. Their journeys have been personal and even difficult at times. Some of their learning has come wrapped in sandpaper and tested them to the very core. Yet, all have fostered wisdom, created hope and stepped into a greater version of themselves by overcoming their greatest test.

Inside the pages of this book, you will read how these women unwrap their gifts, revisit the darkest corners of their lives, accepted the choices they made and found the points where they realized they were worth so much more. The key thing all of these women have discovered is one of the main messages of my teaching. Complete and authentic, unapologetic, self-acceptance. Like me, these women peered into all the dark corners of their lives. They felt the bloody knees, lived through the horrific decisions, the moments when they were unaware, unconscious, or stubborn in their righteousness. When a woman accepts all of her past, she then can find the face of love in the mirror and the space in her heart to forgive every part of herself.

When you can forgive so deeply, so completely, you have the space to have more compassion, when you have more compassion for you, you can step into ultimate love. That's what I believe these women have done and are sharing with you. By breaking free of the shackles of shame, blame, guilt, regret and anger, they are now stepping into the greatest version of themselves. They have become the beacons of light for you to follow into your own brilliance and go after YOUR dreams.

There is so much love, support and wisdom to discover inside these pages. My hope is that they will stir your soul, wake up your resolve while putting that spring back in your step. How you do YOU is the greatest gift you can give the world. That is why you are here. And if your light is too bright for others, just pass them a pair of sunglasses and be YOU all the way.

Join these women in their defining moments when they realized their pasts did not equal or dictate their futures. When they reclaimed their laughter and joy. When they found that 'Ignite' moment in their lives and danced the steps their souls came here to do.

Your sister in success, *Lisa Nichols*

LEARNING FROM LISA:
A PERSONAL INTERVIEW WITH JB OWEN IN BARCELONA, SPAIN

Before I began creating this book, I had the joy and pleasure of spending time with Lisa in Barcelona, Spain. We were there for a powerful week-long mastermind and after a long day, both of us cuddled up under a blanket to decompress from the day. In a rare and life-changing evening, Lisa and I shared, talked and philosophized about her learnings, growth and wisdom. I recorded that conversation so I would never, ever forget what she told me. Her words spoke volumes to my spirit and truly Ignited my soul to always be me and follow my dreams. I wanted to share with you what she taught me, so you too can have the same and wonderful experience and always, always remember to be you.

Lisa: The most important concept to facilitate success in my life is one of the self-care. The first thing I had to learn was how to fall in love with Lisa, I had to learn what loving Lisa looked like and then give myself permission to love me in my unique package. Everything about me. When I began to access what loving Lisa looked like that's when everything began to change. I saw how self-love led to self-validation and that led to self-acceptance... and that led to opening every doorway before me, myself. I could not fall in love with me while I was ashamed of myself or hiding from my past. I had to learn to have compassion with myself and that helped me understand the actions of others. I had to learn how to forgive myself, for all of my mistakes.

JB: How did you access loving Lisa?

Lisa: Through transparency and forgiveness. I could not fall in love with me while I was angry with love. MY forgiveness was my doorway. It was the doorway to compassion and compassion led to self-love.

JB: Was there any particular thing you did to love yourself and grow that self-love for you?

Lisa: I kept trying mirror exercises. I did journalling, I did meditation and I let go of hanging onto who I thought I was supposed to be. Most importantly, I increased my intimacy in-to me. I practiced... In-ti-ma-cy = in-2-me-I-C (into me I see). In-to-me-I-c is a commitment and an action that you've consciously chosen to peel back the layers to find out who shows up in the room when you show up. It's about looking at who else is in the room with you, that isn't the real you. I always ask myself who is in the room when I am in the room? Who do I show up as and be? What behaviors, what mindset characteristic am I open to? Am I defensive? Am I questioning? How do I want to feel in this situation right now that serves not just me but everyone here? How do I see me so that others see that same person?

JB: What's your favorite way to increase inner acceptance?

Lisa: There are a number of different things, but I love to do mirror work. There is one exercise that was the launch of my journey and career. Three sentences in the mirror: I am proud of Lisa... I am proud of you for... I forgive you for... And then I would look her in the eyes and say "Lisa I commit to you that..." Saying those sentences over and over again every day with seven different endings to each one, every day for 90 days was powerful. It helped me cut the shackles I was carrying. I overcame regret and anger and learned to forgive myself completely. When I said I forgive me... I DID forgive me. At first, it was barely audible and I could barely believe myself. I was sobbing so hard and no one else was around. I said stuff I didn't realize I was still mad at myself for from when I was 16! Once I could get through that, I felt more compassion. I started to see the real Lisa with all her pain and sorrow and I loved that person.

JB: Now that you are so far along in your self-love journey, what have you learned?

Lisa: I learned how to be my own best company. I found all the ways to enjoy being with Lisa, and realized that she is good company for me." I also ask myself little things like... Did I apologize quick enough when I was stuck in my righteousness? Did I laugh enough? Forgive enough? Or dance enough? I am always checking in with me.

JB: What's your power quote?

Lisa: Your past does not equal your future.

JB OWEN

"The most successful people make other people successful."

It is my hope that by reading my story you step into your greatest version of you. That despite the path you have taken to get to this moment, you realize there is still more of you to come. That reinventing yourself is possible. That redefining what matters, what makes you happy and what ignites your soul is always available to you.

AWAKENED TO BELIEVE

I remember being thankful my little office had no windows. When I originally saw the tiny, manila-colored room with a small desk and utilitarian chair, I felt depleted. Except, today I was grateful it was tucked away at the end of the hall, with no way to see inside unless you opened the door. My forehead was slumped down on my desk. Tears were dripping off my eyelashes, onto my paper desk blotter. The blotter that was branded with the company's happy slogan. There was nothing happy about me. I was about as broken as they come, and my tears could not be contained any longer.

My normal exuberant self had dwindled down to a shell of a person. The once vivacious woman who took on the world felt reduced, depleted and lost. I had moved to a new town following my latest husband and I didn't know anyone. I had left the support of my family to be with him here, because he said they were stifling, suffocating and intrusive. I packed up my two kids and everything I owned because he wanted a fresh start, a new beginning, and a place that would just be our own. What he really wanted was to get me away from the people who cared about my well-being. To remove me from the influences that knew he was toxic. What he really wanted, was a place where no one recognized him so he could sneak off to buy drugs and drink.

Yes, I had married a recovered addict and alcoholic. He had been sober for eight years before I came careening back into his life. Our paths had reconnected after twenty-five years of being apart. He was my first love, and boyfriend for three years in high school. We were the 'it' couple, the ones that met awkwardly at the first school dance in grade ten and then stayed lip-locked and inseparable till after graduation. We were also the anomaly couple. I was from the right side of the tracks, he was not. I was popular, he, not so much. I was social, he was pensive and brooding. I liked to do things, he liked to stay in, be intimate and always entwined.

As a first love, he was passionate, enthralling and so different from my innocent world. His uniqueness was attractive and intoxicating. In fact, 'intoxication' could have been our theme song. Every weekend his house was a hell-hole of intoxicated parents and drunken relatives. I was his escape from the cops banging down his door at 2 AM to stop beer bottles from being smashed over heads or haul away whoever held glass-shards up against someone's throat. I was the reprieve to the endless nights of his step-dad throwing his mom across the room, the bashing-in of walls and baseball bats pummelling the car. His parents were the quintessential losers and drunks. They were the embarrassments in town everyone knew, and I was the person he ran to.

My parents were the quintessential business owners, the super-successful people in town. Only, their unrelenting climb to the top had eroded their marriage, and their all-consuming divorce left time for our love to blossom. We fell into an intoxicating world of exploration and intimacy, undisturbed by our distracted parents. We were alone all the time to discover and uncover every part of our union and it was magical. For three years we lived in a teenage bubble of doing whatever we wanted, and our parents didn't even notice. Everything was 'Us' until I was accepted to University in the big city and he was not. Where I had options, he had none. I had a support system and he had nothing. We pledged to stay together despite the distance. I'd travel back as much as possible and once he had earned enough money, he'd join me. When it ended, it was bad. He got drunk the weekend before my departure. We fought. He was horrible, smashing in my car window, breaking into my house in the middle of the night, and throwing me across the room. He resorted to all he'd seen and the only things he knew. I left not looking back, appalled at how he had treated me.

Two months later, his mom died of pneumonia due to severe health issues, liver disease, failing lungs from a lifetime of smoking and a bashed-up body from abuse. He begged her to live, but she told him she was done and wanted to end her suffering. He begged me to come back, but I told him I was too busy with school and the flights were too expensive. That left him alone, with his fifteen-year-old brother to take care of and nowhere to live. His step-dad was gone, the bank took the house; he had nothing and was living on the streets. I didn't return for the funeral or reach out to help. I was still mad, hurt and confused. My life had changed, the big city was now way more intoxicating, and I decided to move on and forget about him.

They say unfinished business always finds a way of finishing itself. Who knew the dangling, unresolved anger and the lingering promises we made would come calling two decades later? He popped up on my Facebook page two weeks before my fortieth birthday. I had lived my life as I swore to him I would. I went to design school, worked in fashion, started multiple businesses, and got married. I had had a lustrous career in the film business, working with the biggest stars in Hollywood. I then transitioned into building a highly successful clothing brand, traveled the world, rode high on the hog and had two beautiful, adorable children. But that life had taken its toll, and like my parents, my unrelenting climb to the top had eroded my marriage. I was just four months divorced and lonely, when his familiar face appeared with a message.

Within a week I was flying to see him. By the end of that first night, we were in bed, reliving our childhood love-affair in an insatiable fire of lust, loss and reconnection. Saying we picked up where we left off is an understatement. We were instantly joined at the hip and acting like love-struck teenagers all over again. I remember feeling as if I had been given a reset button. Like I could go back and fix all that was broken due to my immaturity and selfishness. I glossed over everything and only saw the seventeen-year-old boy I fell in love with. I looked past the small stints he had done in jail, the years he lived on the streets and the fact his only friends were drug counsellors and AA companions. I jumped into the proverbial frying pan and married him one year to the day of our reunion.

It didn't take long until I was sitting at that desk, in that awful job, trembling in fear, choking on my mistake, terrified to walk to my car and crippled with anguish and guilt. Two weeks after our wedding, he relapsed and systematically destroyed any semblance of a rekindled, fairy-tale love story. He obliterated the idea of a blended family and massacred any possible future. He went from one rehab clinic to another. Then, stealing my car, robbing things from my house, doing drugs, threatening to throw himself off balconies, getting beat up, driving drunk, hiring prostitutes and bouncing cheques. And, each time they would always call me. The authorities, the bank manager, hotel clerks and perfect strangers who looked in his wallet because he was passed out on their lawn. I was his emergency contact, his next of kin, and no matter how hard I tried to detach, I always got sucked in.

I had hit the worst of the worst. All the people who told me he was rotten, had smug looks on their faces. The ones who knew of his past, just shrugged their shoulders as if I deserved it. I was drowning in self-pity, self-loathing and complete self-defeat. I was single again and everything was crumbling. I was serving a seven-year sentence of credit annihilation due to my bankruptcy. I was taking in boarders to help pay my rent and applying for subsidies to help pay for my kid's after-school programs and sports equipment. I walked the grocery stores skittish and afraid he would come around the corner or be in the next aisle. I would hide in the locker room at my son's hockey practices in case he was sitting in the stands. I was always looking over my shoulder or checking the back seat of my van, in case he was hiding there. I was petrified he'd be sitting on the bench outside my house, holding a gun. I lived paralyzed in the fear of his retaliation, confrontation and some sort of vicious attack.

That day, with my head on my desk, uncontrollably crying, I asked for help. I begged God, a Higher Power, the Universe and all the angels available, to deliver me from the despair I was in. And of course, He answered.

There was a ping on my computer mere moments after my agonizing plea. It was a notice about an event called Awesomenessfest. Through the blurry tears and smudged make-up, I watched the trailer, scoured the website, saw what they were teaching on transformational growth and personal learning. I became obsessed with the notion that this was what I needed. I eagerly completed the application process and hung my hat on the belief that it was going to change my life. I prayed, wished, and promised myself that if I got in, I would do whatever it took to turn my life around and be the person I once was.

Then it happened, I got accepted. I was riding high knowing that it was a sign from God and change was on the horizon. I went to the office feeling lifted, only to be fired that very afternoon. My job performance was horrible due to my awful emotional state and my boss had reached his limit. With four hundred and twenty-three dollars in my bank account, I took my kids to their grandparents and flew to the event in Mexico. I arrived shaking, nervous and holding myself up in a room filled with go-getters and over-achievers. I felt transparent, thinking everyone knew I was the one who'd been robbed, scammed, abused and swindled. I tried hard to hold it together amidst the deep emotional work and inspiring personal growth. I felt cracked open like a walnut, splayed out for my brain to absorb all the new ideas, concepts and possibilities.

My Ignite-moment happened in the front row of Lisa Nichols's transformational speech. I was dead center and throughout her presentation, she looked at me often. Her words were 'intoxicating', inspiring, and motivational. At one profound moment, she stepped off the stage, walked into the audience and right up to me. She kept talking to the crowd but rested her hand on my shoulder. She then said, "don't let anyone stop you from being you," and looked me right in the eye and held it. It may have been a millisecond for her, but it was a lifetime for me. I saw the entire movie of my life rewind right back to the moment I stopped doing just that. Back to the little fat girl, the kid who couldn't do math, the second daughter who should have been a son. In light speed, I saw all the mistakes, wrong turns, smoke screens and blinders I had been wearing. Her touch seemed to wake me up, stir my soul, ignite my desire and rattle me free to be the person I was meant to be.

That night I sat in Lisa's hotel room and listened to everything she had to say. I attended her seminar, read her book, and then worked hard to bring her to Canada to do two events for my community. I saw her at countless more Afests and flew to LA to attend her leadership program. Over the years, we have formed a beautiful and loving friendship. She has become a beacon, and a light I draw on to remind me to shine my own light brighter. She has pushed me, challenged me, cradled me and inspired me. Her gift is the gift of reminding you who you are, and who you were born to be. She believed in me when I wasn't sure and when I needed a lifeline and a life preserver all at the same time.

They say when the student is ready, the teacher will appear. That when you are receptive, the learning is easy. When you are open, all you need will come flooding in. Being cracked open, vulnerable, unsure and empty was exactly what I needed to heal, awaken and be filled with my own determination.

I returned home from that first event to even more chaos and relapses, but this time they were his to deal with, not mine. I stopped living the single-mom syndrome of government hand-outs and limited thinking. I walked taller and prouder one step at a time. I took my life back, my health seriously and my personal growth was at the top of my list. I learned at Al-Anon that it is not one thing that has to change, it is EVERYTHING that has to change. I revamped my life, my body, my mind and my outlook. I made it my mission, that one day I would put my hand on another woman's shoulder and Ignite her. That I would do whatever it took to be a beacon, and a light for someone else. I held my two kids in my arms and promised them a better life and a better mom; no matter what it took. I decided I was going to be a role model for women. I vowed I would change women's lives. No matter what I had to do, I would be there for another woman when she needed to be reminded of who she was, and what she was made of.

Today I can proudly say, I am doing just that. I have overcome a million obstacles and undergone a massive transformation. I've shed all the layers of failure and disappointment I put upon myself. In fact, what was once the most horrible thing, has become the most appreciated thing. I'm grateful for the lessons I had to learn and the pain I had to endure. I respect the broken glass I needed to crawl over to get to where I am right now. I never would have become the woman I am today, if I had not been forced to build myself back up. It was an amazing process and I am thankful for all of it.

I will admit, it took me a long time to ever talk about it. I was afraid to face the judgments and worried about exposing myself too much. Then, there came a moment, when sharing it helped. When releasing the bottled-up shame felt better than holding it inside. A great pain was unburdened, and I found when I told another person, it brought us closer and cemented a bond. That is why I started 'Ignite You'. I have personally felt the joy from releasing my story. I saw how much it helped me, and when I shared, others shared back. When I exposed my suffering, many exposed theirs. That unity and commonalty grew compassion, closeness and deep, deep connection.

In the upcoming pages of this book, you are going to read many stories of triumph and perseverance, just like mine. You will hear about the fires, the pain points, and the 'intoxicating' moments that tore apart another person's soul, only to be propelled back to their highest self. You'll read bone gritting, against all odds, heroines' journeys from other women just like me and possibly, just like you. Thirty-five woman have come together to share the moments in their lives when they needed to shift, to rise, to change and to act. They reveal that IGNITE moment when they became aware of who they were born to be; despite all the hardship and fears.

My wish is that when you read through the stories, you too are touched, and feel all our hands on your shoulder. That your heart opens, and your spirit awakens. That you feel the power of their sharing and the wisdom behind it. Each story begins with a Power Quote, because I believe we all need one. It is that sentence or phrase that you chant when the tears are flowing, yet you also roar when you are riding the waves.

Then, you will read their intentions. These are the author's hopes and wishes of what their story will do for you. It is a personal message, filled with meaning and purpose. They also want to Ignite You to begin living your most enjoyable life. Their intentions set the tone for the story that will both grip and inspire you equally.

Once you have finished their heartfelt stories, you will find an innovative 'Ignite Action Steps'. These are the tangible things they did to move, grow and expand themselves. Each author has explained an easy-to-do, practical idea for you to close the book and try immediately. They are the processes and practices that worked magically in their lives. Each one is different and unique, just like you are.

The actions steps are designed to 'Ignite' you forward in all areas of your life. In fact, that is another amazing part of this book. I have learned that to be happy and successful, you need to address all areas of your life. It doesn't matter if you have the corner office if you feel alone inside. No one cares about a bank statement if you are too unhealthy to climb a flight of stairs. Relationships, families, kids, careers and personal health are all important in a woman's life. Each element needs to be working for them all to be successful. I made sure the stories included exciting possible improvements in the areas of health/wellness, business/finance, relationship/parenting, and personal growth. Instead of buying a book for each quadrant of life, we made sure our action steps spanned them all. Our goal is that this book helps you improve every area of your life, so you can step forward invigorated and empowered. We wanted to offer thirty-five unique possibilities for you to take action and discover the exceptional, magnificence inside of you.

At the back of the book is a list of resources. Many of our authors have taken alternative courses, studied transformational modalities and read books on everything from enlightenment to metaphysics, from numerology to cognitive brain therapy. There is a plethora of ideas to ignite you and additional information to enjoy.

Most importantly, every word in this book and every letter on the pages has been meticulously crafted with love, affection and a deep desire to not just inspire but to heal. The people who are working in the background, editing, supporting and encouraging the authors are some of the most genuine and heart-centered people I know. Their devotion to the vision, the integrity and the message they aspire to convey are at the highest caliber possible. They too, want you to find your ignite moment and flourish. They each believe in you.

If you feel that your story is still unfolding, or you're stuck in the middle, trying to find your way out, we are with you. I can share that once you make that commitment to love and honor yourself full-out, the rest comes relatively easy. Not the task stuff or the learning curves, but the passion, the knowing and the desire. Soon enough, you will get to that place where you can't wait to get up in the morning. You will see the new you and start talking about it with friends. In fact, you will get to that place where it is the ONLY thing you talk about. Ideas will arrive like wildfire, dreams will come true, the right people start showing up and soon enough you are doing, living and completing those things you have always wanted to do.

There will come a time when you look back and see how it all unfolded. What might feel agonizing and hard right now, will subside to allow the golden nuggets and silver lining to appear. That is the richness, the reward, and your superwoman moment. It's where you don your cape because you overcame one of the hardest things in your life and you are a thousand times better for it. Each one of the authors in this book has been through it. We all extend a hand should you need a bit of support, some advice or a shoulder to cry on. We offer ourselves, should you ever want to reach out because something we said really resonated or what we shared was exactly what you needed to hear. Please know we are all accessible and eager to connect, so please feel free to find us.

There are many books on the market and wonderful people willing to assist in your journey through personal growth. I've read hundreds of them and worked with many of them. Each one offers something valuable and any step is a great step if it is in the right direction. My motto is, "what's best for me, comes from me." Be it ideas, decisions, choices, pursuits, or passions, you know deep inside what you need. Trust that voice. That wisdom. That direction. Seek out all the information necessary for you to make a beautiful decision about your own life. Focus on you, your aspirations, and gifts. Highlight your value and shine your brightest light. Give all you can to your expansion because you are worth it. Look past your old conditioned ways and blaze a new frontier. You'll be happier you did, proud you tried and rewarded not when you reach the finish, but when you stop to really bask in the glory of the journey along the way.

I am truly ignited by the idea of you turning the page and reading a rainbow of knowledge, intertwined in a symphony of wisdom. I get excited knowing you are about to ride the roller coaster of elation, followed by a few tears, some goosebumps and definitely a handful of laughs. The stories you are about to embark on are all our stories. They supersede race, culture, age and even gender. They are the human story, the experience of living as a Human Being on this earth. They touch at the very heart of belonging, connecting and sharing. We ask that you please cherish the unique way they are written, the language they use and the colorful characterizations each of them possesses. We did our utmost to preserve the author's voice and personality by saying 'the heck with' proper and perfect grammar or pronunciation. Nothing is perfect in life, so we felt there was no use pretending a book filled with personal stories, written by everyday people, should fit a mold or conformed opinion. They are raw, real and unrestricted... that's what makes them so ridiculously good.

I didn't know I was going to be a collector of stories or a pied piper for other authors. This mission found me. I had once again been asking the Lord to help me make a global impact. I wanted to empower others, do more, share more and spread a conscious positive message to as many people as possible. God was listening, heard me, and handed me this and said, "run!" That collective energy, God, the Universal Power, all told me to go and Ignite others. To let them be heard, share their stories, find their voice and heal their pain. I knew I was supposed to bring people together, offer a way, give back and do something good for the world. That is the mission and purpose behind ME and Ignite You. I found there is power when one person touches the heart of another and a spark begins, may you enjoy that right now and forever.

"May you have many Ignite moments that transform your life into the amazing person you were meant to be." – JB Owen

IGNITE ACTION STEPS

Take a moment to breathe in what it means to be you.

So many of us are told who to be, how to act, what to want and who to love. We are bombarded by pressures, expectations and little boxes we are supposed to fit into.

Stop for a moment and shut all of that out. Go somewhere that isn't you. Isn't filled with all the things you are comfortable with, all the trophies or objects, expensive or broken trinkets that symbolize your journey up until now. Just be somewhere else. Find a new park, a seaside alcove. Drive down a lonely country road or walk to the top of a hill. Just go somewhere away from everything you know. Forget the phone, the bills, the messy desk and heaping pile of laundry. Find a spot where you have never been and that spot has never seen you.

Once you get there, ask yourself if I could be anyone, do anything, step away from this spot completely transformed into the person I have always wanted to be... who would that be?

Ask yourself that question and then write everything that comes to you. No filter, no sarcastic put-downs or negative inner chatter. Just write, write, write. No one knows you in this place. No one will see what you say. Just write everything that describes the woman you desire to be.

Write how she walks, talks and presents herself. Write her wishes, desires and passions. Write what she stands for, what she stands against and what she would fight tooth and nails to make happen. Write what makes her happy. What gets her grooving. What makes her cry and what she'll never say 'yes' to again. Write all her attributes, values and opinions. Write her achievements, accolades and exactly what she has in her life. Write till you can absolutely write no more.

Then before you give yourself permission to leave that spot. DECIDE what you are going to do to become her. If you must sleep there all night, go without food, or cross your legs because you must use the washroom, do not leave that spot until you commit to yourself the very thing you are going to do to bring that woman to life.

Too often we give up, give in, or give excuses why we are not who we want to be. Don't let yourself walk away from her. Don't gloss over her importance or say you'll get back to her. Stay there and commit to her 100%. Stay until you decide you'll do whatever you need to, to find her. Stay there until you discover exactly what you need to do. Stay there and give life to her. She deserves that.

Then, when you step away from that spot, become HER no matter what.

JB Owen, Founder and CEO Ignite You, Lotus Liners and JBO Global.
Ignite YOU. www.igniteyou.life

IGNITE YOU

You are now about to embark on a plethora of stories. Each one has been written around a powerful and impactful IGNITE moment. Everyone has times in their life when something happened that catapulted them in a different direction. An event transpired that triggered a series of other events and had a ripple effect. In reading these stories, it is our hope that you remember one of your IGNITE moments. A time when you promised yourself you would change, you made a clear decision, or had an experience that rocked you to the very core. It may have been an uplifting time beyond all measure or the most devastating thing you have ever felt. However, your IGNITE moment transpired, that moment in some way defined you and what you did next.

Our hope is that through these stories you are prompted to think of a time in your life when something put you on a new path. Where you made a major life decision or turned down a road you have never travelled before. By reflecting on that time in your life you too will be able to see the many outcomes and consequences that unfolded. Some may have been exactly what you wanted; others may have felt completely out of your control. All were meant to happen and lead you to where you are right now.

Taking the time to reflect on an IGNITE moment is a powerful gift. It will teach you much about yourself, your beliefs, attitudes and desires. It can show you how far you have come and just what you have accomplished. It can be a treasured collection of information to help you be the best person you can be. Our gift is that you take this opportunity to remember your IGNITE moments and enjoy your life to the fullest.

STACEY YATES SELLAR

"You have everything you need inside of you."

My dream for you, the reader, is to walk away from this piece knowing you are not alone, you are not crazy, you are worthy and there IS more. By the end, you will have easy, bite-size actions that are surprisingly simple but profoundly powerful.

FINDING 'IT'

I have been an archaeologist of 'IT' for as long as I can remember; digging everywhere in the hope I could uncover the lost 'IT': the missing piece that would complete me, the Rosetta Stone to clarify my purpose, the King Tut of mysteries buried in my soul that would reveal the 'real me'. I always saw my 'real life', the life of my dreams – just out of reach, a bit further on, on the other side of a bridge. (Not one of those fairy-tale ones made of sparkles and rainbows but rather one of those wobbly ones made from rope and half-missing planks hanging precariously above a rushing river.)

All I needed was to find 'IT'! Then I could stop searching. Start enjoying life.

I was born insecure. I have no doubt I came out of the womb worried I hadn't done it as well as everyone else had. Growing up, I wasn't particularly beautiful. Stringy brown hair pulled tensely into pigtails allowing my freckled-pallid skin and buck-teeth nowhere to hide. I never experienced the holy grail of adolescent adjectives: 'popular'. I was neither amazingly intelligent nor wonderfully talented. Naive to the point of stupidity. I was average. I was ordinary.

Only, I didn't want to be ordinary. I wanted to be extraordinary.

But I wasn't.

My adolescent years and resulting inferior self-esteem were scaffolded on comparisons to prettier, better, smarter, funnier, nicer, sportier, *everythinger* friends and siblings. I was pencil thin (before it was trendy), wore big, round, tortoiseshell glasses (trendy in the '70s) and had a mouth full of braces (never trendy). I didn't have a lot- ok... well not any boys choosing me for *Stairway To Heaven* at school dances.

I spent many late hours talking on the phone with my BFF discussing the 'true love' all girls hope to have; the kind of love professed in folded up notes passed between desks during English class. The kind of love that inspires 'me + him = 4ever' heart doodles on peachy folders and 'Stacey fill-in-fantasy-last-name' signatures in math book margins.

When I finally did start dating late in high school, I lacked so much confidence that every relationship was a boxing match between my self-doubt and my boyfriend. Some guys lasted longer than others, but in the end, it was always a knockout and my insecurity would win. The guy would be lying on the boxing ring mat as the count started:

One! "Come on! get up! I really can be fun", I would beg. *Two!* "Please get up. I'm sorry I kept asking 'Why do you like me?'" *Five!* "Please get up! Fight. I wasn't checking messages on your answering machine. It was an accident." *Seven!* "I promise not to cry anymore." *Nine!* "You're not getting back up, are you?" *Ten.*

That insecure-anxious child turned into a teenager with depression and panic attacks who turned into an adult with agoraphobia and unworthiness issues.

But – somehow, I had this feeling – deep down, waaaay down, beyond diffidence, past self-doubt, tucked behind insignificance, around the corner from despair, glimmered a tiny spark of belief and hope I could find what I was missing. I just needed to find 'IT'.

I searched in a broad assortment of therapies: regression, talk, family, cognitive, even angel therapy. I had my stars mapped, chakras aligned, allergies eliminated and energy rearranged. I had my palms, feet, tarot cards, stones and coffee read (I hate coffee). I had my house and wardrobe Feng

Shui'd. I had my handwriting analyzed and my soul retrieved. Horoscope charted; psychic energy contacted. I sought the expertise of yogis, priests, shamans, rabbis, Rempoches, witches, yogis and gurus. I met with psychics, numerologists, astrologists, psychiatrists, hypnotists, manicurists, and hair stylists. I read a book a week on self-improvement, reconstruction, healing, feeling, hating and loving. I found my inner animal to the beat of a drum. I hung my vision board on my refrigerator. I memorized *The Four Agreements*, *The Prayer of Jabez*, *The Lord's Prayer*, studied Kabbalah (complete with red string) and got my secret mantra with transcendental meditation. Acupressure, Reiki, acupuncture, chiropractics, colonics, body talk and cranial sacral? Yup, you name it, I tried it.

I learned my sign (Virgo), my number (6), my animal (monkey), my element (earth), my card (spade), my Enneagram (4 moving toward 1), and my doshic constitution (Vata). I ingested blue-green algae, body balancing aloe vera, herbal teas, mysterious blessed seeds, supplements galore, and every antidepressant on the market. I rubbed essential oils on my feet, wore a red string around my wrist and hung charms from my rear-view mirror. I put ceramic Foo-dogs at my front door and hung red tassels on my door knobs.

At times, I was sure I was a floral housecoat and six cats away from becoming 'the crazy lady upstairs'.

But I wasn't crazy. Just thirsty. Every time someone dangled a chance to quench my thirst for 'IT', I'd drool and pant like Pavlov's dog. And...

– of course, all along, I hoped *Prince Charming* would arrive and make everything all right with one dramatic, cinematic kiss. (Thanks Walt Disney)

When I met Simon, with his movie-star English accent and Euro good-looks, I was instantly enamoured. Although I believed I was not good enough for him, he charmed me into a happily-ever-after-worthy romance. After dating long-distance for a year, I quit my high paying job in California, sold all my belongings, moved across the ocean into a flat with him in London, started a funny blog and lived a glamorous life off the high street in Kensington. Within six-months I had a miserable job, spent all my money on his & hers belongings, cried myself to sleep in that flat in London, stopped the funny blog and questioned my life as I cried in the rain walking the high street in Kensington.

A million ways to beg him to stay ran through my head but I could not utter any of them. I knew I could say nothing to stop him. It was over. He stopped at the door, bags in hand. I rushed to him and threw my arms around his neck, needing to feel him one more time. Tears streamed down our faces as we held each other. When I felt his embrace loosen, I knew it was time to let go. He picked up his bags and walked out the door. I was alone. Again.

After a week of praying (to no avail), packing (I shipped everything but the electric kettle to California) and punishing myself for everything I did wrong (the list was long), I scheduled Black Cab to take me to the airport early the next morning. I withered into the fetal position on the floor of the empty, dark flat. I was so filled with grief that if you had cut me I would have bled tears. My quivering breaths echoed throughout the bare room as tears poured from my eyes, soaking the cold carpet. Knowing he was moving back into the apartment after I left, I wondered if he would feel the agony in the air or the tears when his bare feet touched the carpet.

As I walked through the airport, I tried not to imagine Simon running to catch me (everything else played out like a romantic movie, why stop now); grabbing me just before I handed the steward my ticket, holding me with tears in his eyes, begging me not to go.

I'd be lying if I said I didn't look back a few times as I boarded the plane.

Heartbroken and broke, I moved back with my parents. It was a painful year of checking the empty mailbox and silent answering machine. In the movie version of this story, this is where the time-lapse montage would run, accompanied by the song *Waiting For My Real Life To Begin* by Colin Hay.

Then Sonny Carroll's poem *Awakening* landed in my lap

"A time comes... when you finally get it... in the midst of your fears and insanity you stop... the voice inside your head cries... —ENOUGH!"

It was the bucket of cold water in the face I needed to wake up from the grief coma.

A month later I got a job, moved into a 600 square foot apartment, and began to take action again. I ended up in one of Mike Dooley's first workshops with maybe 14 of us in a small hotel conference room. I learned about clarifying intention and how to make vision boards. I gathered my girlfriends together, put *The Secret* on repeat and pasted pictures of my dream-life on a poster board. I started a daily practice of journaling gratitude and detailing the vision of my best life (in writing, in present tense). I paused looking for external oracles and began digging deep inside.

Over the next year, I lost 30 pounds. My business grew to #1, exceeding all revenue projections. I paid off $20,000 of debt and had money in savings! I had great friends, a loving family and I healed from a crippling back injury.

Plus the handsome, charismatic Scottish man I had met at a wedding in San Francisco. (Full disclosure: I swapped his table card so he was sitting next to me.) After dating long distance for nine months, he moved to California to be with me. My optimism finally outweighed my pessimism. A year later he proposed, we bought our first house and got married in a romantic, 15th-century castle in Scotland. Two years later we had the first of our two gorgeous boys and abundance continues to flow even 12 years later.

My transformation did not happen overnight. It was a Polaroid evolution – gradual and slow. I questioned, "How did all that actually happen?" (I'm a Virgo, we analyze.) Was I just 'one of the lucky ones'? Was it because I was older and wiser? Or had I manifested it through my vision boards? Looking back, I believe it was less luck, a little age and wisdom, but even more, because I did 'the work'.

The 'work' is all of the above. This is not to suggest you have to do everything I did. While I can't really prove a picture on a poster board manifested my house or that a sigil actualized my husband or that putting a healthy plant in the wealth corner increased my wealth, I do believe surrounding myself with positive intention and taking action completely changed my life.

Finally **it** became clear: **'I.T.'** is Intention and Take Action.

'I.T.' was a mindful decision to stop looking outside myself. Stop looking to the other side of the bridge. Stay present. Find happiness right now through gratitude. I was Intentional about what I wanted and *Took action*. It didn't happen as fast as I would have liked. There were many frustrating days. Unfortunately, I'm not perfect, patience was not a virtue I knew well, but living consciously isn't about *being perfect*, it's about *being BETTER*.

Lest you think I now live the perfect life, that whenever I walk out the door, cartoon forest animals scatter to my side and roses bloom as I walk by, let me assure you – I'm not a Disney character. I am human. I have bad hair days and headaches. I get irritated by ignorance and excuses. I still trip on judgment, eat too much of a good thing or sleep in when I should exercise. I cry and laugh (both loudly) and wish I could turn off my busy, analytical, 'monkey' brain. I still look for epiphanies in fortune cookies. I lose more battles with clutter than I win and I am still afraid to fly alone. I don't have answers to why bad things happen to good people. I worry people won't like me.

But these imperfections do not make me better or worse than anyone else. They make me *like* everyone else.

Once I made the decision to be intentional with where I wanted to be and do the work to get there, it took a year for the 'darkness' to fade away, for me to get on this path of abundance. Stick with it, even if it seems impossible to see the light at the end of the proverbial tunnel. Trust. Surrender. Be patient. As you do better, life feels better.

I have curated how to live with intention and what actions to take. Think of this as your *Cliff Notes* for centuries worth of self-help practices and literature. I have been going to 'class' for the past 40 years and here are my highlighted notes.

IGNITE ACTION STEPS

As easy as A, B, C... & D

A: Awareness. This is the START square. You must become aware of your thoughts. Thoughts you think over and over and over – become beliefs. Beliefs influence our decisions, judgments and actions. Pay attention - without judgment. Then start questioning the thoughts and beliefs: - are they true? - are they thoughts you inherited? - are they serving you and where you want to be? - are they kind?

Practice awareness with meditation. Silence all the reasons why you don't think you can do it and just start! Aim for five minutes a day. Then ten. Then 20.

Practice awareness by journaling. Write down the noise, all those thoughts in your head. Get them out, then start questioning and examining their validity.

B. Be Kind. Be kind to yourself and others. Much of the 'work' is reprogramming what you have spent many years programming. It is easier to be kind when you can see challenges as *opportunities* for growth. Challenges also go by the names of: mistakes, illness, annoying people, traffic, a broken heart, bill collectors, irritating co-workers, unhelpful clerks, crying children in the grocery line, an irresistible cupcake when you're dieting, unhappy clients, in-laws, an injury, complainers, those last ten (or forty) pounds, a flat tire, a computer glitch, a headache, a lost earring, a burnt meal... the list is endless.

Practice kindness to yourself through daily affirmations like "I am enough." "I am strong." "I am beautiful." "I am creative."

Practice kindness to others through random acts of generosity, patience, compliments and a genuine interest in them.

C. Count Your Blessings! Gratitude, gratitude, gratitude has been my biggest lesson, which I believe to be the holy grail of happiness. It is also the easiest, quickest way to bring change in your life.

The moment you wake up, take a few minutes – even before you open your eyes, say thanks for all the blessings you have right now. Think you don't have any? Are you lying in a bed? Do you have heat? A blanket? A pillow? Running water? Food in the fridge? Do you have a job (even if you hate it)? Clothes on your back? Shoes on your feet?

I started the life-changing practice of gratitude *before* abundance came to me. I started when I was heartbroken, in debt, overweight, in pain, and alone in a tiny 600 square-foot apartment. This is about finding joy, love, health, and success, regardless of bank account, social level, employment, brand of handbag, marital status or zip-code. This is about finding happiness in what you have, not in what you will or should have. If you aren't happy poor, you won't be happy rich.

When life punches you in the gut, saying thank you for a warm blanket doesn't take away the pain. None of these are 'magic pills'. They are supplements which, when taken each day, will support the "system" you are building to get healthy.

Practice: "Thank you, thank you, thank you." Repeat often! I put a post-it note next to my toothbrush to remember.

D. Do Something! You can't lose weight by merely reading a diet book. You don't become a great basketball player just by watching the game. If you feel stuck and don't even know where to begin, simply do something. Something you aren't already doing.

Get out of bed. Get a job. Get a different job. Break up. Go to therapy. Go to church. Go to Tibet. Volunteer. Travel home. Travel away from home. Go back to school. Write that book. Stop making excuses. Go running. Just Go. Make the phone call. Don't answer that call. Adopt a pet. Put down the ice cream. Say "yes". Say "no". Move. Start a blog. Read an inspiring book. (Oh wait; there's one in your hand now. Check!)

It's ok to be afraid – we all are. It's ok to be insecure – we all are. It's ok to make mistakes – we all have. It's ok to start over again – we all do. If you fall, fall forward.

Practice: Do something new each month that puts you in a different environment, even if it's small.

I found 'I.T.', and now – so have you.

Stacey Yates Sellar, C.A.P.P. Happiness Coach. Happier By the Minute.
www.HappierByTheMinute.com

HEATHER KERR

"Unleash the power of your creativity and watch your life unfold in amazing new directions."

My wish is that some of you will see a glimpse of yourself in my story and experience a nudge to begin your own creative journey. I believe we are all 'artists' in one way or another. If you simply explore the stillness within you, you may be surprised at the unique creative gifts you find to share with the world.

ONE WOMAN'S JOURNEY TO HER CREATIVE SOUL

Whenever I see a group of young children playing together, their imagination in full throttle with joy brightening their faces, I'm reminded of my own early childhood. When I was five, I'd sit with my best friend, Barbara, with a stack of crayons and pad of note-paper and we'd immerse ourselves in colouring. Or I'd convince her to cut up cereal boxes, turn them inside out, colour them and make elaborate houses, forts or, with more difficulty, trees and scenery, to create exactly the right atmosphere for our Barbie dolls. Barbara wasn't as keen on art as I was, so sometimes I had to bribe her with other activities to follow. But I loved everything about creating things, and couldn't get enough of it. When I was focussed on my art, I felt free and easy, which was rare for me.

Even as a little kid, I remember wondering why adults were always saying they wished they could be little kids again and not have to worry. I thought their memories must be poor, because I was an anxious and sensitive little girl. I was always worried about what other people thought and whether they liked me.

When I was in grade five, I worked hard on an art project for Mrs. Hawkins. She circulated through the classroom praising each of the other children's' efforts. I waited in excited anticipation for her reaction. I thought I'd produced something absolutely beautiful to behold and magnificent. I was so proud. But when Mrs. Hawkins stopped at my desk, she made only a few critical suggestions about areas for improvement, then moved on. Not a single compliment.

I had a sudden, devastating realization! My artwork was not 'good'. Flattened in disappointment, I remember going home and crying in bed all night. And the next night. And the one after that. I felt like a piece of me, the part I had always thought was the very best part of me, was not actually real.

I was grieving. That night, I rejected the 'artist in me'. She was drowning, her hand stretched out for me to rescue her. Instead, I pushed her under and walked away.

From then on, I approached art classes at school with a sense of failure and shame. My art materials at home gathered dust on the shelf. I no longer felt any delight or joy in my creativity. In an act of self-violence, I had allowed Ms. Hawkins' criticisms to extinguish my little girl's artistic soul. It took four decades for me to recover it.

By the next year, my sadness transmuted into a constant, seething, but undefined anger. I often didn't feel joyful any more. I had lost myself and all I knew consciously was that I hated to follow other people's rules and I wanted to make up my own mind and choices. I craved freedom.

An illicit back-alley booze episode launched me into teenage-hood. At the tender age of 13, I invited several friends for a sleepover after our first high school dance. On our way to the dance, we cut through the back alley where we consumed copious amounts of Lonesome Charlie, a cheap wine known for its high sugar content. Drinking alcohol felt defiant! Exhilarating! Amazing. I was not only drunk but having a sugar rush!

When we returned to my house, my boozy breath was disguised by an enormous quantity of Scotch peppermints. Which was good. Because my Dad had just been transferred to my school as its principal to 'clean it up'. Dad was known for having no patience for errant teenage behaviour and this made him rather unpopular with the students. I was angry at him for accepting the job, a decision I believed was ruining my life.

I continued to drink to subdue my anger and taste the freedom lost to me. I wasn't so lucky the next time I drank before a school dance. The teachers informed Dad when I was found in the bathroom puking up the beer I always had trouble keeping down. That didn't go well at home. Dad expressed I was ruining his life. There were many repeated episodes. And punishments.

To my parents' relief, when school was finished, I 'settled down', stopped rebelling and conformed to what was expected of me. I went from feeling angry and defiant to anxious and compliant.

Like many other university students selecting classes, I made a lot of 'sensible' choices in order to placate my parents and impress my teachers. They all seemed to have strong views about what I should or shouldn't do. My primary concern was to pick something that would avoid the financial insecurity my parents had experienced as Depression-era babies. I'd given up my art so many years ago; it wasn't a choice I even considered. I had developed a keen interest in psychology, but Dad thought psychologists were 'kooks'. Psychology was not going to fly.

I enrolled in Commerce. Dad thought that was absolutely fantastic! I ignored the uncomfortable pit I felt in my stomach.

This was the beginning of a long stretch of time I spent following other people's advice. I didn't pause to figure out what made ME tick, what brought ME joy, or what gave ME a sense of purpose. These didn't seem to be legitimate questions.

I hated Commerce and felt miserable all first year. I decided to switch to another college. I thought maybe now I could focus on psychology, but my professors countered with strong recommendations to continue my studies in economics. I complied.

Unfortunately, as the subject progressed, economics turned out to be mostly math, a subject I'd always hated. By graduate school, all we did in economics was grind out mathematical models.

My solar plexus burned almost every day, my body signaling me that my choices were taking me off my path. I ignored the frequent rising bile in my throat. At one point, I tried to switch colleges again, but the professors recommended against it.

By the time I graduated, I felt thoroughly stuck. Even though I hated economics, the only direction I could see was to become an economist.

After four years of working in tax policy, I still hadn't mustered any enthusiasm for the job. So I switched directions again. Yet, I still didn't ask myself what I really wanted or what I was called to do.

I canvassed other people for their advice, went to law school and became a tax lawyer, moving still further away from the artist inside me who had died so long ago.

The next 24 years of my life as a tax lawyer, weren't all bad by any measure. My colleagues were fun. We used laughter to ward off our stress. I loved mentoring and helping my staff be the best they could be. I enjoyed serving my clients. I made good money, had a nice house and took my family on exotic vacations.

But I woke up day after day feeling utterly depleted and empty inside. I'd done what everyone had asked me to do. I'd been sensible. I was successful. Yet, I wondered what was wrong with me. Why was I so unhappy? I felt ashamed of my lack of gratitude. I spent my spare time in self-help sections of book stores. I prayed someone would show me how to change things and feel better.

Then one day, everything changed. Something happened that taught me there was a source of wisdom I'd consistently failed to consult. All the answers I'd ever needed were inside of me.

My new life started on a trip to Paris in February. The museums and streets were almost empty. There were only a few tourists strolling about. Window shopping had elbow room and we found our choice of tables in every cafe.

I'd been to the amazing art galleries before, but there had always been a sea of people between me and the Rodin sculptures or I had to peer between bobbing heads to glimpse a Monet. This time I could stop in front of each masterpiece and soak up its essence. I could feel the spirit of the artist as if he or she were standing beside me.

Everyone in Paris was relaxed and happy. I watched Parisians savor their meals. I loved how even the most ordinary taverns served a good selection of delicious Bordeaux wines. Paris became a sensory experience. I absorbed each sight, sound, smell, touch, and taste.

On the fifth day, magic happened. I awoke, still feeling the glow of the day before and a vision appeared in my mind. The image was so clear, it seemed almost physically present. I saw in my mind's eye a large and incredibly beautiful canvas in front of me. I examined it carefully and could see the depth of colour and the texture of every paint stroke. I looked down and saw paint brushes in my hand! I realized I was the artist responsible for that beautiful canvas!

I felt an overwhelming sense of gratitude and I knew that I would recover my artistic soul. I would become whole again. The permanent tightness in my heart released as my chest expanded, filling with air. I took the hand of the drowning little girl from so long ago and pulled her above the water. I was overtaken by a bliss I hadn't known for a very long time.

A switch had flipped. I began to see similar visions every day. Since I had abandoned art in grade five, I was out of practice so, instead, I wrote about the paintings I saw in a journal. I got up to 51 paintings.

When I returned home, everything felt different. I could no longer put aside this deep part of myself bursting to emerge. Everywhere I turned, people who would become my new tribe showed up – artists, female entrepreneurs, teachers, coaches, energy healers, reiki masters and spiritual advisers. They inspired me.

Eight months after my Paris trip, I left my job to pursue art full time.

When I began painting, at first I forgot my newly found ability to find answers within myself, and began replicating my old pattern of looking for answers externally. I enrolled in an acrylic painting class at a local art school for adults. I loved the first few classes. Our instructor taught us how to choose paint brushes, mix colour and create different textures with different media. I was surprised to find everything came easily to me.

But then, the teacher began to introduce limiting principles, "Heather, you shouldn't add a lot of texture to your paintings. The market won't accept highly textured paintings by women."

"Heather, your paintings are too pretty. People want to buy paintings that are meaningful."

"Heather, you shouldn't mix colour with metallics; it dilutes the metallics." And so on. I started to feel trapped and dull again. I was terrified. I had left my job to feel free and get in touch with my inner wisdom. Instead, I was learning how to be successful in the art world, having to follow requirements that didn't make sense to me. It seemed that the art world was just as rule-based as the tax world! I felt betrayed. I sought the counsel of a wise artist friend. She suggested an obvious course of action that freed me, "Heather, just quit! You can teach yourself to paint."

That's what I did. I ignored any advice that felt constraining. I sought my own counsel. I took long walks. I meditated. I went deep. What I discovered was amazing. When I became silent and fully present, I was flooded with ideas and visions – sometimes fully formed paintings. Sometimes just the first steps I should take. I learned that once I started painting, I'd know what to do in each moment.

I painted and I painted some more. As long as I followed my intuition, my paintings always carried exactly the energy I wished them to convey. The few times I forgot to go within and tried to 'think' through the next steps, something contrived and unappealing would emerge.

At first, I didn't understand how I was able to so easily produce paintings I loved, after years of no evidence of my creativity. I was perplexed. Until, one day, I listened to author Eckhart Tolle give a talk. He advised listeners to be still and fully present and allow the creativity within them to emerge. When I heard this, the hair stood up on my arms.

The whole process I had developed on my own was all about dropping into spaciousness and allowing the creativity to arise. Just as Tolle said. It all made sense to me then.

I've since discovered that artistic creativity is no different than other forms of creativity. The same processes work. No matter what we desire to create, the best ideas come when we allow ourselves to not know the answer, but to open instead to our inner guidance. When we learn to do this, we find the freedom to be our best selves and to create something magical in the world!

IGNITE ACTION STEPS

You would be wrong if you left my story thinking that I have a gift that you don't have. I'm not special. I was just a girl who was lucky enough to have an experience in Paris that ignited in me a truth I'd forgotten about myself. A truth you might have forgotten about yourself too.

I believe with all my heart that every single one of us is an artist. We were all born artists. Infinite creative potential is available to us. Somewhere along the way, some of us suffered a comparison, took a criticism to heart, failed in an effort, and we rejected the artist part of ourselves. We defined ourselves as not artistic and we moved on.

Others of us didn't go that far. We continued to believe we are artists. We studied art. We learned techniques. We put our art out into the world. We learned what is valued and what is not, what presents well and what does not. And some of us allowed all the rules, judgments and comparisons to kill our artistic souls and constrain our art.

If you find yourself described by either scenario, I'd like you to consider two simple and practical techniques to reignite your deepest level of creativity.

The first and essential step is to be willing to not know the answer. For these techniques to work, you'll need to look inside yourself for the answers with both openness and trust. If you do that, you'll discover your ability to bring amazing art into the world.

Try one or both of these techniques just before you sit down to do your art:

• Find a beautiful spot in nature. Set an intention to be open to whatever happens. Take a 15-minute sensory walk. Walk slowly with all your senses open. Stop and examine small objects that catch your eye. Notice the little details. See their tiny perfection. Feel their texture.

Continue walking. Relax your eyes and look into the distance. Feel the air on your face. Notice the smells. Listen to the birds, the rustle of the wind in the trees or the hum of traffic in the distance. When you are finished your walk, grab a journal and write down everything that goes through your mind for the next 10 minutes. Then start to paint, draw or sculpt!

• Set aside 30 minutes to meditate. Find meditation music you like and play it or just sit in silence. Sit in a comfortable position with your feet on the floor. Relax. Take three slow, deep breaths. Imagine yourself infused with light coming from above. Imagine the light traveling through you, through the soles of your feet and down through the layers of the earth to connect with a beautiful white crystal in the earth's centre. Let the energy of mother earth flow back up and through you. Let that energy connect with your heart. Bask in it. Let your mind be still. Be open to any thoughts or images that arise. Record these in a journal. And start creating your art!

These techniques will help you step out of thinking and drop into spaciousness. To let go of the belief that you already know the answer, and to allow whatever arises. Be open and prepared to explore what comes up, even if it doesn't make logical sense. Learn how to say "Yes!" to the full measure of creativity available to you. Let your art show up in its full magnificence. If you use these techniques frequently, my guess is that you'll start to see not only your art, but your life transform in amazing and unexpected ways.

Heather Kerr, Life Coach, Artist, Speaker and Retreat Owner.
www.gracedcanvas.com

JENNI WALKE

"You are responsible for who you are today. Who you will be tomorrow is a fantasy."

We are all on our own heroine's journey. It's what we do along the way that makes it extraordinary. I invite you to make the choice to choose. I hope you give yourself permission to stop being who you think you should be; to stop worrying about what you cannot control. My wish is for you to start focussing on who you are today and to recognise and embrace your own heroine's journey.

UNTANGLING THE PATH. MY PATH.

Before we begin, stop for a moment, maybe two, and consider...

What you did today? How much was for you? How much was for your family, friends, pets, others? How much of it was for some 'future self' you're working towards?

Like many women, I go about my day, and do my thing and it is 'just what I do'. I carry the needs of work, friends, family and others, and somehow keep it together. A few years ago, I realised that somewhere along the way I lost myself in this mix. I found myself needing to untangle who I am, from just what I do. Like me, you too may be on a path that needs to be untangled...

My path...

I was in a job I was good at. Great in fact. I had been there for almost four years. I had clients who valued my advice, I had the respect of my manager, and I had freedom in how I performed my job. Then, it all changed. The respect I had was slowly whittled away, the freedom I had was removed and I suddenly found myself caught up in someone else's insecurities and games. It seemed the more competent and valued I became, to our clients and the business, the more threatened they became. The result, I left. I had to. I was at my end – literally and figuratively.

For three months I battled serious anxiety, all while being told there was nothing wrong with me, I was 'faking it'. I would wake with a sense of dread, wondering how I would cope with whatever came that day.

In each moment, my inability to manage my emotions and control my feelings was like a dream. Like I was living someone else's life or watching a really bad movie. I was in equal measure in the depths of despair feeling every raw unbridled emotion, yet detached from the outcome.

When I look back on what happened during this time, I realise how lucky I was. My mother and father had blessed me with love, intellect and fierce determination. I had an amazing partner whom I had just met, who provided me a level of unconditional love and support I didn't know existed. My partner didn't judge me, he didn't expect anything of me – other than to be me. (When I look back, I am where I am today, in a great way because of him).

Having him in my life, at that time was a blessing. Not because he was my love, my partner (I met him at the exact time I developed serious anxiety); rather because this amazing person **gave me 'permission' to be me**. My partner re-empowered a once fierce, indestructible, strong (or maybe single)-minded, pig-headed, there for everyone else, never failing, always together, successful woman - to let everything go. To cry, sometimes uncontrollably, despite telling him on the first date that 'I don't cry'; because that was the only way I knew how to release what I had been holding together. To pivot in the opposite direction from who I thought I was supposed to be (and who he'd initially met), into who I knew I was. Into the Being I had felt deep inside, but never dared release – because release equated to a lack of control.

It was then I developed an understanding and insight into what it was to just BE.

When you are at home all day, sometimes struggling to function as a human, you have a choice to let it control you, or to allow everything to just BE.

It was an interesting dichotomy. **To gain control, I had to let go of control.**

During the time I was unwell, routine was my savior. Now 18 months later, as my business grows, scheduling remains a key part of my day and week. It gives me back time and prevents overwhelm. This is a lesson that I recommend everyone heed.

But I digress!

Taking the leap and building the plane on my way down...

Rather than the planned responses I had practiced so fervently, I felt like I was unravelling, caught in a web of emotional reactions. I felt forced into the situation, out of control and unsure of how I would survive. Then I came to realise this was self-made. I created my environment. I created the situation. I allowed it to happen.

I am not saying, by any means, what I was feeling wasn't true. I am not saying I asked for it. And I am not saying I deserved it. As I reflected, I began to understand and accept that ultimately, I had seen it coming. I had felt the twinge in my gut, heart, and soul. I had chosen to give it power. To allow it. My need for control, for success, for wanting to 'see it through', for not wanting to 'quit' had blinded my vision.

I hadn't stood in my power in any determined way and done everything I thought I could to avoid being hurt; to not be perceived as too strong, or too successful. Looking back, it was like I had been waiting for something to give; for someone to save me all the while unconsciously setting myself up for the upcoming collapse. The lesson. One I would remember and listen to.

Once I accepted my role in my situation, my focus changed. Ever so slightly at first; and then... *like jumping from a plane, with the wind in my face as I fell, exhilaration wrapped in fear, I realised, I didn't pack the parachute.*

I knew logically I had to find and focus on something other than what had happened. And I had a limited time to do it before I hit the ground.

The hardest and scariest thing I ever did was ask for help.

I was living a fairly isolated life during this time. My beautiful man visited between shift work and spending time with his daughter. I was moving towards something. I wasn't sure what. But I damn well knew it wasn't what I had left behind.

While on medical leave, just thinking about the job gave me anxiety. Talking to people I had worked with – even those I treasured deeply – was heartbreaking. Dealing with lawyers, writing submissions, and wondering 'how will I pay this bill' was terrifying. But each step, was a step toward – not a step backward.

People often said to me, 'you'll bounce-back from this'. Somewhere along the way I decided: 'I don't want to bounce-back.' – 'I want to bounce-forward'! I was going to learn. To share. To grow. To become, me. Again.

When I decided to make a change – it was radical.

After speaking with my psychologist, my doctor, my family and friends, I decided I needed to change my state completely. For me, that was realising I couldn't do it alone.

Hence the decision to attend a personal development program in Barcelona. Not having worked for a few months, I was not cash positive. So, I sold my car, borrowed off family and headed to Spain.

Arriving in Barcelona, with a prescription in hand (just in case to manage my anxiety), was incredibly daunting. I had travelled solo before, but on this occasion, in a room full of people I felt alone and isolated. Perhaps it was because I was at the rawest, most vulnerable I had ever been.

On my first evening, there was an event with the other people in the program. I decided I would go. Despite knowing no one else and feeling more on the introverted side of the scale, I decided I would speak to everyone I met. I would ask them who they were, what they did... and boy, did that change everything.

The first time I asked this, I was shot down. "I hate people asking what I do. It's so boring." They'd continue, "I don't work, I travel the world."

To be honest, I thought, 'what a wanker!' instead of letting it get to me, I moved on, and asked another person. While not as obscure, the answer was much the same. My immediate thought, 'what the F@$k am I doing here'? Was this a mistake. But, I'd already ordered food, so I thought I should persevere.

And then, I met three people who would become part of what we affectionately call 'The Australian Mafia;' comprised of three Australians; a New Zealander and an American from South-Carolina. Maybe it's an Australian thing – we can always find another one of us in a room full of people. Maybe it's the accent or our penchant for sarcasm?

Making the choice to stay, to persevere. To be uncomfortable for a moment, to be comfortable for a lifetime – is why I was there.

Looking back, it was in these first moments, encounters, conversations and in the fear, I made the decision to change the way I was thinking. To remember who I was, to... Become the playwright, not the actor...

Despite an eclectic career that included military service, project management roles with the Commonwealth Games, APEC 2007, and World Masters Games, and the Sales Director of a global learning and development company, I realised *I was living the life I thought I should live*

– not necessarily the one I wanted to live. I had GREAT jobs, I travelled, I did what I was GOOD at, I was paid well, I LOVED my life. Well, I *thought* I did.

As we grow, we are taught, through our experiences, family and friends, who we are to become. It starts early. We are asked as a child, "What do you want to be when we grow up?" We say astronaut, pilot, model, race car driver, or artist. As we get older, and depending on our environment, our aspirations change to more traditional endeavours; mother, doctor, accountant, lawyer... roles that provide security and stability. A career.

We lose perspective about what we want and need to fulfil our lives, not just between the hours of 9 AM and 5 PM. We look at everyone else and think, I want that – not knowing many living that life are slowly dying inside.

Unfortunately, it was not until I truly believed I had nothing left that I reflected on my life, what I had, what I 'lost' and what I had gained from the experience. I realised I had become an actor in my own story and not a very good one at that! I had chosen safe options; yearning for stability and a pay packet to reflect my experience and value. Most of the decisions I made had been in consideration of others or what others needed me to do. Rather than what I needed.

When I took the time to stop and consider what I was good at AND what I LOVED TO DO, I realised despite following a traditional, if not assorted path, I had developed great skill in helping others gain clarity about their business strategy, their programs, their communications, and in some cases their life. Doing this type of work, gave me purpose and this purpose gave me direction.

I found me and my genius! I CHOSE to become the playwright AND the director of my life.

In Barcelona, the Australian Mafia would check in with each other daily. Imagine, an eclectic group of strangers from across the world becoming best of friends over wine and banter. Sharing stories and wondering who we wanted to be when we grew up. It was through these discussions I started to talk about who I am, not what I was. About what I was doing and will do, not what I did; the values I offered, not the value I felt was taken from me.

Learning to regain control over my thoughts, actions, and behaviours enabled and empowered me to reconnect to who I was; my generous soul, my love for others, and my genuine desire to help others grow. The reasons I loved my previous job – even when it didn't love me back!

My boundaries were endless; overextending myself in the rush to become something, I had lost my own identity. I began to find my voice and my vision again. It was in these moments I found my joy was helping others find theirs.

Perhaps it was being surrounded by other people who were escaping their current life, trying to find a new one, looking for a new adventure or just enjoying a month in Spain allowed me to reset. But over the course of three weeks, I became me again.

It wasn't easy. There were moments I cried on the phone to my partner; wondering if I had done the right thing. There were moments I broke down in a restaurant bathroom after being pushed just that little too far by a 'friend'. There were also moments of freedom I had never experienced before. They happened when I stopped worrying about who I was supposed to be and allowed myself to be me.

For most women, whether a parent, friend, leader, or community member, putting ourselves first in every decision feels unnatural. It feels selfish and wrong. I learned by putting myself first, I created more space in my heart for everyone else, not less.

It was not an overnight realisation. In fact, it wasn't until a few weeks after I returned when I was speaking with a colleague, that I realised how different I was. Others had noticed I was less focused on the past, and far more present, and our interactions and connection had grown, but I myself hadn't noticed.

For a while after returning from Barcelona, I waited for the sense of freedom I now felt and the lightness to disappear; but two years on, it still remains.

Choice Is A Choice. Not Making One, Is Still A Choice.

I officially quit my job while I was in Barcelona; but in reality I had left it months before. Sending an email to advise I was resigning was the most powerful act I could do for my current and future self. Returning home, I had $43 in my account, and the promise of a new life. A new future. One I would create with passion, energy and joy.

The belief you need to transition from one life to another, keeping one foot inside the plane and one foot outside, didn't work for me. I needed to jump and learn to build the plane on the way down. I didn't just want a parachute. I want the freedom to go anywhere, to be anything.

I didn't understand the freedom and gift I gave myself until much later. But then, most of us don't.

In reading this, I hope you recognise you don't have to be pushed out of a plane to change your thoughts and create the life of your dreams.

You just have to choose You. One more thing, arose out of the writing and my story. At the time, I attached *all the feelings and anxiety* to what was happening in the job. Digging deeper into the writing of this story, I recalled the only other collapse I've experienced in my life, was around the loss of my dad. I had just turned 22 when he became ill. Shortly before this, when I was still 21, he wrote words of encouragement and affirmation on a cheque blank, which I have on my wall to this day. When my collapse occurred in 2017, I was twice the age I was when he wrote that note. There is something significant about this. Something true.

I lived the first 21/22 years of my life with his loving support. 2017 was the anniversary of living 21/22 years without that support. This anniversary, together with having my loving, supportive partner enter my life, were the hidden catalysts behind my 'collapse'.

I invite you to reconsider what has happened as a rebirth for you. What realization and renewed freedom is wanting or waiting for you... In your life.

As you move through your life, I encourage you to look at the significant events and blessings that have been bestowed on you. If you do the math, *and the math, I am told, is always there*, you can strengthen your heart, your soul, understand what has occurred and prepare for what may come.

Ignite Action Steps

I have compiled a list of questions which helped me gain clarity in my environment. They helped me to stop fearing change and to fear not changing.

- When was the last time you let go of something?
- Is this the life you want to live? Is this who you want to be?
- What are you accepting that you know is misaligned with what you want; who you are?
- What choices are you making? What choices have you given others?
- What is one thing you can do now that will move you toward your best self?

I invite you to consider these questions and write down your answers. Look at them. Consider them. Decide if they represent who you are, or someone else. Then, start choosing your path...

Jenni Walke, Business Implementation Coach.
Elephant in the Room Consulting. www.eitrconsulting.com

ANDREA REINDL

"Open your heart and love full out, magic will happen."

It is my hope you open up to experiencing love full out, ditch the fear you might lose something. Oddly, when we fear disconnection, we hold back from connecting. I wish for you to open your heart and love with all you have. You will find magic you can only understand when it happens. Trust and examine where you may be holding back in your life right now. Where can you show up and play so much more full out?

LOVE AND SO MUCH MORE

December 5, 2007, is the day I credit as the day that ignited the experience of love for me. I wouldn't know it though, until several months later.

It seems to me that sometimes we only observe our moments of realization and epiphanies looking backwards. In the moments they are happening we don't know how significant they may be. Hence, when we really engage, we just experience the moment and later are able to reflect and absorb the lesson. While I have many of those moments, this story is one of those for me.

It was the middle of winter in Alberta, Canada (oh that's a polite way of saying - it was bloody cold outside). My Mom had been camping out at my house for two weeks while we all sat around waiting for my baby to come. Two weeks of waiting for a baby to arrive feels like an eternity. We'd nested, cooked, cleaned, played cards, and watched about all the series we had on DVD (ha, remember pre-Netflix days? It was so much harder to binge watch).

Officially, I was nine days overdue and if I made it to day ten, my midwife was legally required to send me to the hospital for induction (which we women know makes the already challenging assignment of having a baby so much more daunting).

I truly did not want to be induced at the hospital - NO WAY! So, under careful supervision, on December 4th around 2 pm, I began taking homoeopathic remedies, specifically one that is used to induce horses. Turns out, they work on humans too. By 10:30 that night I was in gentle yet serious labour. Around 1:30 am on December 5th, submerged in a pool of warm water, with dim lights, in my own home, my beautiful daughter, Melaina, entered the world. It was basically a perfect birthing experience, truly it could not have been better.

I think one of the pure, true joys, and surprises left in life is finding out the gender of your baby at the moment of birth. Hence, I didn't know I was having a girl. I REALLY wanted a girl. I craved it as much as my body wanted food. I will eternally cherish the surge of emotion when I drew her out of the water, pressed her squirmy, slimy, wiggling body on mine and just cried tears of relief that 'my baby' was finally in my arms. Time slowed to a crawl until I remembered we didn't know if 'it' was a boy or a girl. (Oh, the high of childbirth!) I glanced down and even more tears flowed as I examined her perfect little body and saw she was a girl.

Little did I know that less than 24 hours later I would face the most terrifying reality and that perfect little girl would change my life forever.

The hours after birth she was healthy, good Apgar scores, strong as a baby can be, the midwife was happy with how good both she and I were doing. We were basically the perfect story of 'Mom and baby doing well'. This delightful little bundle was swaddled in her blanket and trendy little outfit I'd purchased with the anticipation of getting to buy pink after 'it' was born. Both blanket and outfit were in neutral colours of course. Tucked between her father and I, she was resting peacefully.

When the midwife came up to say her final goodbye before she went home for some sleep she noticed James and I were giggling at her perfect little sigh on each exhale. Like she was just happy it was finally over and she was here. The midwife noted that sound wasn't completely normal. It alarmed her just a tad, she left to take a nap saying she'd come back and check on us later in the day.

The day passed, Melaina met her brother who thought she was pretty cool and shared his favourite blankie as his first act of love. We all ogled and cooed at her since she was the perfect baby and so damn cute. We called the people who we cared about and let them know Mommy and baby were healthy. I think I even slept a couple of hours.

Around 9:00 pm I nursed her. That part of the day hadn't gone all that smoothly. She didn't take to it with ease as my first had. Shortly after feeding she began to lose her strength and become more like a cabbage patch than a strong healthy newborn. Thank God my Mom was there. She knew something wasn't right and called the midwife. The midwife wasted no time telling us she'd meet us at the Children's Hospital. Tired, frightened and in shock I sat plopped at the bottom of my stairs and packed my perfect miracle into her carseat. Later, my Mom told me she was sure that was the last time she'd see Melaina alive.

We arrived at the Children's hospital 20 minutes later. The car ride seemed to take forever as I sat in the backseat with her. She had been shrieking the entire trip. In a daze, I jiggled her seat (not sure how I thought that would help) and tried unsuccessfully to calm her.

When we arrived at emergency, I jumped out of the car and took her and the entire car seat into the waiting room. Just as I drew her dusky blue, tiny body out of the car seat, a nurse came barreling down on me and with a whoosh, tore Melaina from my arms. No paperwork to sign. No names asked. We were raced to the back of the emergency room with people rushing about, calling out phrases that felt like 'code words for someone is going to die' (I still have no clue what they actually said). I'm still pretty convinced in all the hysteria one person may have dropped out of the ceiling like Spiderman.

For the next eight or nine hours a team of angels known as emergency room doctors and nurses kept my daughter alive. One was even breathing for her. I still remember watching her pumping the device that kept fresh oxygen going to my baby's lungs.

Several specialists were woken up and called in to figure out what was wrong with my baby. No one could figure it out. I will always remember the befuddled look on the cardiologist's face while he used the ultrasound machine over her tiny chest.

Three nurses who surrounded him all had a look I couldn't interpret and could only guess they were the faces of those who were equally as lost as their leader. All I could sense in the room was dread and confusion. All the faces reminded me of hospital emergency room television shows where there isn't always a happy ending. I was terrified.

During most of this time, I was off to the side, unable to touch my baby that had been so safe inside of me less than 24 hours before. The longer the night went on, the more tired I got, the more I could see and feel what I had never felt before. It was like the more tired I was, the more I was waking up deep inside.

Slowly, it began to sink in that she might not make it. I might have to say the ultimate goodbye to my perfect baby after only a few hours. Like a fast-paced recap of a movie, I imagined this being the end, her little body lifeless, us picking an urn, having to select flowers and saying goodbye to her forever… just like that, it all became so real and so possible.

I don't remember the exact instant it happened but I do remember that I started to pull back my love, pull back my joy that I felt earlier that day and began to come to terms with knowing I might have to say this goodbye and let her go. After several hours her Dad and I were finally allowed to move close enough to touch her.

I remember feeling so very terrified to love her, she might disappear the same moment I let myself fully love her. It was then I realized that it's true I might fully love her AND she might die shortly after. However, there was a small stirring inside of me that knew that if I didn't fully love her (and somehow be ok with letting her go at the same time) she would for sure die. It's as though my heart knew it wouldn't be just the doctors and treatments that kept her alive. I knew somehow she needed me to love her full out to make it and live past the next few days.

Remember how earlier I mentioned sometimes we only realize things looking back, not in the moment. So much of what I experienced and learned that night came to me as lessons in the months that followed, not right in the moment. It wasn't until later when I became so very aware I really hadn't ever experienced that depth of love until that night. Loving with the real possibility of letting it go in the same moment. That is a whole different kind of experience. For the first time in my 27 years on this planet, I let go of fear and connected, really connected where love and loss and power collide - where the unexplainable magic happens.

This story has a good ending. It was discovered she had a somewhat rare condition called PPHN. Wikipedia says this about it: Persistent pulmonary hypertension of the newborn (PPHN) is defined as the failure of the normal circulatory transition that occurs after birth.

For seven days I didn't leave the hospital or her side. I took a few naps, periodically I would go to the pumping room to fill bottles with the abundance of milk I had. I avoided eye contact with the other Moms, flooded with guilt for having three or four bottles of milk for my baby who couldn't use it, while the Moms of preemies who really needed it could barely get ¼ of a bottle. I felt like passing over my bottles and saying 'here use this'... but that would have been awkward.

For a week I sat over my baby, hovered my hand on her little abdomen and sent her every ounce of love I had. The more I gave the more I had. The love just expanded.

One of the nurses told me on our last day in the ward, every time I would leave to nap or go to the bathroom her vitals would drop. As long as I was in the room she was strong. No one told me this till she was fully out of jeopardy and recovered.

After so many terrifying days of being monitored every two minutes and receiving effective treatments, my precious baby was eventually given a clean bill of health and sent home. Just like that... one week, seven days, it was the ultimate roller coaster ride. First perfection, then nope, it's all about to be taken away, and then oh now you have a perfect baby, take her home. It still feels surreal and like a movie script in my mind.

I know, I still don't realize all the gifts this experience has given me. What I do know for sure is that until that first night at the hospital I had never allowed myself to fall into love with anyone or anything for fear I might get hurt or I might lose it all. I had never given my heart over fully, knowing all that what I adored might be ripped from me in the same moment I surrendered to love.

Going through this allowed me to open up in a way I never had before and take risks. Risks to love fully, be fully captivated and give my heart over, you know, go all-in, even knowing it might end up in heartbreak.

Since those days and that experience, I now know what it feels like when I bump up against going all in. I know what it feels like to push past the comfort zone of staying safe instead of playing full out for love. Since then I let love happen more often. I love my kids more fully, I take more risks with work and I let myself fully feel what is true for me. Since then I've allowed love more. It's not about falling, it's about choosing love and then letting it happen with a sense of knowing it's ok to love and let go at the same time.

I guess what I'm trying to say is I think we've all had moments and experiences like this. I don't think I'm all that unique or this is that original of an experience. It's just we don't usually connect to the moment and the lesson until after it's well behind us.

My experience is we just need time to connect to and process them. I hope you are able to use your own experiences of connection to ignite the spark of the best you inside of you.

When you reflect on your own life where and when have you had to give all of your best self to create magic? I'd like to suggest our work while here on this planet is not to look for love, but rather to simply open to the fullest expression of ourselves where love lives naturally.

Ignite Action Steps

This is all fine and well. Maybe you are wondering though, how does one actively connect to these experiences? What is an action step you can take to practice noticing when you have magic appear in your life. I have found that small daily actions of focusing on the present moment connects me to the experiences of wonder every day.

While you are digging deep into the feeling of loving full out, commit to something fully and follow what truly feels right for you.

For many of us the challenge is staying in the moment and loving full out. Good news is this is something you can practice intentionally. Here is a daily practice I've adopted and adapted from one of my mentors, Marshall Goldsmith.

It's simple. It will take you, less than an hour to set up and then less than five minutes a day and after a month you'll start to notice you show up differently because you've checked in daily.

What you are going to do is every day at the end of the day, preferably the same time every day, you'll simply ask yourself a few questions and answer them honestly. Sometimes you'll like the answer, sometimes you won't. You want to design these questions to help you stay in the moment, experience the feelings that make you feel alive and live the life you want. Below I'll share my questions, you can use these if you want and I really suggest you at least add a few of your own.

Before creating your own questions, think about the way you want to spend your days and the way you want to feel every day. What connects you to the fullest expression of yourself? What allows you to feel love fully? Make a list of those moments in your life up until now. Next, think about how you can daily ask yourself questions that will force you to watch for the moments of feeling fully self expressed.

After you know your questions, you'll want a way to track them so you can see progress. One easy way to do this is just open a google doc, set up a spreadsheet and answer them yourself everyday filling in the blanks. Another way (and what I do) is to have someone call me and ask the questions and fill the spreadsheet in for me. A third option is to set this system up with a friend, and ask each other the questions. However you do it, the idea is you want to actively think about the questions then answer each one honestly every day saying 'yes' or 'no' and watch the magic that happens as you will begin to look for ways to answer 'yes' more and more every day.

A ninja tip is that it's a little harder to cheat when a real person is asking the questions requiring an answer. So, do your best to find a way that you have to answer to a friend or someone who is holding you accountable.

Here are the questions I use. You can borrow them and/or make some of your own.

- Did you do your best to stay true to yourself?
- Did you do your best to show love?
- Did you do your best to be kind?
- Did you do your best to stay present?
- Did you do your best to stay patient with those who matter to you?
- Did you do your best to let those you love know you love them?
- Did you hug your children for one minute?
- Did you love yourself and were you kind to yourself?
- Did you find something to be grateful for?

I know, it seems so simple. I challenge you to try it for six weeks and watch what happens when you just do it. Change the questions as often as you like and use a google doc to track by the month. If you are working on a new habit, put a question in that will support the positive habit.

Remember, amazing results come from small actions and progress on a daily basis.

Andrea Reindl, Legacy Creative CEO.
www.AndreaReindl.com

LOURDES
ALDANONDO

"Connection is the basis of all happiness. When you connect and listen without judgment, you can hear your soul whisper."

My words are designed to give you wings, to invite you to live your life unapologetically and to break the illusion of separation. I want to inspire you to reach out and connect with others in the knowledge that the truth in you can never be unmade.

THE ILLUSION OF SEPARATION: TRUSTING THE UNIVERSE AGAIN

I grew up in a matriarchal society, where my mother ran the household with the power of a dragon. I love dragons, by the way, even if sometimes they burn.

She, along with my older sister, made me believe I was a strong, independent girl, with the same rights as any man …and a few more responsibilities. In the Basque Country, women are not seen as delicate feminine creatures. Actually, I had to learn to fall in love with my feminine side much later in life.

I remember clearly understanding that women had to go through childbirth, carry most of the responsibility of their upbringing as well as being in charge of the household, maintain a career, and be the backbone of their family and home. Their opinions did matter, they were heard, yet being strong had its price.

To my young eyes, in comparison, men's lives were less complicated. My dad and brother enjoyed that advantage while being warm, loving and fun. So unsurprisingly I used to go to bed every night asking some higher power to "please, please let me wake up as a boy." Of course, my pleads were never met. As I approached the crazy, hormonal, teenage years, I watched my boobs grow in front of my body as part of the irrevocable change into womanhood. I decided to let my hair grow long and make the best of this thing called 'being a girl'.

For most of my life, I had fulfilled the expectations I carried with me from my upbringing. I travelled the world, had a wonderful partner, two amazing kids and a steady career. My job as a therapist was my passion. My interest in complementary medicine came from my Basque roots. I have wonderful memories wandering in the mountains, picking medicinal herbs with my father that later my mother would turn into some remedy or salve. I don't ever remember wanting to be anything other than a health professional.

My fundamental support team were the close women in my life, my sister, my mum, and my Scottish sister-in-law and mother-in-law. They were my role models and my safety net. They provided me with the unspoken feeling that, whatever happened, I could count on them, I wasn't alone, I was part of a sisterhood. They gave me that precious, golden treasure: unconditional love. We didn't agree on everything. Who does? However, fundamentally, primitively, I knew they had my back, always and forever.

Then things changed radically for the worse and insanely quick. My sister was diagnosed with cancer and passed away. My mum, sick with grief, couldn't take the pain and retreated from the world into the hazy blur of dementia. In a cruel short time, we also lost my mother-in-law and sister-in-law. In a few years, the most important women in my life, my female tribe, my solidity, were gone.

I read that grief comes in waves. First you feel as if you're drowning in an ocean of pain. Each wave hits you with such a force you're gasping for air. It feels like it can't possibly hurt any more, but the next wave is even more painful. No time to catch your breath, no place to grasp safety. I felt as if everything that grounded me had disappeared and I was in freefall, with nothing to hold on to and no one to catch me. The fear of living without their supportive, unconditional love was paralyzing.

I knew I was a strong independent woman, so I had to pick myself up and keep going. I had kids to look after, a job to do and a household to run. On the outside everything looked fine, life didn't change much. My mind did a very good job silencing my heart. But on the inside, I was numb, anesthetized, I couldn't feel anything. If I allowed myself to feel, I knew the pain was so strong it would make me collapse.

Still, I refused to ask for help. I didn't know how. I didn't realize I had permission to do so. I was scared that if I showed my vulnerability I wouldn't appear strong enough by some insane, abstract standard. Showing myself as powerless to the world would shatter the pre-imposed ideas I had about myself. The ego plays its role so well when your heart is shattered, it only thinks of its own survival. I closed myself off and was blind to the love I had around me. I didn't trust life anymore.

Then I cracked.

The inability to share your pain with others can make you feel isolated and detached from your life. How many times have you felt alone in a crowd? How many times did you feel lonely even in the company of your loved ones?

The biggest fear we have as human beings is the illusion of separation, the idea that we are not part of the whole. In a time of great loss this becomes incredibly real. We have the limiting belief that individualism, independence, freedom and strength are incompatible with showing our vulnerability and our need for connection. In the modern world, disconnection is the biggest killer in our society, and I felt as if my pain and grief was killing me.

I learned that every traumatic experience needs to be RECOGNISED, VALUED AND ACCEPTED… because, the truth is, our body doesn't know the difference between an emotional or physical attack. The biokinetic forces that create trauma can be either physical, spiritual or emotional. When these forces are too strong, happen repeatedly or are prolonged over time, our system is unable to deal with them. It doesn't have the ability to absorb them or digest them and they become stored somewhere inside our body. With time, this 'energetic cyst' develops into an ache or pain, a knotted muscle, or even something more sinister. This compacted emotional energy we've suppressed will sooner or later cry out for attention, because it yearns to be recognized, valued and accepted.

You see, the symptoms we experience as 'dis-ease' are the best way our bodies have of manifesting and expressing unbalanced health, and protecting our whole system from internal harm. For example, the pain of losing her first-born child to cancer was too much for my mother to bear. She dealt with the suffering by retreating into her own world with a form of dementia. She literally tried to forget. I'm not saying her disease was caused by her loss. Maybe she would have succumbed to it sooner or later, but the onset was definitely accelerated by the tragic event. Her body decided dementia was the best alternative she had to avoid facing the loss and the pain.

In the same way, my continuous headaches, sore neck and back problems could not be solved by any osteopath. I had to stop and really listen to what these symptoms had to say. After reaching rock bottom emotionally, I decided to stay still. Someone told me, "if you have a broken leg, you can't go swimming in the ocean or skiing in the mountains, you have to wait until your leg heals. Your heart is broken; it also needs to be nursed back to health." I held on to this thought and allowed myself the time and space to heal.

The fundamental path I took to be happy again was to surrender to the pain. I let it breathe out of my every pore. I didn't dwell on it. I wouldn't let it become part of my identity, but I let it talk, let it have its say. I stopped pretending that everything was ok, I allowed myself to cry without feeling shame.

My body took a big role in this transformation too. A friend of mine took me to a spinning class in the gym (believe me, not my favorite place on earth) and as I was trying hard not to pass out and fall off the bike, part of me was connecting to my sister's strength all through her gruelling chemo sessions. I could feel her resilience and her will power, her ability to just power through with a smile, never complaining.

I kept thinking, "If she could do that, I can get through this too." I found out that in moments of distress, when I wanted to run away from everything, I could tap into my sister-in-law´s formidable charisma, my mum´s protective warmth, my mother-in-law´s zest for life and my sister´s compassion and will power. They were still very much present to me. I just had to reach out to them to feel their love and help carrying me to the next step. Was I connecting to the collective force, the universal qualities that unite us, the sea of emotions we all share?

I remember one clear sunny morning, tears pouring out while sitting in my favourite meditation spot, a secluded rock on my hometown beach. You see, my sister wanted to go back to the sea, she wanted her ashes to become part of her favorite ocean bay. As one of my young boys said at the time "that way, we can be with her wherever we are in the world, because the sea is one".

I often went down to the beach to talk to her as I had that day. I was getting lightly splashed by the gentle Mediterranean waves, I realised my son had a point. The sea water, my tears, the fluid that we are all made off, is the element of connection that unites us all.

Gradually I began to treat my pain as a mother holds her little girl when she throws a tantrum. She naturally goes down on her knees and holds her tight until she calms down, not ignoring her, not shouting at her, not distracting her, just accompanying her and letting her go through the storm while holding space. I became my own mother to my inner child, the one that felt abandoned and terrified of not being loved. I slowly started talking to people about how I felt. Not necessarily my nearest friends and family, they were too close to my pain, and I knew the burden wasn't fair on them. Sometimes we expect our closest ones, a partner, a brother, a daughter or our best friends, to somehow heal us and make everything better, but it's not their job. Only we have the ability to heal ourselves. We can't put that responsibility in anyone else's hands.

As I connected with other people's journeys through their pain, their courage inspired me. I began to see my loss as an opportunity for renewal.

I didn't experience a single glorious epiphany or a particular moment that changed my world completely. Life doesn't usually work that way. To expect a sudden change can be the cause of great disappointment and frustration. Life is made of little 'aha' moments that slowly create the change you seek. Every little moment of happiness adds up, like building a mountain with a grain of sand at a time.

Gradually I opened up to new learning environments where I felt safe. I invested in personal growth, learning everything I could find from theories and teachings about who we are in the world. Once I realized I needed to share my vulnerability to decompress, incredible, magical souls appeared on my path. People that could hold me without judgment, without expectations, who just listened. I started to trust the Universe again.

Even though I no longer had those four wonderful women believing in me unconditionally, once I opened my heart's eyes again, I could see there was so much love supporting me on my journey. When I was open to the possibility, every hug, every encouraging comment made me feel I was enough the way I was. The pain and underlying fear of being abandoned, lifted. Loving my perfect imperfections, being strong in my vulnerability. I started to forgive myself and became flooded with gratitude for my life, and the love around me.

I always believe everyone on the planet has a message to share, their own unique way to express their particular manifestation of the source. My message is that this life is not a rehearsal. It is here and now, now or never.

In my therapy practice I changed from doing to being, from actively working on my clients' problems to accompanying them while they regain their personal power. Teaching them simple, effective ways to rediscover the best version of themselves. My new focus led to founding MindTouch®, a beautiful form of physical mindfulness that integrates Biodynamic Craniosacral Therapy and Bodywork. It is a powerful and effective method for everyone interested in improving their relationships with themselves and others. It helps us to actively listen without judgment or expectations, whilst simply holding the space for one another in gratitude.

CONNECTION is the basis of all happiness. We need nurturing, safe contact with our loved ones as much as we need food and water to live. It's as simple as that. Our yearning for belonging is deeper than any other emotional or physical need. The pain that damages us most is the pain suffered in isolation.

I remember telling my mum when I was little, that I was here to have fun. She insisted that this world was a valley full of tears, a notion ingrained into her psyche like so many women from her generation and religion. I had the feeling life could be much easier and more joyful than the way the grown-ups explained it. I knew then, like I know now, that life is a game and we are here to play! I am grateful for that childhood wisdom.

To this day, I still feel the warmth of my dad's hand holding mine while walking up the green Basque hills near my home. I can smell the fragrant medicinal herbs in my little fingers, and feel the sun stroking my face. Lying in the grass with him, looking up at the sky made me feel like I was invincible and in perfect union with life. Closing my eyes, I can still capture that feeling and connect with it every day. It allows me to feel truly safe, filled with gratitude for the little things in life and have complete trust in the universe. When I allow myself to fully decompress this way I feel the rivers of life run through my body in a perfect state of flow.

The healing powers of nature are the healing powers in us all. Our inherent health, our true essence, is the intrinsic intelligence of the universe. I may not have my sister and my mother by my side, but all the women in my life now are also extraordinary warriors that nurture my soul. I can see my sister's strength in their eyes, I can feel my mother's warmth in every hug and their lightness in the laughter we share. I'm surrounded by amazing Goddesses wherever I look, and along with them, some wonderful men make up my loving tribe. They push me to grow, to enjoy every moment as a unique, exquisite, experience, and for that, I'm eternally grateful.

I finally understand that we are pure manifestations of love. When life's struggles throw us into the fire of fear, we need to pause and remember that our soul is not in a hurry and that the truth in all of us can never be unmade.

IGNITE ACTION STEPS

Midline meditation: becoming your own lighthouse. I practice this exercise every day to make me feel strong, peaceful and have clarity of mind. I become my own lighthouse: rooted to the ground, sending a universal message of love and connected to the light. I hope it helps you deal with the storms in your life.

Ideally you will practice this meditation in a relaxed environment whilst in a comfortable position, sitting or lying down. You can also use it in moments of distress to bring you back to your centre. Additionally, these exercises can be done with a partner, which will magnify the results.

We have three main energy centers in our body: CORE, HEART and MIND. Our CORE gives us strength, sense of security, is the connection with our instinct, our blood, the family tree, our identity and survival mechanism. The HEART has the biggest electromagnetic field in our body, expressing our emotions and communicating our message of connection and love. Our MIND is the perfect tool to create our reality through thoughts of wisdom and clarity. Each one of them has its role to play and all three have to be aligned in order for us to live in a harmonious way. We need to connect with our instinct, express our love and use our wisdom.

Close your eyes, become aware of your Midline. Your Midline is the central axis that we all have. It runs from the base of your spine to your head. It's your system's focal point. Now connect with your breathing.

• Place your left hand on your abdomen below your navel. Connect with your core, feel the strength of the earth, your ancestors, your community and tribe. Trust your instinct. Remember a time when you felt strong and safe. Breathe this feeling of security into your every cell.

• Place your right hand on your heart. Connect with love. Bring forth a moment when you felt unconditional love, when you felt an experience of connection and total harmony with life. Breathe in this sense of peace and gratitude into your every cell.

• Place your left hand on your forehead. Connect with your light. Remember your intrinsic intelligence and wisdom. Recall a moment of total brightness and certainty. Breathe in this sense of clarity into your every cell.

As you transition between energy centres, go back to your Midline and your breath. That's your home. Welcome every cell in your body. Visualize yourself as the best version of yourself and repeat: I am strong, I am love, I am wise.

Lourdes Aldanondo, Health Practitioner & Educator. MindTouch®
www.mindtouchbarcelona.com

JADE GREEN

"Life is a Choice. It is what I Choose!
My past does not define me! "

I am sharing my journey from trauma to triumph to show you there is a way forward, and you can live your own dream life. Are you going to be the victor or the victim? The choice is yours. What you decide will shape every aspect of your life.

NEVER GIVE UP AND NEVER GIVE IN

It started in Penrith, Sydney where I was born to my 21-year-old mother, Judy. My Dad, an ex-sailor turned mercenary for the Red Cross rescuing child soldiers in the Congo, was serving a sentence in Long Bay Prison. He'd been involved in an accident while driving under the influence. Although to be fair, the other driver ran a red light and T-Boned him. His best mate, asleep on the back seat, died at the scene. Dad was locked away for vehicular manslaughter.

After his release, Judy and Dad were married in a backyard in Mount Druitt, a super-f@*king, classy suburb of Sydney where you wouldn't dare park your shitbox of a car, or walk down the street alone.

When I was two, we moved to a shitty little caravan park. When the owners went on holidays, Dad managed the property. When I was 4½, the owners left, never to return. We lived in the kiosk (reception building) and ran the place until I was six. Dad, being entrepreneurial, managed to get someone to front him to start building transportable homes. He made spectacular mobile homes. He was doing so well, we entered caravan competitions. When one of our homes won the mobile home of-the-year award, a media mogul ordered 19 mobile homes. Mass production began.

My sisters were born: Holly when I was six and a half and Ely three years later. Judy, aka Mum, got postnatal depression and went proper bat-shit crazy! She rang up our creditors to say we're going bankrupt. They stopped all credit! No working capital! No building! She then told the clients we were going under. They stopped their payments! The business was history.

When this was happening, Dad was working seven hours away in a rural area called Scone, with his best mate, Doug whose wife was nine months pregnant. Dad told him, "go home before the baby comes." Instead, Doug shacked up with Judy AT OUR HOUSE! One of Dad's friends, John,caught on. Not one to let things slide, John came round and gave Doug a proper hiding.

We were locked in Judy's room in the mobile home for 24 hours with my friend, two-year old Holly and Ely with just a potty, no food. I had to pry the security screen off the corner of the window to crawl out through the bougainvillea bush to go around and unlock the door to let us out while the adults had gone to hospital.

Mere months later, Judy came to fetch me from school, "We're leaving!" "Huh? Where are we going?" Our house was packed up. We were off, driving to Tasmania with Doug of all people, who'd abandoned his wife, four kids, including his newborn baby! Doug was a total douchebag.

It took Dad three months and a private investigator to finally find us. Cops tried and failed. Even though Judy had effectively kidnapped us, the courts said we still had to stay with her. No court gave a Dad custody of the kids, let alone three little girls to a man with my Dad's history. So we had to move back into our mobile home. Elaine – Judy's mother (even crazier than her) moved in and things got worse. After one of our access weekend visits with Dad, I took Holly back inside, raced back out to climb back in Dad's truck. "I'm not going back!"

"Whaddya mean you're not going back? You're not staying with me; your mother got custody; if I take you, I'll go to jail."

"You've got two choices." I told him, "You either take me or I'll live on the street! I'm not fucking going back." I was nine! That was the defining moment of my life: life is a choice, it is what I choose. I was ready to live on the street. There was no way I'd live in that house with that crazy b-i-t-c-h! Legal proceedings followed. The courts tried forcing me to go back, but I wouldn't. Except for access weekends to see my sisters. On my 12th birthday, I remember sitting and waiting for hours for Judy to pick me up. It was her access weekend and I wanted to spend time with my sisters. She just never showed up. Even then, I was still a girl wanting a mother. I felt so gutted.

When I'm 13, Judy birthed Alyssa, my youngest half-sister. Doug's sixth child. Before putting Alyssa up for adoption, Judy let Holly and Ely hold the baby; like WTF?! Then things truly went sideways. Judy went completely bonkers. She locked my sisters in a cupboard, got blind drunk, stood on the balcony naked, hurling abuses and ashtrays at a priest down below. The police took her away. Child Services said "just maybe, you shouldn't have kids"... about bloody time ! My Uncle called Dad; we drove 12 hours nonstop to get my sisters. At 14, I became their signatory, assuming the mother role.

By this time, Dad had been seeing a woman for a few years. Crazy times there too. Her kids would pour petrol on cane toads, light them on fire and other crazy shit! It's weird that their psycho behaviour just seemed normal at the time. The bizarre things we did as kids maybe gave us a sense of power when we were powerless. Looking back, I see how off-the-wall-crazy life was. There was always an undercurrent of anxiety, the threat of impending violence. What was going to happen next?

Dad found us a scout hall to rent for only $25/week. The owner had his brains blown out by his missus in what ended up being Ely's room....after the renovations of course. We moved out after it got condemned a year or so later. Eight under one roof: Dad, the girlfriend, three of her kids, Holly, Ely, and me. Of course, Dad and his girlfriend constantly exploded into drunken arguments. Like the time his girlfriend wanted to leave. She'd been drinking, so Dad didn't want her to drive. Attempting to stop her, Dad leaned in the car window to pull the handbrake.

She yelled "I'll fuckin' run over you". She ran over his foot, pulling him under. His shoe flew 20 meters, hitting our house door. We ran outside just as she reversed and flattened his legs again. She sped off, leaving Dad mangled, his knees twisted and mutilated. Want more crazy? About a week later, Dad was released from hospital with his drip. Drip in tow, they went partying as a couple. People inquired: "She ran me over"– nobody blinked. That was my life at 14.

Just before turning 15, we moved to the beach. A government Study Allowance grant for underprivileged kids became my collateral to buy a portable caravan. Parked out back, I lived there so my sisters could have their own rooms in the house.

I got jobs; we needed money. But also because I wanted to drink dark spirits, not cheap wine. By 17, I'd been working for three years: a nanny five nights/week: a waitress one evening/week; a short order cook on weekends. During holidays, I worked in a factory making school uniforms. In my spare time, I was a surf lifesaving instructor. I'd wake up super early to go surfing before school. It's still my normal to rise early and seize the day. It's quite clear my work ethic arose from choosing to be responsible for keeping our family together. Nobody forced me, I decided.

In school, I had no boobs. I had broad shoulders from surfing meant I had to wear a bigger one to prevent them from ripping all the time. All public schools had hideous uniforms. The girls' tops were like tea towels with no shape in yellow, black and white checks. Mine gaped open enough across my chest that boys could stand either side of me and talk through the front of my uniform blouse from one side to the other, teasing me I was so flat, the walls were jealous... I wore a boy's school uniform instead. They threatened to kick me off school council and reject me for captain. I still rejected the girls' uniform AND dyed my hair purple...

I told the Headmaster, "The rules say you must wear 'a school uniform'. So screw you, I'm wearing the boys uniform." Before I graduated, I had the entire uniform changed. Everyone wore the same polo shirt and could choose shorts, skirts or culottes. My younger sisters were stoked! Moral of the story? Don't follow bullshit rules, just because someone tells you.

Finally done with school, university only accepted me for teaching; my grades were too low. A teacher asked if I wanted a traineeship, running her surf shop. "Get paid to work in a surf shop. Sweet!" Except the job only paid $17,500/year. Trainees were supposed to go to school to get certified in small business management. But she just handed me keys, along with an $80,000 budget to spend on clothing for the store.

I toughed it out for a few years running the surf shop, but it wasn't paying the bills. A friend suggested travelling. So, we quit our jobs and headed to Darwin. We drove three days straight to have my 21st birthday in the big smoke, only to find Darwin was another small town – much like the little towns I grew up in. I was totally bummed!

I brainstormed and came up with another plan. As a barmaid, I can travel and work anywhere. I started in Darwin. That led to a lady asking, "Would you work as a V8 supercars promo girl?" "Hell yeah! I love cars." One day, the promo uniforms weren't going to arrive on time – so I offered to make the gear. Fast-forward four years. I inherited a dressmaking business. Ironic!

As a kid, I dreamed of being a fashion designer – despite, being a tomboy who mischievously ground Barbie's boobs off.

We made outfits for every liquor company in town – swimmers advertising booze on national fishing magazine covers. Swimsuits in every colour of pre-mixed vodka for bikini comps. Having successfully launched my promo agency, Bundaberg Rum approached me, "come onboard as sales rep". I could run my agency on the side as long as I didn't wear other brands or do promos for other liquor companies.

Tragedy interrupted my run of luck. My boyfriend's grandmother got sick. A friend was eaten alive by a crocodile. We decided: time to leave Darwin. We packed our bags. Someone wanted to buy the business, but I couldn't sell it in good faith: no contracts with suppliers; everything was paid in cash; staff loyal to me... So I closed up and moved to Sydney. Another lesson: set up your business properly from day one!

Looking for a new job in Sydney, I was drawn to recruitment and interviewed with a few agencies. The company I decided I wanted to work for told me, "no". I kept trying. After 10 rejections, I called them, "you have five minutes to send me a contract, otherwise I'm gonna work for the company across the road and steal all your clients!" I got the job; worked there five years, helped them grow their team from 4 to 50 staff, and started a new Melbourne branch. The owners were early 30's, snorting/drinking their millions away. Then the Global Financial Crisis struck! It hit recruitment hard.

Fast forward, I've been married 3 years and I have started my own firm: Velocity Consulting. Around the three year mark, The Entourage invested intending to grow our agency – $25 million valuation within five years, starting from $1 million. It was a big ask! My husband cautioned "Don't take the deal. We'll end in divorce... the company will go under..." Within a year we were split! Two years later, I closed the company. God I hate it when he's right!

Those last two years running Velocity, I hit burnout. Like rock-fucking-bottom, hardcore burnout. My mentor recommended reading Neale Donald Walsch's Conversations With God. Sometimes in life, there are those moments when everything changes, just like that. This was one of them. The light switched on and I was ready to live a new life.

After 13 years together, now divorced, I sold my stuff to embark on a personal journey to Bali. Everyone thought me crazy, in a reverse-midlife-crisis when, instead of buying a fluro-coloured sports car, I sold it.

I became a self-help junkie – travelling the world, learning from the best entrepreneurial educators – leading me to start Business:Engineered in 2018. Restoring the dream I had for Velocity Consulting: to support and educate founders of fast-growth startups to become happier humans. After reading numerous books, I realized that we are spiritual beings here having a human experience. Many of us, me included, had bought into the bullshit rules of society and we were just going along – like sheep. Building businesses and lives that we should, and that none of it really mattered. What mattered was living life and experiencing the world: enjoying the sunshine, nature, sex....

I started Business:Engineered and created my Life:Engineered program as a reminder to myself to not be one or two dimensional. Life:Engineered is about the six core areas that make you a five dimensional human. Business, Relationships, Wisdom, Health, Adventure and Spirituality. I want to help entrepreneurs and A-type personalities, like me, escape the grind of building businesses based on 'brules' (bullshit rules) and ego.

I have been on a quest for the last two and a half years, to learn how to break the cycle of hustle and learn how to create and cultivate flow. After all, I 100% believe that happiness is the greatest hack to productivity and profitability. If we can build lives that are more aligned with our soul's true purpose, everything we need in life will be realized.

I still struggle daily with the nagging mean-girl voice in my head telling me to be better and that I have not achieved enough. I am a constant work in progress and I have to make sure I'm surrounding myself with other awakened humans, who are willing to have real conversations. The ones who also have the drive, but need the reminder that life is but a game, one that we are meant to enjoy and to LIVE.

The key, I believe, is in the balance. Do the things to build the life you choose but also remember to do the things that truly set your soul on fire.. like dancing in the rain or surfing in the sunshine. Laughing uncontrollably over too many wines or stepping onto a stage to share your message with 600 souls.

It doesn't matter where you've come from, your upbringing, the mistakes you've made or the opportunities you've had. Fact is: "Life is a choice – it is what you choose! Your past does not define you." Nobody else is responsible for making you happy or successful. We all get the same 24 hours in each day – so, go out, grab life by the balls, take hold of what you want, and make it happen. Here's how I put it: JFDI

"Just fucking do it!" I know you can do it, so go DO IT!

IGNITE ACTION STEPS

It's important to set goals and have dreams, but we often look at where we want to be and don't take action. So, how do you go from struggle to success and transform your life? It starts with the first step, just one step at a time. Make a small commitment to yourself and tick it off. Then take another small step. Then another. You should be learning and acting, not always planning for the next 10 years!

Start small and make the commitment to change your morning routine for the first week. The day starts when you open your eyes. To own the day, you need to start in that same moment. When you hit the snooze button, you don't wake up properly. It messes with your sleep cycles. Brain fog hampers your energy and productivity throughout the day.

Just get out of bed. It helps to move your alarm clock to the other side of the room so you need to stand up to turn it off. On the first morning, just aim to get up and have a glass of water. Keep it simple – don't try to go from zero to hero immediately.

The next day, get up, have a glass of water and stretch, have a cold shower, or do some exercise. Do something small you can easily commit to. Getting the dopamine rush from making it happen, means it becomes easier each time you do it.

Add an extra activity to your waking pattern each morning. Before you know it, you'll have a morning routine that energizes and inspires you to make the most of your day.

Once you have a rhythm going, it's easier to show up; step up; find your flow. Find your groove. Create the time and mental space. Take actions towards your dreams.

The hardest part is starting. Most people would get out of bed for $1000. But what's the rest of your life worth? What's your ideal dream life worth? Surely it's worth more than $1000? So it's just about making that commitment. It's about saying "I'm drawing a line in the sand. I choose to get up and do these things."

Where you draw the line in the sand is over to you – life is a choice, it is what you choose!

Jade Green, Chief Life Engineer at Life:Engineered.
lifeengineered.academy

CATHERINE
MALLI-DAWSON

*"The ordinary life we live is an extraordinary adventure if only
we can see the gifts sent to us along the way."*

**My intention in sharing this story is to challenge the concept of good or
bad situations. The labels we apply to our experiences directly influence
the outcome. I encourage you to evaluate the lessons gifted to you from
the Universe in all the myriad ways that those messages come through
and embrace the journey.**

EMBRACING GIFTS FROM THE UNIVERSE

"Is that scale accurate?" I asked timidly and a little hopeful.

"Yes, we have it calibrated monthly," replied Susan, Dr. Adams' Nurse
as she tapped, tapped, tapped the weight further down the scale.

Dr. Adams was a bit nonchalant explaining my results as I sat in stunned
silence. Her words were a fuzzy murmur as she told me I'm 254 pounds
and borderline diabetic, but my blood pressure looked good. Somehow, I
couldn't take solace in that small fact.

Being 6'1" I was able to 'hide' it, but when I look back at pictures
from that time, I realize the only thing I was hiding was my shame and
insecurities. I knew I needed to do something, but I was clearly incapable
of making the changes on my own. The next morning, I stared at myself in

the mirror observing my pale, bloated features, puffy, bloodshot eyes and let my tears fall. I realized I was slipping down the same slow path to an early death my mother had tread. Then I heard my father's condemnation of what I'd let myself become. Fat, bloated, obese, grotesque. "I thought you were better than this. How can you let yourself get so ugly when you were such a beautiful girl?" He would have condemned me with his judgement. I sat down on my bed, curled into a fetal position and sobbed into my pillow.

Then I meditated. I asked the Universe for help, guidance, and poured all my fear, shame, sadness, and anxiety out into its hands. After my tears dried, I put on my 'game face' and drove to work.

About two weeks later I awoke around 2 am, violently ill. Diarrhea, vomiting – yes, at the same time. Knives of pain ripping through my abdomen. My first thought was food poisoning, but not like any I'd encountered previously. I thought back to the lovely dinner I'd enjoyed with my friend. We had cooked our meal at his house, opened a bottle of wine and didn't even finish it, so I knew it couldn't be the food or wine. It must be the flu. It was going around at work and I'd heard it was pretty bad, but I hadn't appreciated just how bad it could be. Yes, I told myself, it must be the flu.

I muddled through the weekend and by Monday, I was feeling good enough to go to work (the diarrhea and vomiting had stopped at least). I'm fairly certain it was due to not eating anything for two days. As I was still having severe cramps in my stomach, I phoned my doctor and made an appointment for the next Friday. After the exam, she noted my blood pressure was a bit elevated, but couldn't find anything obvious. So, as any good practicing physician will do, she ordered blood tests.

Early the next week I got a call with the results. She asked me if I had had anything to drink the night before my blood work. 'No' was my answer. She then proceeded to tell me everything looked normal with one exception. My liver was showing signs of what she described as an 'allergy to alcohol'. She asked me a series of questions all directed at how much alcohol I consume. I could see where this was leading and assured her I've never been a heavy drinker. Not that I didn't go out to have a good time, but I never drank excessively and rarely drank hard liquor - a Sipsmith's Gin and Tonic was the occasional exception. So, this allergy thing was a bit perplexing. I admitted I had noticed, over the past several months, that I was a bit more sensitive to alcohol. I would have one beer or one glass of wine and then have a migraine or intestinal cramps the next day, but I just put that off as stress.

She asked me to abstain from drinking for four weeks and come in for another test. "No problem," I said. Four weeks later, I returned for more tests. The results were actually worse, and I had started experiencing more abdominal cramping around my pancreas and gallbladder. Now she was concerned. She ordered an ultrasound to rule out any abnormalities. No fatty liver, normal spleen, happy pancreas, and smooth gallbladder. All seemed well and normal. She again requested I abstain from alcohol for another four weeks and return for more tests. The end result of all of this testing, poking and prodding, was my liver had stopped processing alcohol. We believe, but can't confirm, that it was the result of taking a prescription medication that had been originally prescribed in 2013 when I had plantar fasciitis on both of my feet (also very painful and a direct result of my ever-increasing girth). I had continued to use the medication because it was a low dose and really helped the pain in my knees, feet, back, joints etc. I had tried several times to stop taking it, but the pain and discomfort were just too debilitating. No label warnings said anything about liver damage, just to watch your kidneys. Apparently, it wasn't my kidneys that needed watching.

Throughout this four-month period, one of the things I had thought would be a silver lining out of the 'no alcohol' situation, was that I would lose a few pounds and step out of my mother's footsteps. However, after four months of continued testing, abstaining from alcohol and really starting to think about my diet, I had only reduced my weight by five pounds which didn't even equate to half a dress size. This left me feeling even more depressed. This whole liver thing clearly wasn't the answer to resolving my weight issue and I again appealed to the Universe for guidance.

The Universe, having a sense of humor, sent me a new gift in June when I came down with an upper respiratory infection. I was so ill, I knew I needed to see a doctor for medication. Working in the healthcare industry, has taught me one thing - you only go to the doctor when you are really, really ill. Everything else can be resolved with chicken soup. I dragged myself into an urgent care clinic, trying desperately not to touch any unnecessary surfaces and avoiding the children in the waiting room. Once in the exam room, the doctor came in, shoved a scope in my ears, peered down my throat and up my nose. He declared I had an upper respiratory infection and handed me three prescriptions. It turns out the antibiotic was one of the 'end spectrum' drugs (meaning it was really powerful and usually only used when all others fail). My doctor instructed me to make sure I take all of them and not to do any exercises, because one of the side effects was torn tendons. I assured her exercise was not on my agenda. I completed my medication and recovered from the infection.

After I had 'recovered', I noticed food was tasteless. Coffee tasted strangely like water. Peanut butter was gooey, oily, and bland. I put it off as congested sinuses from allergies, and side effect over from the infection. Another two weeks later, I was wishing for that bland, tasteless experience. It seemed my taste buds had gone a little wacky with all the medication. Not only could I no longer taste things correctly, but the taste was truly horrid. Well, to be frank, everything tasted like putrefied, like rotten meat. Not what you expect when you stick your favorite snack of celery with peanut butter in your mouth hoping for delectable creamy goodness, only to experience horrible, cloying, sticky, rottenness. I can tell you trying to get peanut butter out of your mouth without swallowing is not an easy task. It involves fingers, gagging, napkins, and ultimately, a deep cleaning with a toothbrush.

I completely lost my appetite and found the only things I could 'safely' eat without gagging was plain lettuce, salmon, and tomatoes only because they all tasted like nothing. I stopped making my morning Starbucks run because the smell was so nauseating, I nearly vomited just getting near the door. My husband, being a coffee aficionado, even had to give up his morning barista duties because I just couldn't stomach the smell of him making our morning lattes. Going to the grocery store became a tortuous exercise. Not only were the smells so overwhelming (I actually left several times without completing my shopping), but nothing was appealing. I didn't know what was 'safe' to eat and what wasn't. Every bite of food was an exercise in curiosity, fear, frustration, anxiety, and rarely relief. I welcomed foods with no taste, because at least I could eat them without gagging.

I muddled through this for a while thinking it would pass. I told myself it was just a lingering effect from the congestion. My husband wasn't sure what to think. While he was very supportive, I'm sure he thought I was having a mental breakdown. After a few more weeks passed and still no change, I again phoned my doctor.

More blood tests, no clear indication of illness. She referred me to an Ear, Nose and Throat Specialist. Another exam, more poking and prodding, again no obvious signs of illness.

Next steps, an MRI.

"Why?" I ask, not really wanting to know.

"Well, it's likely your nasal nerve pads are damaged from the medication; however, we also want to make sure there's no brain tumor or anything…"

"Brain tumor?!?!" "What?" That hadn't even entered my mind as a possibility.

Fortunately, the MRI results were normal. However, this left me with no direction.

"What caused this taste distortion?"

"It could be any number of things. You're 50 years old, it could even be menopause related."

"When will I get my sense of smell and taste back?"

"No idea. It could be three months, six months, or maybe never. Make an appointment in a few months and let's see how you're doing."

I drove home. Tears streaming down my face and fear pounding in my chest. Was this what my life was going to be like from now on? Lettuce, salmon, and tomatoes? Dry - no dressing. Dining out at a nice restaurant was pointless. Cooking was diabolical. What had I done to deserve this and how am I going to survive? Do I really want to live like this the rest of my life?

I carried on for the next few months, testing various food items, spitting most of it out. Returning to my doctor for the follow-up visit, I finally found my silver lining. I stepped on the scale and the nurse only tapped the weight half as far as the previous times. 20 pounds lighter! That's one dress size! Although I hadn't really noticed a difference in my clothes, all the enforced food restrictions had resulted in a calorie reduced diet. Everything again checked out OK and this time as I drove home, I felt a sense of liberation. Instead of thinking about all I had lost (except for the pounds - for that I was celebrating), I started thinking about how this experience had forced me to really examine my relationship with food. My addiction to coffee, sugar, and dairy had been shattered. Mainly because putrefied, rotten meat and rancid baby puke, just aren't that tasty.

As I meditated on this new-found freedom, I reflected on the previous six-month odyssey and realized it had all started when I asked the Universe for help. What I hadn't done was be specific! I decided to embrace the situation, learn from what I was going through and start taking better care of myself. I had already reduced my weight by 20 pounds. I had no idea how long this was going to last or if this was my new normal. I decided it was time to stop feeling sorry for myself, put my big girl pants on and embrace this imposed diet for the gift that it was.

I started exploring healthy options. I doubled down on my meditation practice and became a certified Primordial Sound Meditation instructor. I reconnected with my fitness routine. Then I discovered Eric Edmeades and the WildFit program. When his talk started, I was prepared to see it as just another fad diet trend. However, when Eric explained the WildFit program will recalibrate your taste buds, I took notice. Having been through a distorted and tasteless year of hell, the principles of WildFit really resonated with me. Wanting to at least maintain the progress I had achieved, I started the WildFit 90-day program. Having experienced the previous year in frustration, desperation, and finally inspiration, I was completely open to everything taught in the program and fully embraced the principles. The outcome has given me a new perspective on everything and a desire to share it with others.

Becoming a WildFit coach was a natural progression given all I had been through and could now share with others. WildFit did help me recalibrate my taste buds and while my nerve pads were healing, I was continuing to feed my body healthy, nourishing, fresh options instead of the typical highly processed, plastic food I had been accustomed to. My sense of smell/taste have mostly recovered. Interestingly, I find the things that were the most disgusting during my ordeal, were the things that are the least healthy - dairy, bread, coffee, sweet treats, etc. My body was obviously trying to tell me something. I just needed to learn how to listen.

I've now released over 70 pounds (50 attributed to WildFit). I have more energy than when I was 30 and my husband thinks he's won the lottery with a new and improved wife. I think the new sexy bras and panties help. I meditate daily and have learned to ask for guidance with more specificity, as well as not being attached to the outcome. I've forgiven my mother for not being the role model I needed, knowing that she couldn't give me what she didn't receive herself. I've forgiven my father for his judgemental love and trying to protect me in the only way he knew how. My anger and frustration with my parents were released with 70 pounds of shame and guilt.

My journey started in April 2017 and has really only just begun. The Universe gifted me with an opportunity to renew my life and regain my sense of self. While this experience was incredibly painful and depressing, I now see it as a rebirthing of my true self. I am more confident, healthy and clear in my intentions. Forgiveness and acceptance helped me to shed the 70 pounds. WildFit is helping me move forward and maintain the progress. The Universe is there ready to gift me with guidance whenever I need it.

IGNITE ACTION STEPS

I encourage you to open your heart and mind to all the gifts currently present in your life. Examine the lessons in both the good experiences alongside the more challenging ones. Observe your reactions, thoughts, and feelings to adverse events. The tools that helped me survive were key to my success.

• Forgiveness - for myself and those who love me; letting go of perceived past hurts.

• A strong support system of family and friends - I included them in my odyssey without becoming a victim.

• Meditation - I dug deep to understand the lessons gifted to me through this experience and sought solace when there was little to be found.

• WildFit - I found a health program that resonated with me and helped me truly transform my life so I am now able to make mindful, conscious decisions about my health and nutrition.

Without these four elements, I'm afraid I may not have survived my tasteless year. I encourage you to find the tools that will help you survive any adverse situations, take control of your life, be specific in what help you're asking for and be open to what comes. There are always positive lessons in every experience.

Catherine Malli-Dawson, Founder & CEO of LifeWhys LLC.
www.lifewhysllc.com

SUZANNE HALL

"When your heart feels fractured, be open and curious.
It lets the magic flow in"

Our worst and most helpless experiences, if we are curious, can be the catalyst that propels us into the life of our dreams. My hope is that my story inspires you, that whenever you're struggling, be curious, be open, wait for the light and the magic to find you. Even if it's a flicker, stay open and it will flow right in and transform you.

THE MAGIC OF YOU IS ALWAYS IN YOU

It was the early 1980s. I had a huge vision for my life. I'd be an artist, shocking people into new ways of thinking. I'd be a modern-day Joan of Arc, or Boadicea, a fierce red-headed woman who united the British tribes against the Roman Empire. I wanted to heal the world.

My reality was somewhat different.

At 20, I'd become unexpectedly pregnant with a man I didn't love or know very well. Just before the birth, it became clear that there were some serious issues and a total lack of support. It wasn't looking good. The stress and anger directed towards me just before, during, and after my baby was born were unlike anything I'd imagined.

Two weeks after my baby arrived, I lay sobbing on the floor, a new mom at 21, with a choice to stay with a difficult, unsupportive partner, and still have to create a living, or be a solo mum on welfare.

I thought I could somehow fix the unhealthy relationship, even fix the hints of violence and lack of support. After all, I had set out to heal the world; why couldn't I heal my relationship? I was bone tired as only new mums can be and I felt deep, deep sadness and utter hopelessness. This was not what I'd planned for my life. The awful feelings overwhelmed me. Every pain I had ever felt welled to the surface, all together, bubbling over in a confused mess. The deep love I felt for my child brought forth a comparison, and the realisation of how I felt such a lack of love from my parents, and now my partner. The pain amplified with me seeing my many mistakes, bad decisions, laziness, and stupid careless things I'd done to friends. It all spilled over in agonising hurt. My whole body was shaking, I'd never sobbed so loudly and deeply, ever.

Thankfully, my baby slept. As the sobbing subsided, I felt this spark inside... a tiny light that slowly grew and became brighter, with sound and colour that permeated every cell of my body. I felt like I was shining and glowing with light. I remember so clearly hearing my inner voice say, "Okay Suzanne – what are you going to do about it? Life has changed. You can wallow or you can take action! You are exactly where you led yourself, so find out why!".

At that moment, something awakened that I'd never felt before – something that has never left me – a fierce sense that there is always a way; there is a calling within us all that leads us to our true destiny. I don't think I could have explained that at the time, but something shifted within every part of me.

I grabbed a big piece of paper and wrote down every skill I had, what I was curious and passionate about, all my personality flaws, everything I could think of that was part of who I was. Over the next four hours, things intersected, a picture started to form.

What poured in was magic. It was in that moment, that day – the idea to create the world's most natural skin care began. My first business was born.

My beautiful baby woke, and the world had forever changed for me.

From that moment in time, I've never again had to find motivation; despite exhaustion, every part of me suddenly had purpose. Being that frustrated, angry, fearful, and allowing it, somehow opened me up. The awful relationship was one of the sparks that ignited a whole new path for my life.

What followed was massive action, fired up by the vision. I took every moment I could, to work towards this idea. This was before home computers, cell phones and Google. So, I explored. Asked many questions. Little did I know, I was in a flow state of soaking up as much knowledge as possible.

This passion of creating, dimmed the difficult relationship and made things somehow bearable. He was a devoted dad and for some time things stayed calm. I was still trying to fix things and make us into a happy family and thought if we had another child somehow it would help. Along came my second child, a beautiful daughter, alert and smart right from the start. With a baby and a two-year-old, sometimes carrying one in a front pack and the other on my back, I kept working on bringing my business into fruition.

The relationship just kept getting worse and the violent episodes closer. Everyone around knew what was happening, but I felt unable to leave, not wanting the children to come from a broken home, not understanding that our home was already broken. One side of my life was so toxic, while the other with my children and business, was filled with joy. Things were starting to bloom in the business, and somehow (truthfully I don't know how because by this stage we hardly talked to one another) I was pregnant again. Three kids under five, a business taking off, and I wore a mask out in the world, pretending everything was ok. Most nights I would work in my lab formulating, while the children were asleep, which gave room for the light inside to grow bright again. Hearing the magic in the night, allowed me to feel the certainty of my path.

It took 11 years to leave the toxic relationship. I struggled on a daily basis to hide how awful it was. I put my energy into my children, and the vision, holding onto an idea that somehow I could make everything right. I wonder now how many women are doing that? With my children 3, 5 and 7, the nightmare of custody battles, and sometimes even fighting for my life, began. The business was sabotaged, and I had to start again hiding what was happening in my personal life from the world.

My story isn't about a bad relationship, it's about the gems that came from a difficult situation. If he had been a loving supportive partner, I may never have had that first "ignite-moment". The situation created a perfect storm for me to evolve and set me on a path that has felt so right. I developed a much deeper compassion for women and sometimes men, trapped in such situations. I understand how people can stay in violent situations, I understand some people's (usually women) need to fix everything. These have made me a much better person. As well as my children, many valuable things were born from that difficult decade.

I so often see women being the best mother they can be, juggling parental responsibilities, while building a business. Especially in a world where so many parents are single and trying to manage everything.

I still have so many moments of guilt and to this day my adult children still hold my feet to the fire. No financial support, no good parenting role models, a partner with a mental illness, and trying to build a business that would provide for all of us – it was really hard. If I had to do it again, I'd have bundled up my children sooner and ran for the hills.

Once I left, I realised how much of a shadow I'd been living under. Now there was freedom to forge ahead. I'd forgotten how to laugh. The vision for the business kept me moving forward, despite massive financial challenges. I have so many dear friends who helped, who had seen the struggles, and were so happy to see me begin again. Their kind deeds were like a lifeboat in a really stormy sea. I hope those friends still know how much I value them and how without them, I would not have survived. Those friends who were amazing mums were my role models. It inspired me to create a world where single mums could thrive and those in hard relationships could have an alternative.

I started everything again and built the world of Living Nature into a rich company. The teams we built, the majority being single mums, were strong. So many people advised that having so many single mums was dangerous and what an unreliable workforce. The opposite was true! The main thing that created the success was the amazing work ethics of those women; their humour and staunchness. Together we created something really special. We were pioneers.

Over the next 20 years, the business gained global recognition and earned international awards. We exported to 14 countries, achieving a 20 million turnover with a staff of over 100. However, the greater accomplishment was staff and management creating a culture of personal evolvement. That culture was just as important as the growth of the business, if not more so, as it was the foundation of the success.

Holding the vision is my best quality; I had no management skills or experience. Although I struggle with consistency, I'm a great problem-solver and love to formulate and design. Everyone in the business had an important role and knew they were valued. The next 10 years were some of the best in my life. Our success just kept growing. Help turned up when I clearly asked the universe for it. The first god-sent shareholder gave support on many levels; I will forever appreciate how they added to the vision. After this first experience, more mentors came into my life, who had their own huge visions.

After 20-plus years, I was happy that the business had grown. I made a decision to leave at the peak of success; to see what other ways I could impact the world. By this stage, I had a cocky attitude that I could do anything. I just had to apply the same formula, and everything would work out.

Another life lesson for me!

After exiting, I had planned to have a year off, but within a few weeks, there was a new puzzle in front of me. One of the banks called and asked if I would be interested in contracting to help them build their culture. They were doing a lot of engagement activities and weren't getting the traction they expected. Having read media accounts about how the human resource culture funded the success of Living Nature, they wondered if any insights could be transferable. Once again, I had no skills, but I was fiercely interested, and immediately said "Yes!"

I'd never worked in a corporate situation. I soon discerned the bank people were swamped, stressed, and exhausted. The more the company tried to engage them, the more overwhelmed they became. They were willing, but not able.

The challenge was clear. How could we build tools that could help build resilience; small habits that could increase energy, motivation and health? How could we put those tools at everyone's fingertips? Technology seemed the obvious choice. This was nearly 10 years ago, before smartphones and apps – it's so hard to imagine those days now.

The compassion and empathy I developed in my first business became a trait of my second business.

My life at this stage was really happy; I'd created a beautiful home; my children were almost adults; I'd exited well from my business, and I had this new challenge to solve. I'd got back that spark I'd had as a teenager and thought I could heal the world. I had no idea that some of my biggest challenges lay ahead. While I'd began Living Nature with lab skills, a good sense of design, and a passion for natural health, starting a technology company was complex. I didn't even know the language.

I created a new vision called Be Intent… an app to give people a tool that made it easier to be their best selves. I wanted corporations to acknowledge that staff are, first of all humans, sometimes fragile, with complex lives. The challenges of creating and building a skincare company were simple by comparison. In many ways the success I had just come from was a stumbling block. Looking back, I abandoned the process and wisdom I'd applied to my first venture. If I had to do it again, I would find a coach to help me build a new set of muscles and skills.

I'd put out into the universe that I wanted a challenge, and she sure delivered. Technology was changing faster than we could develop; people were not open to mindfulness and positive psychology; I needed changing skill sets within the team. I'd used the same process for choosing key staff I had with my first endeavour, thinking we'd learn on the job together, but that didn't work. My lack of knowledge of the industry just hobbled our progress. This business idea needed the best in the business; it took me years, and all my resources to figure that out.

I felt this burning vision more strongly than ever for Be Intent to succeed, but it kept being just out of reach… three steps forward and four steps back. The global economy had crashed; my target market of corporates was not spending on wellbeing. I was funding the business out of dwindling savings. At the same time, I was fielding some amazing business opportunities, that didn't always come to fruition, (though just enough to be tantalizing). The more we learned, the more complex the tool became. It is now a world-first platform that on a daily basis, is a pulse for how people are feeling, how they want to feel; a raft of incredible data that enables resources to be used more effectively.

Amongst this fascinating challenge, I was really struggling on so many levels. Everyone thought I was mad to continue. Each day I would meditate – the answer would come back strong – I was on the right path. There is a fine line between holding the faith and knowing when to let go. I knew we had something worth holding onto.

I am ever thankful for the shareholders who came into the business. Who shared the idea of a tool designed so corporations could have compassion built into how they operated? Even now, I struggle under the extra pressure for the business to perform, not realising that earlier we were well ahead of our time and I hadn't assembled the right team for each stage of the business. Getting a return to shareholders can be a heavy burden for a founder to carry. It's something that I was and still am aware of with every action, every day. When your business is growing and evolving, at a slower pace than anticipated, satisfying shareholder expectations can be a constant pressure that impacts on the business. I wonder; how many great ideas fail because of this?

If I had to do things again, of course, I would do them differently, so the best I can do is share my learnings with you. I've even begun another skincare company called 'Power', but that's another story.

It feels like I've gone through the dark ages and have come out into the light. As the world is now actively looking for resilience and mindfulness tools, our years of testing and positive results have become the foundation of a tool for change. The breadth of our reach is from school age to all ages and life paths. We are like a kind, wise friend helping people make better small decisions each day towards building their best self. It's like a manifestation of my early years, wanting to help the world, but now even bigger and clearer.

We are working with the innovative New Zealand government, who are focusing on youth mental wellbeing and suicide prevention, combined with our desire to disrupt ineffective patterns and create social change. The vision has become even stronger and I know we will be part of a brighter future for humanity.

As I look back to 45 years ago – to that girl who wanted to heal the world – I'm proud of her and how she grew from the many challenges she has overcome. As a grandmother of three amazing beings, I'm still on that track to create social change. I have a whole raft of loving, inspiring and hard-working people around me sharing that vision. Many of them are in this book. My journey so far has been a blessed one. Every hardship or obstacle is a gift of understanding that helps me shine a light and guide others on their journey to a life well lived. My hope is that even in your darkest hour, you too find your light and magic.

IGNITE ACTION STEPS

Here are a couple of daily actions that really make a difference:

At the Start of your Day: Dedicate a minimum of 20 minutes a day to yourself, even if you have to get up earlier. Decide carefully what you do in that time. Use it to center yourself and be totally present, whether it's gently breathing; looking at the sky; dancing to your favourite music; writing in your journal. Value yourself and give yourself that time. It signals to your subconscious that you are important.

At the End of Your Day: again, take a moment to check in with yourself. What are two things you did well? What is one thing you will do better tomorrow? Write them down or use our Be Intent tool to keep a record. Your brain recognises success and feels good. When you switch off for the night, you will feel prepared for constant evolution.

We've spent 10 years identifying all the small actions you can take each day to achieve peace of heart and solid success and built them into our Be Intent tool. Which you're welcome to use – just login to the business area with the code ignite and enjoy.

Suzanne Hall, MNZM. www.beintent.com

HELLE BRODIE

"Freedom is found in what you believe. Choose to be free!"

My intention is to reveal that many of our beliefs – most of which were instilled in us by others, can prevent us from feeling true internal freedom. We must embrace our authentic selves and find our internal freedom by releasing old beliefs that no longer serve us. My story here is one of many of my life's freedom journeys.

BOYS ARE BETTER THAN GIRLS. OR ARE THEY?

I grew up with the belief 'boys are better than girls', without even knowing it! This belief held me prisoner for 45 years. I am eternally grateful for the journey of awakening that has crumbled this belief giving me the freedom to be who I really am.

As I was growing up, most world leaders were men. Men held all the 'important' jobs. They were the breadwinners, decision-makers and leaders.

I remember my mother saying:

Look at what your brother is doing

Your brother is good at so many things

Your brother is so smart

He is so strong

He has so many friends

It's true he had all of these attributes. I didn't take this as him being better than me. He was older and I aspired to be more like him. The undertone to these praises seeded the belief: boys are better than the girls. I wanted to be like that too!

Laura, a teenage neighbour ten years older than me had beautiful long hair; she was pretty and sexy and really cool! She gave us (the neighbourhood kids) a Beatles record that we cherished, just because it was Laura's. If she listened to Eight Days a Week then that's what we wanted to listen to. We gathered a few neighbourhood friends to form a rock band. We had hours and hours of fun learning the lyrics and pretending to be a famous. We played that song on our cheap record player, until the old 45 started to skip from being overplayed!

These were the days before the internet, so we had no idea what the Beatles looked like or who was in the band. Of course, the lead singer and the other musicians were all boys. The girls were only there to dance, play the tambourine and look pretty. This seemed in synch with how the world worked: you had to be a boy to do important things.

I remember, when things didn't go well in my family it was always my father who made it right. He was the one to please, the one to fear, he made the rules, and was our provider. He was our rock. He was larger than life! He was our leader.

I had no idea that these experiences were all creating this belief that boys are better than girls.

I felt inadequate and un-valuable, just because I was a girl. The adults seemed to praise the boys, and the boys teased us for being sissies. I wanted to be as good as they were. I certainly didn't want to be a sissy! I became a tomboy. I wanted to play boys' games, so I joined a hockey team. I became very competitive. I learned to walk and talk like the boys. I even learned how to fight like the boys. I took it one step further. I learned to hide my emotions or to pretend they didn't exist because that's what the boys did. I became tough on the outside. I hid my softer, more feminine side.

No more frilly dresses. I shopped in the boys' section. I bought clothes that made me look like a boy. I even shopped in second hand stores for that tough and worn-in look.

When I went off to University, I met the man I would marry. We played broom hockey. We drank tequila on Friday nights with his buddies and played billiards at the pool hall. We always hung out with the guys. Great for him! He hung out with his friends and enjoyed benefits on the side. I didn't see any great women out there. I wasn't exposed to them.

Then he was accepted into the Optometry program and I was expected to join the 'Optometry Wives Club'. These women spent hours talking about how they supported their husbands in school. They prepared meals, did the cleanup and helped with their studies. They worshipped the ground their husbands walked on with no visible identity or personal goals. Their entire purpose in life was to support their husbands. No way I was going to participate in that. I had a brain AND goals. I was more like the guys. I wasn't going to cave or conform to these women's ideals! I was NOT going to cave to the pressures of fitting in with these women! I was not like them.

I embarked on a career in a male-dominated industry: the design and construction industry. There are many more women in this field today. It wasn't always that way. Despite the significant design component to Landscape Architecture, it was still about strong men building things. I thought they were strong in the early days.

I started my own business when my son was born – again, not the typical path, but then I was not typical. I was grateful my clients didn't know I was a woman. I thought because they didn't know my little secret, my firm would have more opportunities for growth and success. When my clients found out later that I was a woman with an unusual name, they would already know I could get the job done, so my gender wouldn't matter. Clearly, my belief was very deeply ingrained. I was doing a great job of fooling myself.

My daughter was born 16 months later, four weeks early. I remember calling a client from the hospital, telling him that I could not meet his deadline. I heard an unmistakable tone of disappointment in his voice. He clearly would not have had this problem if he had hired a man.

I finished the work, meeting his deadline when my daughter was 2 weeks old. She slept in a crib in my office. I ate when she ate and got back to 'real work' when she was ready for a nap.

After 20 years of marriage, I left my husband. My mother insisted my life would be difficult. I would be cast out. I would be poor, and I would be lonely. Surely, I could put up with whatever was wrong as long as there wasn't an affair - her only justification for leaving a marriage. That was her pain, not mine. I wanted equality! Not just housework and cooking and raising the children on my own, while working on my business on the side.

I moved myself and my two wonderful children back to my hometown. I purchased a 'handyman special' (a phrase for a house needing immediate renovations) and ran my business out of the basement apartment. It was all I could afford. Mom was right in some ways. It really was tough. I needed to be close to my young teenage kids. They needed their mom and some sense of security: to know that somehow, everything was going to be alright. I juggled being a mother a breadwinner and an entrepreneur. I was tough. I could do this!

As my business grew, I began to hire people. I remember interviewing someone who could help take my little business to the next level. I was ecstatic! I made the job offer and prepared myself for incredible success. She turned me down!! She didn't think I was serious enough about my career because I was running the business out of an apartment in my house while being a mom to my two kids who were upstairs. It felt like she took a wrecking ball to my dreams! So much for support and comradery from other women! I felt betrayed. I withdrew even further from women.

It seemed women were trying to gain success at each other's expense to get ahead in this man's world. There was so much cattiness and backstabbing everywhere.

I learned to keep my communications brief, to the point, and void of emotion - just like the men. It was all about business and getting the job done. I wore suits or pants because dresses and feminine things didn't belong on construction sites. Job sites were about work boots, construction hats and safety gear. I drove an SUV – it suited my image. I was the breadwinner of the family and I had an image to uphold.

On a personal level, I renovated my 'handy-man special'. I taught myself to use power tools, to hang and tape drywall. I even did most of the plumbing and wiring. There was nothing that a man could do that I couldn't do. Though I felt strong and capable, I didn't realize then, where I was headed.

Despite all my achievements, I began to realize I really wasn't happy. I got in touch with wanting someone to be there for me and to help with some heavy chores. I was lonely and alone. Even more so as my male friends were getting married. They feared their wives/girlfriends might become jealous. My wonderful children had left home for University. Sure, I had career success and raised two incredible kids. I had feelings and emotions, a need to connect with people and a softer side I was afraid to show anyone. Because of course if you're strong, you don't have those softer sides.

I tried to connect with other women. I found that they were busy with their husbands or their work. It seemed they didn't have time for someone like me.

A male friend of mine suggested I join a women's club where successful women, business owners and entrepreneurs connected. At first, I was excited! I would finally make some new connections with like-minded women. After rejection, criticism and being let down by women, I had some serious doubts and no faith or trust. Was it really going to be as good as I imagined? Would I finally have a place where I fit in?

As I got involved in activities at the club, I saw these powerful and successful women expressing their emotions: happy, sad, excited, and everything in between. I noticed how they supported each other and how they could talk about anything! I started to connect with emotions that I had buried for so many years! Joy and happiness, support and comradery, pain and sadness – I felt it all! As I began bonding with the more feminine side of myself, I even bought a few dresses. Suddenly it felt awesome to be a woman. Feminine, emotional, sexy, supportive, and successful. But it also felt so very unfamiliar. Was it really OK to be this way? To be free with your emotions, to be authentic to these emotions? To be intuitive and creative and supportive? To just be? Could you really be successful and do all of this too?

I connected with other women while working out in the mornings at the club gym. We would talk about life and work, about challenges and successes. Always supporting without judgement. Knowing the more we helped each other, the more we would all grow and the more we could support each other. I even learned it's OK to cry. These women had no shame in displaying their emotions. I started to believe it was possible! I awakened to a side of women I had never seen before. A combination of independence, trust, intelligence, support, and community. These women had my back, and I had theirs.

Together we were creating the shift in consciousness in the world that is so needed for us to live in peace and harmony. We don't have to do everything with force. We don't have to compete for everything. We can take action and create change by working together in powerful, peaceful, loving, supportive ways, simply by being who we truly are.

I now know these women exist everywhere because they just show up in my life. The crazy part is they have always been there. I just didn't see them. The best part is that we are growing in numbers! Successful women who feel the need to connect and support each other, instead of competing, doubting, and outdoing each other. So, my life continues to transform, feeling the freedom to really be myself, the woman that I am.

I now know my mistaken belief was so deeply ingrained in my being that it affected almost every corner of my life. I'm on a freedom journey and will continue to grow for many years to come. I now recognize that little voice in my head that used to criticise women for being weak and helpless - all the things I heard when I was young. I can challenge that voice with acceptance of my feminine, loving, supportive, and caring side.

Boys are not better than girls. We are just different. My mother taught me the values that had been instilled in her: that men are stronger than women. Yet she was an engineering technician, my grandmother was a lawyer. (Unheard of in her time.) Two strong women in the man's world. Yet they grew up with these crazy, mixed up beliefs – society's beliefs. Beliefs so strong you might even think they were passed down through our genes! I now see how strong they actually were to achieve what they did in their time. Yet they still carried the mistaken beliefs that somehow, they were not as good as the men around them.

I followed in my mother's and grandmother's footsteps taking on a career associated with the construction industry. In fact, it was encouraged that I do something 'important' with my life. Even though they were so strong, they had no idea that they were passing on beliefs that we are second best. Beliefs I'd have to challenge and resolve for myself.

I'm now changing the cycle that has been established for the women in my family for three generations! Maybe more. We all need to change this cycle. As women, we often don't even realize that we have that deeply ingrained belief that somehow boys or men are better than we are. That we must compete with them and each other to prove ourselves. And so, we perpetuate that cycle without even knowing it.

It doesn't have to be that way. We can embrace who we are. We can challenge those beliefs. We can create support and community and connection. We can bring humanity back into the world.

As women, it's time for us to take that leadership role. To share centre stage and really create a shift in the Universe. I'm not talking about pushing men aside or making them out to be bad or wrong. I'm talking about loving them for who they are and taking our rightful place in being co-creators of this world through embracing our womanhood. It is only when we do these things that we become truly free.

We've moved into an era in which emotional intelligence and building community are as important, or possibly even more important than the hard skills. We are shifting from the competitive model to a cooperative model in this connected age. In other words, these feminine qualities are what we all need for the healing and growth of society. These talents come so naturally to women, if we allow them. In order to succeed in all areas of our lives and to be truly free, we all need to accept and embrace our softer sides and to let go of misguided beliefs.

It's only through changing ourselves that we can help those that we love and those that follow us. We owe it to ourselves to understand and free ourselves so that we might change and accept ourselves in a truly authentic way. We owe it to our daughters, and our daughter's daughters. We also owe it to our sons, so that each generation can live in greater harmony than the last.

IGNITE ACTION STEPS

• Set for yourself a task: listening to your inner voice. It's so simple, it can be done 24-7. Whenever you are doing something where your mind can wander, check in on your inner voice. Listen to what it's saying. Is it supporting the beliefs that you value or the beliefs that no longer serve you? Is it telling you that boys are better than girls? Or is it telling you we all have strengths that we should honor?

• Whenever you start feeling uncomfortable or stuck in a situation, tap into that inner voice. Maybe it's showing you the way to uncover yet another belief that no longer serves you.

• Ask Yourself: Is that voice telling me the truth? Or Is it telling me something I have been led to believe is true? Is it supporting beliefs I value?

It's so simple I found it hard to believe it could work. I listened and challenged that voice and transformed myself and my life. You can do the same.

Step on your path to true freedom. Embrace the journey!

Helle Brodie, Mentor, Coach, and Speaker. Freedom Journeys.
Freedomjourneys.ca

SHANNON SILVERMOON

"Face your shadows, stare them down, feel into them.
Break free from the silence and cycle of repression."

Sweeping important issues and emotions under the rug will create the very thing you are hiding from! I am passionate about showing others the power of healing the past by changing patterns and beliefs. Surround yourself with supportive people: trained professionals, ministers, witchy friends...and God. End the cycle, heal yourself, your ancestors and your future generations.

REPRESSION LEADS TO AGGRESSION

"Stop it! Leave her alone! Stop it, leave her alone!"

It was the first time I had ever done Ayahuasca, a powerful South American healing medicine used under the guidance of a Shaman. I was expecting colors, fractals, insights and instant healing. Instead I laid on the floor on a mattress in the pitch-dark room with six other women feeling the plant medicine mildly coarse through my body. I felt warm and fuzzy, my head was light and airy. It felt like I was on mushrooms but without the intense psychedelic colors and giddy hysterical laughing; all I felt was a sense of bewilderment.

Who was saying this, why were they saying this, is this voice just going to say that all night? It was the voice of a child, an echo from the past. A memory I had repressed for almost 40 years seemed to be bubbling to the surface. I was in shock. How could I have not looked at this memory before? how could I just forget it that easily?

That's exactly what I was taught to do. Don't talk about it. Sweep it under the rug. Move on.

Most of my memories are hazy and faded. However, I remember the beginning and the end of this trauma clearly; only the middle is fuzzy. I was 5 years old at the time. Mom had left Dad for the first time, embarking on a 13-hour journey to my Grandparents home. Devastated, I stared out the back-seat window of the car watching the familiar street fade away. I wasn't even given the option to stay with my Dad.

My sister and I spent that summer playing around my grandparents' neighborhood. I met the boy across the street and started spending time with him, even if I was teased by my family that I had a boyfriend. His house had a large treed backyard that was fun to play in, but I felt less comfortable inside where it felt dark and dank, smelling like stale cigarettes and mold.

On the day we went in to play in his room, I remember the second floor smelled better. His bedroom had more light. He suggested we do what they do on TV and lay on each other naked. I took off my white summer dress with small purple flowers on it and he laid on top of me. We had no idea what to do next, but we didn't have much time to think about it, before his very large and enraged father burst into the room.

At one point, I remember hiding under the bed but at another I was in the closet peering through the slats of the door at a mad man with long scraggly grayish, yellow hair, beard and a large bare-chested pot belly. He looked like Santa Claus gone wrong. I don't know what he did but it was violent, and I blocked out whatever that was.

Suddenly, I was in the kitchen having an out-of-body experience. I saw angry Santa use his blue phone with the long blue cord mounted on the wall to call my folks across the street saying I was a bad dirty girl. I was being sent home now! With my head hung low, I was kicked out of the house feeling so much shame.

My five-year-old self walked across the street, only to find no one seemed to care. I don't remember being asked what happened, only that I was teased for having my pants down with the neighbour boy. It was swept under the rug. Like everything else.

The only processing I had was sneaking away with the little boy the next day; we just sat side by side on a flight of abandoned cement steps leading to nowhere in the overgrown lot next door holding hands, our heads bowed comforting each other. I felt so sad for him, I never once thought about myself.

Suddenly we were back where we started, back to the drinking, the instability, the yelling and partying. Mom would give Dad the silent treatment. Dad, instead of beating his wife found it easier to push around and bully a child. That was me. When my fragile middle sibling was born 15 months after me, she became the novelty, the petite prettier model. I was pushed aside by my mother. When my third sibling arrived, Dad had his 'boy' and I felt even less like I belonged or was wanted.

I became the family scapegoat. More of Mom and Dad's frustrations came my way. Mom shamed me for waiting hours at the front window for Dad. I resented her for sending me to my room, excluding me from my sister and mother's bonding activities. Her excuse for hitting me with the plastic spatula, was that physically disciplining me worked for Dad. I was seen as the rebellious one, the independent, strong one. Now I see I was acting out my pain, masking how I felt inside.

Worst of all, Mom never talked to us about anything. No one did. No one talked to us about how we felt with the separations or how was school today? They knew I was angry but just passed me off to a counselor or two because they didn't know how to talk to me.

My parents dulled their pain with drugs and alcohol, eating and sex, moving and moving and moving again. I attended 13 different schools in 12 years. During March break in my grade six year, Dad technically kidnapped us kids, Along with five German Shepherds and Dad's girlfriend Faith, we drove across the country in a Ford pickup truck.

The one constant I had was my sister. She was my only friend; the only one who never bullied me. Someone I could talk to. I was always the fat new kid in every school and either I had my jacket stuffed in a boys toilet or was shamed by the whole class for my weight. I took it out on the other kids by throwing rocks at boys who bothered my sister or punched a girl in the stomach for calling my dad a drunk. How she knew, I will never know.

As much as I hated the repression that was passed down I became my own worst enemy; I ended up doing the very thing I hated in my parents. I ate, drank and smoked. I did drugs and brought men home from the bar or worse; just had sex in the car outside the bar. I felt my only worth was through my sexual prowess. I didn't know how to communicate with men. I didn't know how to communicate with anyone. Dad warned me that men only wanted one thing and to keep a nickel between my knees, whereas men were all assholes in the eyes of my mother.

So, I did the opposite, I put every man on a pedestal, gave them what they wanted and was crushed when they turned out to be exactly what my parents predicted. After an abortion at 17 and pregnant again at 19, with rainbow hair and tattoos, I did the best I could at being a single mom. I read to him every night, took him to soccer, scouts and the park regularly, laughed and went camping and took road trips as much as we could, but my selfish wild ways and deep insecurities were always present, and my own repressions caught up with me. I finally had to look at how I was carrying them forward.

It came to a head when a painfully deep incident happened in the family. I had to look at who I was in my role as a mother, sister and daughter. My family was torn apart; sides were taken. Court and counseling ensued. My heart was broken. My sister and I could barely speak to each other, our bond now severed. My brother disowned my son and I. Most everyone else was stunned and shocked and tried their best to support us, some more than others.

On the first-year anniversary since the incident, our father died. He wasn't found for three days. They said it was a heart attack due to drugs and alcohol, and the stress of northern, winter long-haul truck-driving. I personally think grief from his family falling apart and guilt from his past haunted him which played a big part. It was all too much. After his death, it was all too much for me as well. Not only had we been shunned, I had now lost my father who I loved, hated and yearned for, yet was one of my only supports.

It was time, I was lost, I was broken, I could barely keep it together... I went to counseling. The repression had to stop... NOW!!

I have no idea how I got her information, but she sounded good and affordable and I was desperate; I needed something for my sanity. She was a minister through the Centre for Spiritual Living Science of Mind, a church I never knew existed.

When I was eight, I joined a Christian after-school youth group, although we never went to church or had any spiritual teachings growing up. The most I remember was my father saying all you need to know from the bible is to treat others how you want to be treated and to respect your elders.

I was always curious about God and the metaphysical. In my late teens, early 20s my curiosity was ignited again when I came across powerful spiritual books. However, being a young single mom surviving on her own was more important than finding God and so God took a back seat.

My counsellor and I spent two or three years getting to the root of the dysfunctions in my past, so we could see how they carried into my present. The first time she guided me into a meditation where we went looking for my inner child, I was so disconnected. I could hardly look at my young self; she was so far away... we had a lot of work to do to heal the hurt.

She got me through those very difficult years of my breakdown. I kept it together enough to get by with work and responsibilities but my relationship with my son was deteriorating. He was bringing his shame, regret, worthlessness, rejection, and sadness into his teenage years.

He eventually dropped out of school because of his depression and guilt. It was difficult to watch but since I was still not fully healed myself, we fought regularly. I'm grateful to have him alive today, thanks to his counselling and programs. He also knew I was doing the work and would be devastated without him. I needed to show him another way. I needed to learn how to talk to him. I needed to learn how to talk about our family and all of the hurtful things. I couldn't bear for him to have to endure silence and avoiding issues and repeating the same patterns as I had in my family. I didn't want to pass one more minute of repression on to him!

My counsellor introduced me to the S.O.M. church and eventually I became a pop-in attendee on Sundays. I began looking at the centre's classes and workshops which propelled me into my real transformation and growth. This was the year I arranged to marry and commit to my own self. My S.O.M. counselor and my witchy Pagan friend jointly officiated the ceremony for me on my 39th birthday. My friends watched my son walk me, arm in arm, down the aisle with my father's ring on his pinky finger as I recited vows, walked around the fire, cut cords and honored the commitment I was making to myself.

As I write this, I am in awe of how God works as I am coming up to the five-year anniversary of my wedding to myself, when this book will be released. In those five years of commitment, I was shocked to learn how the power of my thoughts and beliefs ruled my world. I did intense inner child work crying, wailing, screaming and throwing journals across the room.

I traveled the world staying in hostels and hitchhiking across Israel, Jordan, Cambodia, Thailand, Ireland, Scotland, as well as all of Central America to find out how the rest of the world worked and who I was in this world.

I lived in my camper van for three years being the hippy I always wanted to be. I became a hot yoga junkie, painted, hosted meditation art workshops, and face painted at festivals. I did multiple soul retreats, sweat lodges and ceremonies around the world to still and calm a mind that was out of control and self-absorbed.

Through hardships on the home-front, adventures on the road, head-under-the-cover days and singing from the rooftop days I have found God. The Source of all that is – is working through me, as me and in me.

I found God as I rolled into Guatemala at 9 pm, with only $1 and nowhere to stay. I found God following my heart to Bridgids garden in Ireland when it was closing in five minutes, only to crash an Irish wedding that night before my 6 am flight the next day. I found God within myself, while Meditating for ten days. I was rewarded with a private Thai dance on the balcony at night over the lights of Chaing Mai. I found God in Thailand, feeling my Harley-riding father's spirit with me, as I repeated over and over, "I am safe. I am good." while riding a scooter down steep treacherous roads. I found God in sunsets and unexpected interactions with strangers. I found God in unexpected money, when I signed up for a class I couldn't afford. I found God in a lover showing me who I am in relationships. I found God in challenging ego-busting situations and in sweet, peaceful moments.

I am working from the inside out, not the outside in. I take responsibility for how I experience every moment now and the Universe rewards me. I let go of my illusion of control and my expectations of, -how a loving family unit should be, -how my son should act, -what society says a relationship should look like. Releasing allows me to focus on the present not what I think the outcome should be. Now, I accept myself for who I am – not allowing myself or others to peg-hole me into a role that no longer fits.

I needed to be brave. I faced my ego. I faced how I judged others and how I thought they judged me. I used bravery to reach out for help. I found healthy professionals and non-judgemental friends who allowed a safe space to grow and heal so that I could do some serious inner reflection and awareness.

Passion fueled by my hatred for ignoring the elephant-in-the-room has made me look at everything! I feel proud and strong, knowing I'm doing my part to break the cycle of repression, healing the ancestral line for past family and future generations to come. You have that same power, passion and desire to make an impact - make the change. Stop the cycle.

Ignite Action Steps

1. Automatic Writing: (Buy a journal that is pretty and appealing to write in. Invest in yourself!) Be alone, really alone. No distractions, no electronics,

no lovers. I had to dig deep and really feel my hurts and wounds. Sit and really listen to your inner child asking her how she is feeling and what she needs and wants. Meditation is a good start to clear the busy mind. The best way I found to communicate was through journaling. Write, write what you can't say to the world, write all your taboos and secrets. Record your dreams, they are subconsciously speaking to you. Stuffing the thoughts, emotions and feelings is repression; this is a safe way of releasing the damn! Next, ask yourself how you are feeling. Stop. Switch the pen to your non dominant hand and wait. It may be hard to write but get your mind out of the way. The ego will try to control your response, don't think-write!

Use your dominant hand to ask questions, "How are you feeling, I'm sorry you feel that, what do you want or need?"

Let the non-dominant hand say whatever comes up. No judgement. This is a safe space. If she is angry, give her space and love her no matter what. Use the dominant hand to reassure and nurture her that it's ok to be angry. If she is sad, find out what she needs at this moment. This is an ongoing conversation between you both. A conversation that you may never had had as a child.

Are you having trouble getting it out as words? Grab a paintbrush. Let her pick the colours with your non-dominant hand and only use that side without any judgement as to how the painting will turn out. Ask questions and don't be afraid to let her angrily slap the black or red paint everywhere. Be prepared to get messy! This is your child after all. You are giving her a chance to speak or express herself in ways that you or other adults may not have allowed her to. This is her opportunity to be free and wild. Be loving and gentle with her.

2. Travel: Get lost!Traveling is a mirror for how you show up in the world. How are you when a flight is delayed for ten hours? How do you make friends with 19-year-old German co-travellers? What do you have in common? Are you easily flustered in a crowd or do you confidently bargain for that silk scarf?

Preferably travel alone. It gives you the opportunity to listen to your intuition, be spontaneous and not have to worry about a travelling partner's mood or itinerary. Travelling alone breaks down your walls to connect with the locals, take risks and follow your inner compass.

Find your bravery! Get out there and blaze your own path. You will find exactly what you are looking for.

Shannon Silvermoon, Inner child guide. www.shannonsilvermoon.com

Karyn
Kerr Pettigrew

"If you live at your radical intersection, synchronicity,
serendipity, and grace become your faithful companions
making life a beautiful, wild ride."

**I want you to understand that it's possible to live an extraordinary life
– on your terms. I believe choosing to live at your radical intersection,
that point where your loves, gifts, strengths, callings, and wonder converge – is where you reclaim and activate all aspects of your most powerful self.**

What's Wrong With Me?

Apparently, I was supposed to die at 17; but I was not included in
that conversation.

So, I lived.

My Mom, while really great in many ways, completely avoided
sensitive conversations. Although she remarried when I was eight years
old, she essentially raised me as a single parent. My step-father might as
well have been paint-on-the-wall, for all of the influence and direction
he provided. He was a nice enough man but contributed very little to my
upbringing.

I was 16 when I finally started menstruating, three years past the usual age, which had me wondering, "What's wrong with me?" I never dated in high school and again spent years wondering "What's wrong with me?" My biological father had not been in my life since I was an infant. Most of that time, I wondered, "What's wrong with me?"

My mother and I never discussed any of these topics. So, when I developed Hodgkin's Disease while still a minor, at age 17, it shouldn't be a surprise that any serious medical conversations were conducted without me.

I had no idea my prognosis was death. I found out accidentally after my mom passed away. I was 45, at a high school reunion, when one of my favorite teachers called to me, "There's my miracle child!" I gave her a big hug and asked, "What?"

She told me, "In your senior year, the doctors gathered all your teachers and closest friends. You weren't expected to live past the holidays."

No one told me they didn't expect me to live.

There are times when ignorance is bliss; or at least, helpful. Not being aware of what everyone else seems to have known, I continued to live like a girl on a mission. I was also very practiced at pushing down sensitive topics and redirecting my energy to other things. I was a senior, an athlete, a leader - and I had plans for not only college, but for my life.

Looking back, there were two diametrically opposed things happening. First, all the stuffing down of important, sensitive subjects may have catalyzed my illness. Louise Hay cites the probable cause of Hodgkin's as "Blame and tremendous fear of not being good enough. A frantic race to prove one's self until the blood has no substance left to support itself." Interesting.

Second, while this seems evident to me now, it is also true that my behavior of stuffing down sensitive topics and focusing on the future starved the illness of its power. In the end, I believe my will and focus on what I was creating is why I am alive today.

After a year of chemo, I left to study at Wellesley on schedule, with no evidence of cancer remaining. I had an amazing experience at college. In my senior year, I was accepted into Harvard business school.

I chose Wellesley and Harvard because, as a black woman, I didn't want my right to be present, at any table, to be questioned. I thought that with the right credentials I would be respected and allowed to live freely. This was a life lesson in the making.

I graduated from business school, got married to the first and only man I dated seriously, and took a highly-coveted job all in the same year. I worked on a high-profile brand, flew to exciting places and events, and met amazing people. While I learned a lot about marketing, I learned more about myself and how I felt about being confronted by institutional racism, glass ceilings, and my drive to live freely.

About two years in, I found out senior management had forced my first manager to accept me for the position, although he had not initially wanted me for the job. He later became an advocate, but learning how he felt in the beginning still created a barrier. So again, I wondered, "what's wrong with me?"

Four years later, serendipitously, an alumna mentioned a marketing opportunity. At the time, I thought I'd go back and see if anyone at my current company was interested. That was the same week I had my annual review, which went well. I received a five-out-of-five rating. I thought that would set me up for a brand-manager opportunity. Instead, I was offered a position in promotions, with no guaranteed timing to return to a brand. I was furious. I was the only person in my cohort to be made this offer. In brand culture, staff positions are not considered to be as prestigious as the brand positions.

A month later, I had quit, and found myself working for the alumna who had been looking for a marketing director. She happened to be a black female; I was now second in command. With a $20 million marketing budget and more than a handful of direct reports, I had complete marketing responsibility. I was free to be me!

For 12 years, I helped build other people's brands; but by the time I was in my late 30s, I had two young children and was beginning to experience a work/life imbalance.

I had been studying metaphysics and was feeling called to use my talents in a different way. For a few years, I resisted the call. I continued to show up for work and my family while continuous cortisol spikes cut my appetite and burned away 20 pounds. I became anxious and sensitive to everything.

Ultimately, I hit a wall. My husband and I decided that I could quit. My intention was to open a wellness center in the heart of downtown Chicago – the frontline of work/life dysfunction. My mentor received another insight – intuitive direction. She thought I should be helping people through intuition. That was both surprising and inviting.

Instead of opening the wellness center, I wrote my first book, which began my exploration into following our hearts to work that feeds us. I wondered, what does it take to design an extraordinary life on my terms? Ever since then, my work has been dedicated to answering and sharing what I discovered.

I now believe that extraordinary living, however we define it, occurs at our radical intersection. That place where our loves, gifts, strengths, callings, and wonder converge.

Standing in the clarity of a radical intersection may call for life-enhancing actions. I didn't foresee the disruption coming my way, the road I was about to take: Blowing-up my life, as I knew it, to save my own soul.

Following 18 months of loss including the sudden deaths of my mother, father-in-law, and my recently reconciled father, I ended my 23-year relationship.

The marriage looked perfect from the outside, and for all practical purposes it functioned that way; except that I didn't feel right. I had lost myself. I didn't feel emotionally safe or understood. Over the years, the connection eroded like death by a thousand cuts. I acknowledge that there are things I could have done differently. I compromised and shut down my needs in deference to the family's needs, which I know now was the wrong thing to do. There was resistance all around. With all of my heart I wanted to break the cycle of divorce in my family, but I was dying inside. The decision to end it was more devastating than I could have ever imagined.

Leaving my former life has been excruciating, at times, and the grieving process long. The ensuing battle burned away the plaque that had accumulated over my self-expression, stifling it and preventing me from recognizing myself. I was raw but born again.

Forging new communities and relationships, I now live at my radical intersection feeling more insightful and more aware than ever before. I no longer ask, "What's wrong with me?" I simply choose to interact with people and be part of communities that understand me as I am.

Every aspect of myself that I reclaim - the buried, the denied, the forgotten, the ashamed, the repressed, and the guilty – is converted to fuel.

This energy that we carry, the negative stuff, can't go anywhere. Energy is neither created nor destroyed, it can only be transformed (first law of thermodynamics).

Choosing to live at my radical intersection actually transforms the negative. As I assimilate all parts of myself, I return to a type of internal balance, homeostasis.

I know that the opportunity is to catch low vibrations as they emerge and consciously redirect them. Life-altering.

My radical intersection, the convergence of my loves, gifts, strengths, callings and wonder, looks something like this:

- Travel as a loving observer
- Creative expression
- Affirming people (adjective; verb)
- First-time experiences
- Problem-solving
- All art forms
- Rom-Coms and Sci-Fi
- Sensuality
- All kinds of dance
- Empathetic healer
- Teacher
- A love for the soul
- Design
- The sun on my skin
- Freedom seeker – expression, self-determination

These aspects combine to support me in my life and two businesses: My current coaching and consulting practice, Beyond Blind Spots, and my new clothing line, ZoeGoes, focused on women who love to travel. My loves (i.e. travel, women, soul) intersect with my skills (marketing, business), my strengths (teaching, empathy, articulating ideas) and my wonder (how do we manifest?) to create these two businesses.

As a result of living at my radical intersection, I also better understand what I want and need. As I live more in this space, I reduce the gaps in my confidence and integrity such that more and more of what I want is manifesting in my life. Synchronicity, serendipity, and grace are my faithful companions, making life a beautiful, wild ride. It is through this process that I believe you, too, will find your greatest power.

IGNITE ACTION STEPS

Exercise: Would you like to live at your radical intersection?
The questions below are from my Soul Code program. Answer them quickly. Write down your first thoughts without censoring. There is no "right" answer. Get your phone and set the timer for three minutes for each question.
- YOUR LOVE LIST: What do you love? Make a list and just let the thoughts flow.
- YOUR ADMIRATION LIST: Think of someone you admire; living or not, fictional or real, and then list why you admire them.
- YOUR CREDENTIALS LIST: List your credentials – degrees, certifications, years of experience, etc.

EXERCISE EXPLAINED

1) LOVE LIST: Now go back to your love list. What is written on this list are the things that feed you, provide stamina, heal you. You need these things in your life in copious amounts. Circle three things that restore you quickly and three things that give you a deep sense of renewal.

From the six items you circled, decide which you can work into your life on a daily basis.

2) ADMIRATION LIST: Nothing resonates with you that is not innately, inherently part of you. When we admire, we are actually summoning a mirror. The traits you admire in someone else are operating at passive levels within you. Noticing who you admire and what you see in them is your opportunity to activate those aspects in yourself.

Choose to bring those traits into your life at an active level.

You already have it, now bring it to life!

Circle three to five of the attributes that stand out the most to you.

These are your core values.

3) CREDENTIALS LIST:
Your credentials are the door openers. These are the things most people use to decide if you should be given a shot. They are the least effective of determining whether someone will be a good fit for anything.

Your job anytime, you're given the opportunity, is to flip the conversation from these factual items onto what is special about you; your loves, core values, and how you get things done.

Your responses to these questions are a written prescription for action that you can take right now. In answering these questions, your soul has offered you specific direction. Go ahead, step into the plan you agreed to before you came to exist on this planet. It's your life. Take it.

Your responses can be very powerful tools to help you with discernment: your true north star, of sorts. Any of the attributes you listed or the things you love can be converted into questions so that you can determine if a person or opportunity moves you closer to or farther away from where you're going.

For instance, freedom to express is a core value for me. As I'm interviewing a new collaborator or new hire, I ask questions that help me understand how they feel about self-expression and how they feel about having freedom to express. Whether you use these tools at work or at home, your answers are part of you and go everywhere you go. Now notice where they intersect.

This entire exercise takes just a few minutes, including reading the explanations. Now that you know that, you can't unknow it. All it took to get a refreshed message from your soul and a blueprint for where to go was a few minutes and a willingness to discover the radical intersection in your Soul Code.

Continued blessings on your journey. Enjoy!

Karyn Kerr Pettigrew, Founder / CEO of Beyond Blind Spots.
BeyondBlindSpots.com

KATARINA AMADORA

"Kintsugi: Learn to love your shattered pieces
and fill them in with Gold."

My intention is to show that a personal practice of self-knowledge and cultivating resilience are the primary tools for even the most perilous moments in life.

MENDING MY CRACKS WITH GOLD

Have you ever felt broken? Have you ever wondered whether you will ever feel whole and complete again? I think that we all feel this way from time to time. I take inspiration from the Japanese art of "Kintsugi" whenever those voices start to creep in that tell me "I am not good enough" or "I will never fit in." Each little ego-death is like another crack in a fine clay pot. Yet, it is through each successive breakdown that I have emerged ever more beautiful, vibrant. and more exquisitely unique than before.

There are few things in life more difficult for a parent than to watch their child in deep struggle, knowing there is nothing you can do to help. My daughter 'R' inspires me every day. I will forever be grateful for her resilience as she perilously navigated her teenage years through tremendous challenges. I could have lost her so easily. I am so grateful she is still with me, now a junior in high school. I am in awe of the young woman she is becoming. There were too many days when I feared we would never reach this point.

The first time 'R' tried to kill herself, she was only 10 years old. We were living in Shanghai and she had been diagnosed with Type I Juvenile Onset Bipolar Disorder. One of the most difficult aspects of this for her was that her memories were fragmented. One of our favorite anime series from that time period was 'Princess Tutu.' In it, a young Prince had to go find and reclaim lost shards of his heart which had been scattered throughout the mystical realm. In much the same way, my daughter's spirit was splintered and fragmented. Like a broken piece of pottery, her psyche was fractured.

She would often report to me that she could not remember things. As I asked her about this, a pattern emerged in her dystopia. At any one time, she could only remember memories that had been encoded when she was experiencing emotions congruent to her current state. If she was manic, she could only recall manic episodes. If she was sad, she could only recall memories of being depressed. While angry, she could only recall memories associated with rage.

This was so disorienting for her. Her memories were disconnected, there was no continuity. This was frightening. As her mom, I felt powerless to help. It was like an image of a fractured mirror where each shard reflected a different unrelated scene. Nothing fit!

I can't imagine what it would be like to live a life with such fractured memories. It was excruciatingly and devastatingly painful to witness her battle with self-loathing, as she fantasized about morbid scenes and escalated her own self-harm. She was hospitalized after another suicide attempt at the age of 11, when she tried to hang herself in the garage. This began a series of hospitalizations, until a few months later she was referred to a Dialectical Behavioral Therapy (DBT) residential care facility.

Thanks to DBT, my daughter gained new skills and improved control over her thoughts and actions; however, things were far from okay. She could not attend public school. Instead, we had to enroll her into a special program. She could barely concentrate, and it was difficult for her to get through the day. Unfortunately, this program was very expensive, driving my husband and me to argue. He would belittle my opinions, hurtfully disregarding my experience as a trained physician. This triggered the hell out of me! In turn, this triggered 'R' and led to more self-harm. I was in constant fear that I would discover more new red cuts on her body despite doing everything possible to lock away anything sharp in the house.

This was the darkest and most traumatic period of my life. My marriage was falling apart; and in a strange way, this reflected the state of my daughter's fragmented memories. Nothing I did seemed to make a difference. I could not fix my daughter or my marriage. My husband moved out the day after Christmas. A week later, on New Year's Day, 'R' tried to take her life for the third time. This time she had done research. She searched the internet to find the lethal dose for lithium. She took over twice that number of pills, spacing them out over an hour to make sure that she wouldn't throw up. I am grateful that her stomach had other plans. She came to me after her third bout of retching into the toilet. By that time, the contents of her stomach were a thick white slurry of partially-digested lithium.

She threw up two more times before I managed to get her out of the house, into the car and to the hospital. After so many solo vigils, I was grateful when my husband came to relieve me. For a change, he was the one to sit at her side! I could rest. This was the very first time that she had done anything destructive to herself while he was in town. All of her other hospitalizations had occurred when I was alone.

After this failed attempt, 'R' was placed in long term residential treatment in another state. She was away from home for the next 2-1/2 years, first in a residential treatment program, and then in a boarding school that served as a step-down program for kids who had graduated from other residential programs but were not yet ready to transition home.

The bright spot in all this chaos was that I was given a break from living in constant fear. I could not heal her, but I knew that I needed to find the strength to be there for her. The only thing that I could do was to work on healing myself. While in the midst of all this, I read *The Four Agreements*, by Don Miguel Ruiz. I had purchased it five years earlier, because it called to me, but it had been collecting dust on my bookshelf ever since. As I read, tears streamed down my face. I viscerally felt the impact of every word on the page. I recognized so many ways in which I had been living an illusion. I had frequently blamed my husband, always pointed my finger outward. I routinely took things personally as he reflected the worst parts of myself back to me. I hadn't always communicated clearly, and I made assumptions. Too often, I saw only in judgment and fault, failing to give validation when someone was doing something right. The author's words stung as they carved deep into my soul. I grieved that I had made so many mistakes. What if I had read it earlier? Would it have had any impact on how I communicated in my marriage and to my kids? Could it have made a difference?

So many times, we look outside ourselves at other people. We judge them for how they don't measure up to our expectations. We forget that anything that we see in another is usually just a reflection of something we need to heal in ourselves. In my case, I now see how my husband mirrored back the ugly parts that I disowned about myself. The things that he criticized me for were exactly those things that I judged in myself, even though I did not want to admit they were real. It was precisely because I disowned these aspects of myself that the things he said hurt so much.

My daughter's fractured world mirrored the fractures in our relationship. Our constant fighting about R's treatment contributed to her downward spiral. The silvery crisscross scars upon her legs serve as a visual reminder of how toxic our environment had become. Like the Kintsugi pot, her scars are a testament to the massive transformation that was required for her to heal during her years of residential treatment. In much the same way, every iteration of my own transformation has come from each successive breakdown, as I repeatedly find the strength to work on myself and to fill the cracks with unconditional love. My journey has given me the strength, compassion, empathy, and understanding that enable and drive me to help others find their way out of their own darkness.

Sometimes, moms get so focused on their kids that they forget all about themselves. What kind of example does that give to their children? The entire family benefits from a mom who is whole and complete in spirit. Self-care is not only deserved – IT IS ESSENTIAL! Just as you are instructed at the beginning of every flight to put on your own oxygen mask before assisting others, it is vital to take personal time for yourself. We must each do the self-work that is required to come into our relationships as a whole and fulfilled individual. When you neglect your own self-care, it sends a message to your kids that you don't value yourself. If you can't set boundaries that prioritize self-care, you teach your kids that they don't need to take care of themselves either. It is too easy to snap at your loved ones when you have been running on empty.

I recently read 'The Telomere Effect' by Elizabeth Blackburn and Elissa Epel. In it, the authors talk about the impact of chronic stress on the caregivers of chronically ill children. The greater the stress, the greater the shortening of one's telomeres. Shorter telomeres lead to a lack of progenitor cells which are important for a wide range of restorative functions in the body. This results in premature aging. Curious about the impact of all of the lifestyle changes that I have installed, I recently had my telomeres tested.

The results were remarkable. I am 53, but I amazingly have the telomeres of a 39-year-old! This validates the powerful impact of the changes that I have made for my own well-being, and I would like to share these strategies with you.

Over the past five years since my daughter first went into treatment, I not only prioritized self-care, I embraced personal development as if my life depended on it. I started meditating, practicing yoga, and doing Shamanic Fusion and Ecstatic Dance. I learned Bodywork, Tantra, and was Ordained as a Priestess of Isis. Most important of all, I surround myself with community every chance I get.

Body, Mind, Spirit, and Community. All are essential to being a whole and balanced individual. I nourish my body with healthy food as well as with dance, yoga, and movement. I nourish my mind with learning each day, and I use RTT (Rapid Transformational Therapy) to rewire my critical thoughts. I walk the spiritual path of a priestess. Tantra has enabled me to inhabit my body more fully than ever before. I embrace community, intimacy, and partnership; and I prioritize taking care of myself so that I can be a better mom for my two daughters. They might not always be able to see it, but I know that I am doing my best and that is what counts.

This long journey has really been a road back to myself. In dealing with these challenges, I had to be strong for both my girls, but more than that, I needed to learn to be strong for myself. I needed to discover my own value beyond my role as a wife or as a mother. I will always be 'Mom,' yet I cannot live my life for my girls. They are but arrows that were launched from the bow there dad and I created. Our bow may have broken, but I trust that we have at least pointed them in the right direction. They will have to find their own way from here, just as every person does as they transition into adulthood. My love for my girls is eternal. Now my role is to love and accept them as they are. I must let go of the need to guide or control their flight. Any attempt to control them now will only be met with resistance.

My DNA lives on in my daughters; and in certain respects, we share aspects of karma which have been passed down from generation to generation. Thanks to our current understanding of epigenetics, research has shown that this is not immutable. I am responsible for healing myself. This karma stops with me. It is not theirs to carry. Healing myself is the greatest gift that I can give to them because this sets an example of how much they should love themselves, and of the importance of doing their inner work.

Through this learning I surrendered into the chrysalis and became the grey mush of potential. In order to heal myself fully, I realized that my next step was to let go of the last vestige of my previous self, my married name. I chose to surrender the name "Katherine L Potter" because it is a remnant of my past and it no longer resonates with the person I have become. I embraced the name 'Katarina Amadora,' which represents a woman who lives in alignment with her highest self. As I emerged from that chrysalis with wings dripping wet, I connected with my radiant essence in the sunlight as I prepared to fly. I am grateful for each difficult moment that has led me to where I am today and to the person I have become.

This moment represents a new dawn in my life. I am determined that these new chapters will be lived in alignment with my higher self. It is up to me to create my future, free of the past yet remembering the lessons that I have learned. I believe the world lies open before me, like a fresh canvas waiting for paint. Your Universe has also been patiently waiting for you to step into your embodiment – so that you, too, can do your best work in the world. Let go of the limitations which you previously placed on yourself. I know now that I have nothing to hide, nothing to prove, and nothing to protect. I have a purpose that I am here to fulfill. I know that I have always been a healer. I give up the need to prove anything. I am here to journey with people, to inspire them, and to help them see they are better than they think they are. I am here for you.

IGNITE ACTION STEPS

Social Connection: Joining an online circle for support was the first bread-crumb which led me out of my isolation. Social connection is the single most important predictor of health, happiness, and success in life. More significant than obesity, smoking, or high blood pressure, loneliness represents a greater health hazard than smoking a pack of cigarettes every day. Find a tribe you can connect with and get involved. Reach out and connect with like-minded persons who resonate with you. Let go of any toxic associations from your past because they no longer resonate with who you are becoming. You become like the five persons you spend the most time with, so choose wisely both your inner circle and those whom you choose to love from a distance.

Physical Health: Prioritize taking care of your body. A huge part of this for me was doing WildFit in 2016. It is not be an exaggeration to say that it changed my life. Today, as a WildFit Coach, I am helping others to make the same transformation that I experienced. I have gone from a size 16 to a sexy size 8. I now love how I look in the mirror. Changing your nutrition is the single most important thing you can do to transform your health. You are made from the foods that you eat, so choose wisely. Find physical activities which you love, and which make you feel so alive so that you look forward to moving your body. Level-up your fitness so that you can experience the vibrant physicality of a healthy body.

Spirituality: Through my spiritual practices of Tantra and meditation, I have learned to be more present and open, and I am able to step into the role of the observer when stressful things happen. Finding your own spiritual practice is important in creating peace of mind and regulating your nervous system. Find a spiritual path that resonates for you, whether mindfulness practices, meditation, yoga, ecstatic dance, or belief in a higher power. These practices have powerful physiologic effects to calm the mind and give you a sense of purpose, meaning, and connection in the world. Don't allow someone else to tell you what that path should be. Find your own path, and blaze a trail for others to follow.

Mental Health: Another important piece for me was rewiring the subconscious beliefs which were keeping me stuck in old habits of thought and behaviors. Through learning and practicing Rapid Transformational Therapy (RTT), I have supercharged my own development and growth. Working with the subconscious mind can be an incredibly powerful way to rewire faulty belief systems. If you think about it, all of your programming was laid down when you were just a child. You did your best to integrate all the sensory inputs coming at you from your parents, peers, culture, religion, teachers, and other influences. These messages can often be conflicting and random, and none of your programming was consciously chosen. You can choose to let go of old disempowering beliefs and to take on positive new beliefs. Whether this is done through RTT, through self-love practices, journaling, working with plant medicines or other modes of therapy, it is important to keep doing your self-work consistently – to allow yourself to grow and evolve into the highest expression of you: The self that you were always meant to be.

Katarina Amadora, Holistic Health Coach. Amadora Transformations.
www.AmadoraTransformations.com

DR. JUDY GIANNI

"Fears are just stepping stones on the road to empowerment."

My intention is to share with you my journey of facing my fears head-on and overcoming self-limiting beliefs. Through my moment of triumph, I began to live my best life. In doing so, I wish to inspire and encourage you to reclaim your power, face your fears and live the life of your dreams.

NAVIGATING AN EMPOWERED LIFE

The road from feeling limited, fearful, and disempowered to one of boldness and courage has allowed me to live a fabulous life without limits with multiple opportunities to express my gifts. But this road was once filled with stumbling blocks that threatened to trip me up until I learned how to use those blocks as my stepping stones.

Where did my fear and learned helplessness originate? I am the youngest of three girls and the youngest of an extended family. I was the quintessential baby. I learned to be cute and helpless. Everyone would just step in and take care of everything. As a child it worked for me and in my marriages (yes, plural) it worked for a while as well. Manage finances? Oh that's for my husband. Travel arrangements? Oh he does that! Common household repairs? Not my territory! Big road trips? I'm in the passenger seat!

I also watched my mother, who didn't work outside the home, once a confident city girl, who upon moving to the suburbs, found herself out of her element. I can remember seeing vintage 1940's photos of a girl trip to Chicago, my mother's head tossed back in laughter, appearing wild and carefree with her friends, but once she was married and settled down in the beautiful house my father built, in the wooded neighborhoods of Fairfield, Connecticut, her social life and sense of independence disappeared. She focused on raising her family. Over the years, outside of tending to us, her three girls and my father, she ended up isolating at home, lost in books or TV. I watched as she relegated any activity that required complex thought and action to my father and how she let her fears and lack of confidence make her world smaller and smaller. I had no idea how much what she said and how she navigated in life caused me to second guess myself and tend towards playing small and playing it safe. It wasn't really who I truly was, but it was learned behavior. I have had to spend most of my life busting out of the shackles of self-imposed fear and self-induced limitation.

Now with that awareness I have my freedom. Yet, I am shocked to recall the times I questioned her small, suburban housewife stereotype even as a young child. I can recall clearly, one day when I was nine, in the backseat of my mother's car as we drove on Black Rock Turnpike. We were having a conversation and I asked, "Wait, you mean you don't have any of your own money?" I thought about how my parents argued and didn't seem happy at all. I remember feeling a silent outrage, thinking "no way will that be me!" Vowing at that moment, I would always find a way to have my own power, money, happiness, and independence.

I am grateful to that nine-year-old me. Even though I fell into the patterns of my mother for the first part of my life. That vow helped me avoid drowning in that same isolation and empty dependent life of my mother. I became a successful naturopathic physician and business owner for 24 years, and ran my own small real estate investment company. I operate four Airbnb's, have four grown children, and 5 grandchildren. I've raised my 14-year-old granddaughter for most of her life and almost completely on my own. But I wasn't always this accomplished. Discovering my hidden adventuresome spirit came to me much later.

Travelling of any kind was limited by my invisible handicap. Although all my limbs are intact and my five senses work adequately, this handicap has threatened to limit me in a very real way. I have absolutely zero sense of direction. You laugh, but I am here to tell you it inhibits my ability to go to new places or even places I've been multiple times, and to me, that is no laughing matter.

I can describe this extreme level of being directionally challenged to the likes of a brain dyslexia. Which is not really an official thing, but as close as I can get to describing the crippling effect of not being able to orient oneself spatially. I can't tell you how many times, after moving into a new home, I turn the wrong direction down the hall in my own house. There are hundreds of times over the years that I have been lost in the maze of hallways and stores at my local mall or in hotels, resorts or hospitals. Places like those throw me off badly; I get completely turned around. I can tell you from experience, a six-level parking garage at night in the cold is not a fun place to be. After two hours of panicked searching on foot, I conquered my embarrassment and asked a parking attendant to drive me around to find my car. This lack of orientation made me feel too vulnerable to do any traveling on my own, until one day when I didn't have a choice.

In 2009, after two trips to Europe with my then husband, we had an upcoming trip in June. Paris was our first destination and favorite city. From there, we'd take a train through Provence and ultimately head to Milan where we would meet my older sister and my dad to celebrate his 90th birthday. This was an important trip as it would most likely be his last. We wanted to take him to Lake Garda, home to the maternal side of his family. My husband Ron was an extreme planner. Anything short of a six-month lead time was considered 'last minute' and he would refuse to go. He was extraordinarily intelligent and great with details, which made it easy to allow him to take the reins on most of the things in our lives. But as we were drawing closer to the time of our departure, only our airfare was booked. It was surely out of character for Ron to not have the hotels chosen and booked. By now, train tickets should have been purchased, and tours explored. I knew things had been very bumpy for a while. We were arguing a lot, but my denial was keeping me from seeing the reality – that our almost five-year marriage was truly disintegrating.

After days turned into weeks of pleading with him to sit down and make some concrete plans, he finally told me, "You should just go on your own".

What?! Terror ran through my veins. I felt faint. "What do you mean?! I can't do this on my own?! I can't navigate the Paris subways without you!" I pictured myself in the station, cowering in a corner, rolled in a ball, lost, crying and terrified. Not an empowering sight! No! Although I agreed we were not getting along in just about every department, there was just no possible way I could go on this trip alone! I couldn't cancel. This was my dad's special trip. I begged Ron to come and after days of appealing to him in every way possible, he reluctantly agreed.

Doing our best to hide our discord for my dad's sake, the tension between us and the disconnect did not make for an enjoyable trip. Two weeks after our return, we separated and eventually filed for divorce.

The year following, reflecting on my state of disempowerment, I realized it was time to truly grow up and take back my power. I started with growing and managing my business. I got savvy about real estate, investing and my personal finances. I took solo road trips and learned simple household maintenance and repairs. I went to the movies, to restaurants and hiking on my own. All these served as stepping stones toward a greater sense of self-empowerment.

Then it was time to take on a bigger challenge. I knew what I had to do! I booked a trip to Paris by myself for the following summer. I'd never been in a foreign country alone before. The whole concept of making it into the country, lugging my suitcase by myself, getting through passport control, figuring out the money exchange...the situation robbed me of sleep on countless nights. But my biggest fear of all – navigating the subways!

The subway system in Paris is a marvel. The rapid transit system of the city's metropolitan area is 133 miles/214 km long, has 302 stations with 62 transfers between the lines. There are 16 lines numbered 1-14. Sixteen million passengers use the service each day – a busy, bustling, frenetic scene. It is a maze of winding halls, multiple levels and staircases with symbols, color coded and numbered signs. Mind-boggling to say the least! Taxis are super expensive, the streets are congested, filled with traffic jams. Anyone who's visited or lived in Paris will tell you that they walk more in a week than you would elsewhere cumulatively in a month. Paris is huge, sites are spread far and wide, so to easily and affordably traverse this magnificent metropolis, the subway is the best way to go.

I don't speak French... ordering butter, they hand me a beer, so not knowing the language makes it particularly challenging. But feeling the terror at the very idea of it, I knew I had to take it on or give in to the closing walls of safety and small-worldness.

It was Paris in July, hot but not stifling, just as magical as I remembered it, with its quaint cafes, art nouveau signs and delicious food. I arrived without a hitch, went through passport control and got my luggage. The previous year we had picked up our luggage and headed for the B Line train and arrived in the transfer station at Chatelet. Lugging our heavy suitcases up steps would be a physical impossibility to handle on my own. I wanted to face my fears, but I didn't have to be a masochist! It cost me €50, but I took a taxi directly to my hotel, the École Centrale in Le Marais, just across the street from the subway entrance.

I got my subway map, mapped out my route, memorizing in my head the color, the number and direction (defined only by the identification of the last stop on that route) and set off on my daily adventures. It was intimidating and challenging at first, but every time I traversed successfully, I got more and more confident. And other than one quick freakout for heading in the wrong direction, I recovered and calmly got off to take the stairs to the other side, and board the next subway. Disaster averted! I felt triumphant!

I made the most of this solo trip and really enjoyed myself. I pushed past many fears and experienced a lot of 'firsts'. I signed up for a cooking class where a group of strangers (facing another fear) of several ages had to meet up at a designated spot that I successfully found. We went to the local market to pick out fresh vegetables, herbs and went on to make a tender, flaky, white fish with a velvety fragrant red pepper sauce. Cooking that delicious meal, with new friends from all over the globe and of all ages created not only great food but for made for interesting cross-cultural conversation.

I took a bike tour, each time traversing the city bravely, with my subway map in my back pocket, to get to the meeting spot. It was so beautiful, pedaling along the Seine River, viewing the gothic architecture of Notre Dame.

The success of that trip fueled my urge to continue pushing past perceived limitations, expanding and accomplishing new things. Paris on my own gave me the confidence to take anything on.

I have since traveled to 25 countries, in the last four years and often by myself. I have had amazing adventures including a white-water rafting trip down the Ayung River in Bali, volunteering at an elephant rescue in Thailand, luxuriating in an ancient steam bath in Istanbul to hiking the majestic peaks of Machu Picchu in Peru, just to name a few.

My pinnacle experience in my journey to push beyond my limits was participating in a Seven Day Darkness Retreat in India. Arriving in New Delhi the day after the festival of Diwali, the air was filled with smoke from the ongoing fireworks and celebration, but I made it to my retreat center on the outskirts to enter into seven days and nights with a group of 14, completely surrounded in pitch black darkness. We did yoga, chanting, ecstatic dancing (a new spin on "Dance like no one is watching!") down to eating all meals, showering/dressing, all in complete pitch-black. Hidden fears, insecurities and anything else holding me back in any way that needed to come up, this was the cauldron that could boil it to the surface.

It was both immensely peaceful and deeply connecting, but I have to report my sense of direction never improved in the dark! I would often find myself bumping into the wrong corners looking for the bathroom, patting down empty walls, looking for the door with an increased sense of urgency. Eventually I made my way around and felt triumphant.

So, these days, it's not like I have it all figured out. New challenges present themselves weekly, if not daily, as opportunities to choose to shrink back, to take the easy way out, to play it small and safe. But with every decision that I make to deal with things head on, to bravely face each challenge, to refuse to go back to a state of fear and powerlessness, I give rise to my best, most fearless, confident and unstoppable self.

IGNITE ACTION STEPS

Do you want to push past limitations and find your brave, unlimited Self? Here are some journal exercises and action steps you can take:

*Some people will start with a specific goal in mind (ie. "I want to have my own business and create my own program, service, etc." or "I want to enter a marathon", or "I want to write a book"). Others may not have a defined goal but know how they want to feel (ie. "I want to feel free to express the true me"., "I want to live an abundant life and experience true financial freedom", or "I want to feel confident in my body and move with ease"). It doesn't matter if your goal is tangible or a feeling state. Just choose it and write about it in a journal.

* Picture yourself achieving your goal and view it in your head like a mental movie. Notice where you feel caught up, where your stomach tightens, or your shoulders tense up. Listen to the negative thoughts telling you, "Oh, I can't do that". Breathe, stay present, get curious about your reactions and resistance. Write down what they are and if you have an insight, note where the feeling or sentiment came from. Did a parent tell you this? Or did a teacher or society give you this message? How old were you? Write it all down.

*After you have made an exhaustive list of your fears or negative messaging and documenting them in your journal, take a moment, close your eyes and breathe. Ask for guidance in answering, "Is there anything else, any other message unconsciously holding me back?". If you get something right then, great! Write it down. If not, just ask for it to percolate through you and maybe pop up at a later time so you can write it down.

* Now for the next step, grab another colored pen. Next to these limiting messages and fears, write down a challenge to this. For instance, you can write, "Is this really true? Is there another way? Why not me?" Sometimes, just taking these unconscious fears from the dark recesses of our minds

and pulling them into the light of day and challenging them can deflate the power they hold over us.

* Break down your goals in several small steps. Instead of seeing the whole goal and having it overwhelm you and threaten to paralyze you, take small, actionable steps. Take time to inform yourself (ie. watch a YouTube on "How to write a book proposal" or read blogs about train travel through Europe). Empower yourself with ways to overcome the series of small obstacles and start using them as your stepping stones.

* Form a habit of challenging your fears. Look for opportunities to push past your comfort zone in little and big ways. When thoughts like, "I couldn't possibly" come up or you find yourself shrinking with fear, use it as a chance to push past it and grow. A few months ago, I was in the Yucatán with my 23-year-old son, his girlfriend, and my 14-year-old granddaughter. We were going to go swim in a breathtaking cenote or freshwater deep-water hole 30 feet below the ground. It was cerulean blue and inviting with a very long rope swing that people were lining up to use. Mostly kids, fit men, and young people were jumping off the wooden deck, propelling high into the air and dropping into the pristine water below. I was terrified but I knew I had to challenge myself to do it.

So, I stepped up onto the platform, around 20 people watching and despite my complete fear, I grabbed the rope and jumped, swinging out into the center of the 50-foot-wide natural pool and let go. As my body sliced into and hit the cool water, it stung my legs a bit and water went up my nose, but I felt triumphant! I didn't love it, but I felt brave and unstoppable and even took a second leap, which I actually enjoyed much more! Little wins build confidence.

* Celebrate your little and big wins! Acknowledge yourself when you have conquered a fear, made a positive step, got some traction. Soon you will be feeling more and more courageous to achieve your goals and make new ones. Enjoy the process. Be kind to yourself if you get tripped up. Each step leads to learning. Ask for help and support along the way. Use available resources. Be creative in how you navigate your course; you get points for creativity!

Enjoy the process on your road to empowerment.

Dr. Judy Gianni, Naturopathic Physician.
www.naturemedica.net

VALENTINE OWEN

"Forgiveness is contagious. It starts with you
and easily transpires to others."

**My intention is that you find the gift in my story to unravel life's myster-
ies. That you look past your fears and beyond the things that might be
blinding or binding you. My hope is that in solving your own mysteries,
you find the treasure to live your best life and stand up for what you
believe.**

UNRAVELLING THE MYSTERIES

I have never been one for mysteries. Since I can remember, I have always
had the desire to know things. As a child, I endlessly pestered my mother and
grandparents to tell me the truth about everything. Only, that was difficult
during the war. They didn't have the answers to why the soldiers came.
Why we had to keep running from Hitler's army. They couldn't explain why
there was so little food in the refugee camp and why some of the men were
gathered up and taken away. As my family and I fled across Europe seeking
safe haven, no one seemed to have the answers. I never understood why my
mother lied about my age to the passport officer. Nor, why I had to cut my
hair to look like a boy, as we took a lengthy voyage across the ocean from
London to Halifax. Why when some of the people died on the ship, did they
throw the bodies overboard. There were always so many questions in my
mind.

When I first arrived in our new country, there were mysteries all around. Like why was my father not with us and a new step-father was coming instead? Why were we indentured to a man who owned a farm where we had to work day and night? Why were we not free? Why did we have nothing? My mother and stepfather were required to do hard labour when we immigrated into this country in exchange for food and shelter. Except the house we had been given was more like a chicken coop than a home. The farmer had cleaned it out and installed two makeshift beds. There wasn't much of anything. There was no explanation for that.

My mother and step-father worked day and night picking sugar beets out of the hard, black dirt under the unrelenting blazing sun. For two years we lived like prisoners, even though everyone said the war was over. I lived most of my childhood in a tiny shack, with a dirt floor and the local kids teasing me endlessly. When I went to school, they made fun of my accent, my odd clothing, and they called me a DP (displaced person). I didn't know what that meant? Why couldn't/didn't they just see me as a person? I never understood why things were so different, but I made a vow to balance them out. I worked as hard as I could on my grades. Took odd jobs, taught myself to sew and make clothing. I began nursing school right out of high school.

I was driven to answer the questions of life. I studied, read books and educated myself. I learned finances, business and lived modestly in hopes for my future. I got a loan at nineteen and bought my first tiny one-bedroom house. I made sure I would never live with dirt floors again.

I worked hard to support both myself and my mother after she divorced my abusive stepfather. I sent funds home every month for her and my brother who was nine years younger and my sister a year younger than him. I vowed to always unravel the mysteries of life by making good choices and wise decisions. I married a man who was strong, competent and I felt would be successful. With his determination and drive, I knew together we could live an enjoyable life. My dream was to one day have children and that they would live a much better life than I had, with a much nicer home than what I grew up in.

It took close to twenty years, but we achieved it. Having our own business helped and I worked day and night to unravel the mysteries of payroll dedications, equity loans, building codes and city zoning. I also learned how to parent two beautiful daughters. One loved drama, while the other loved academics. I supported them both endlessly. The youngest in her creativity while the older earned tops marks and became valedictorian at school. Life was busy, non-stop and all consuming.

I am sure it was all the times my mother told me to stop complaining that bore its way into my mind. When my back ached and my fingers bled from picking beets, she had little sympathy. When garter snakes or worms were found in the house, she told me to stop complaining and be grateful that I was lucky enough to live this country. I didn't change when I got older, I was very accepting and did not complain about much. Even when my husband seemed less interested in our marriage and spent more time working out of town, I said nothing. I trusted him implicitly and did what I always did – just kept working hard.

Only the years were stacking up. I was forty, putting in eighty-hour weeks, managing twenty-six staff and going full tilt. Looking back, I was on autopilot. I don't remember feeling anything other than the pressure to just 'do'. My husband had expanded our business and that meant he was flying to the coast weekly. He had fulfilled two of his boyhood dreams. One, by becoming a pilot and buying a small cessna plane. He'd fly himself each week to the coast and enjoy his second dream; a boat large enough to live on. It was also a vacation place for us and the girls in the summer and his home away from home when he was out of town. Success had graced us. Everything 'looked' good. I guess I'll admit in hindsight, I had my blinders on. I didn't see the cracks in the marriage, the clues or that things were falling apart.

I don't remember much of that day when my ignite-moment happened. My oldest daughter was attending University. It was my youngest daughter who was there that day; she could tell you more. What I do remember is I woke up early in the morning, needing to go to the washroom. Except, I couldn't move! For some very strange reason, *I could not get myself out of bed*. I slid off the side and landed on the floor. Nothing was working. I couldn't stand up or use my legs, so I crawled on my belly to my daughter's room. Like most fifteen-year olds, she woke up grumpy, until she noticed me lying on the floor. I asked her to help me stand up. I don't know why, but I couldn't seem to get my feet to move from underneath me. My daughter reached under both my arms to help stand me up. That is the last thing I remember. I blacked out.

I was rushed to the large speciality hospital an hour away from our home, and instantly seen by numerous doctors. When I regained consciousness hours later, the prognosis was not good. The cartilage and disc in my lower back had ruptured. They had to do emergency surgery and there was only a 20 percent chance I would ever walk again. I called my husband – utterly terrified. He was at the coast… on the boat… "Very busy!" he said. When

I told him what the doctors had reported, his response was short. When I explained I needed to have a major, and possibly life-threatening operation, his demeanour seemed unfazed. He hemmed and hawed and listened to me, but in the end came the words… "You don't really need me to fly home, do you?"

Like the good non-complainer, I had been trained to be, I said "No, it's fine. I'll be alright," and hung up the phone. I'd like to say I handled it well, but I didn't. My mind went wild, my emotions erupted, and I fought the biggest inner struggle of my life. I could not fathom, understand or comprehend why my husband would not race to my side to comfort me. What could possibly be stopping him from driving to the airport, and flying his OWN plane home? The nurses had to pin me down as I tried to get out of bed. The doctor raced in to sedate me. He had to call my family doctor in my home town to talk me through my emotional hysteria. I didn't want to have the surgery. I was gripped by fear. What if I never walked again? What if I died? I didn't know how to handle this all on my own. What possibly could be preventing a husband from coming to be with his wife in her hour of desperate need? It was a mystery and I needed to find some answers.

Of course, the sedatives won. With no one at my side, I was wheeled into surgery, not knowing if I'd ever stand up or walk again. I made a vow to myself in that moment that I would do whatever I had to, to regain the use of my legs. There was no reason in the world that could explain my husband's decision not to be with me. I prayed to God to let me walk again. With less than a 20 percent chance in my favour, I knew if I could heal and walk, I was walking right out of my marriage.

When I awoke from the surgery, my oldest daughter was there with a family friend. I wondered why no remorse, obligation or love had kicked in, as my husband had still not done anything to be at my side.

Despite all the warnings from the hospital staff, I swung my legs over the side of my bed and attempted to stand. Two orderlies caringly held me up as I begged them to let me put my feet on the floor. I NEEDED to know. I had to be sure… When I felt the cold linoleum on my feet and the wobbliness in my knees I knew. When I could feel my body weight on my heels and the pinching of the stitches in the skin on my back, I relented. I let them lay me back down knowing there was sensation. I knew in that second, I was going to be okay. I could heal – I WOULD walk again. The surgery had been successful.

It took me nearly a year to recover completely. According to the doctors, my healing was dependent on laying down; I was not to sit under any circumstances. They marveled at the fact I could even move; they warned me I might forever be handicapped or best-case scenario, walk with a cane. *I refused to believe them.* I had things to do, along with a mystery to solve.

While I was recovering, I was also *uncovering.* Peeling back the layers and the reasons. That first month I did everything possible to heal and took a few steps. The second month, a few more. We lived on the edge of a spectacular park and each week a new tree, bench or scrub became a goal for me to take a few more steps, go a little further, strengthen myself a little bit more. I was determined to not just recover but be stronger than before.

I said nothing to my husband. I catered to his hollow excuses and routine of leaving me each week to check on things at the coast. I started studying our bank statements, checking visa slips, looking for clues. All the while, I was organizing my finances, restructuring my affairs, and setting things up for me and my girls. I refused to stay home despite my condition, so I had my husband purchase a large station wagon. We took out the back seats and slid in a mattress. My youngest daughter had her learner's permit, so I had her drive me to work and do errands.

When my husband was in town, I was recovering. Staying home, walking in the park and healing. When he was gone, I was busy; making phone calls, planning my exit…looking for clues. I secretly bought a small one-bedroom house and then flipped it. I needed to build up my own wealth. The vigil finally paid off. One day I got a tip, that led to a name, that led to a phone number, that led to a woman who lived on the coast. At 2 AM, I called her number pretending to be a nurse from the hospital (I'd recently learned a lot about hospitals). I said one of his daughters had been in an accident and to please put him on the phone. In her half-awakened state, she did so, and when I heard his voice respond, I knew I had the answer to all my many questions.

Mysteries can always be solved if you are willing to look for the clues and wait for the pieces to fall into place. My mind was clear, my suspicion confirmed – I left the very next day. I had waited patiently for over twelve months to make sure I was okay, that I could take care of myself and my girls. I set things up not to hurt him, but to never let him hurt me. I walked out of that marriage stronger than when I walked in. I didn't listen to all the advice, the fear, and the ones who didn't think I could do it on my own. I listened to myself, my inner knowing, the will I found in my own God-given strength.

On my road back to optimum health, and once I had left, I decided to do some emotional healing. I started studying to become a religious minister. I had a new journey that I needed to undergo; one of forgiveness. I had to forgive many people in my life: my mother for not protecting me from my step-father for being so abusive; the soldiers who killed some of my family; the kids who bullied me in school; my husband of course; and most importantly myself.

It is ironic that my back needed to collapse to make myself important enough to finally stand up for me. I received my degree and was ordained. I ministered in church and began teaching forgiveness seminars. I knew part of my healing was letting go of anger, resentment and the pain I carried in my heart. I knew I would never be healthy if I kept all that rage inside.

I now teach people how to forgive, not just others, but also themselves. To find the peace that lies in every situation; to trust in their inner knowing; to look past the human failures and see through the mistakes of others. Emotional pain and mental discord can store itself in the body, leading to physical health issues and mental unrest; all factors in my injury. Seeing past the injustices and forgiving whenever you can, will free you of any suffering you may feel. Looking beyond the circumstances, to see the good or find the silver lining is more for you than for anyone else.

I have learned that the mysteries of life are gifts. They help you discover who you are and what you value. We may not uncover them all, but in looking for answers, we find the ones that matter most. Your life may have a mystery that needs solving – you may need to search to find some answers. Whatever it is for you, do it with love and peace in your heart. Think clearly, be smart and let go of falling into blame, or reaction. Respect your physical health by being in optimum-mental awareness. Believe in what matters to you and when push comes to shove... always stand up for yourself. Swing your feet off the bed, put your feet on the ground and walk when you need to walk.

IGNITE ACTION STEPS

Learning to forgive is one of the greatest things you can do for yourself. Many people believe that by forgiving, you let the other person off the hook, or you accept their behaviour. Forgiveness is *not* about condoning or permitting. It is about freeing yourself from the mental anguish and emotional pain that lingers when you harbor resentment towards someone.

Make a list of all the things you are still holding onto and having trouble forgiving.

Then expand your list by adding to it all the POSITIVE things that have happened to you from that situation and use a positive affirmation sentence to help you truly see the gifts that have come from it.

For example, "I choose to forgive those who teased me, because they made me a stronger person." "I choose to forgive those that bullied me because I went on to make something of myself." "I choose to forgive those that rejected me because they taught me to never be like that." "I choose to forgive those that abandoned me because it inspired me to be kind to others."

Write a letter to the person who hurt you. There is something special about putting pen to paper. Take some time to write out all the things you need to say to that person. Don't hold back. Get it all out. Put down all the ways that you feel and how it has affected you. The important part of this letter is to say how you feel. To own all your emotions and only talk about you. By unloading all your feelings, you will release the pent-up discord inside of you. The letter is for you – *your healing* – it never needs to be sent. It is a way for you to release what needs to be forgiven. The hurt and anguish is inside of you and that is what needs to shift. Negative feelings create negative experiences, illness, or dis-ease in the body and that is what needs to be released.

You can save your letter, burn it, or rewrite it again and again. The benefits that come from doing this are for you. Part of forgiveness is in the process. It has little to do with the other person, the work is to remove the anguish inside of you.

Say a positive prayer to the person who has hurt you. There is a saying that 'hurt people hurt'. When someone is hurtful, it is usually because somewhere inside of them, they are also hurting. It took many years for me to recognize the pain that must have lived inside my abusive step-father. As an adult, I was able to look beyond all his transgressions and see that his actions arose out of deep hurts in his heart. It did not make his behaviour acceptable, but my forgiveness allowed my heart to find compassion, empathy and understanding. Expanding my heart in this way fueled me. I felt better. I felt more in control of who I was and the person I wanted to be; one capable of forgiving. Holding so much resentment towards him was only hurting me.

Create a mantra to say to yourself. Mantras are sentences you repeat to help reprogram the brain. Shift out of the old messaging that has consumed you till now and find a new, positive mantra to chant in your head or out loud to send a different message to your brain.

Here is a simple one: I forgive you. I forgive me. I choose to be free. I forgive you. I forgive me. I choose to love me.

Forgiving will free you and heal your heart. You will be happier, and your life will improve. That is the joy in forgiving and being grateful for all of life's gifts. I wish that joyous peace and happiness for you.

Reverend Valentine Owen, Ordained Minister. www.cslreddeer.org

SHIRLEY WHING CHOW

"The heavens gave you a voice to reach for the stars.
Believe it and send it soaring."

Obsessed with the happiness and success of children and young women, I have been put on the stage to help them Sing, Shine, and Succeed. In sharing the story of voices lost and found, I intend to share with you some tricks I use to elevate my inner voice to the frequencies of Confidence, Courage, and Compassion. The SOUND of OUR highest and happiest MUSIC is just a few breezy 'whistles' away. I hope you will make the loveliest music every day.

RESILIENCE RHAPSODY

Are you one of the lucky souls who sing and 'jive' along to Bohemian Rhapsody or Happy in total surrender on your commute?

I am. My dad would be one as well. I owe my musical, humour, people-loving, and leadership genes to him. From twenty-five years of memories, I fondly recall when he played the harmonica. Dad and I were just beginning to get close when I left Hong Kong for graduate studies in the U.S. If he had not subconsciously resigned to the belief that after retirement at age 55, a man can only await his inevitable end, I would be able to hear his singing voice today. In waiting for a liver transplant, his finale came too soon.

For Mum, she probably would not act 'silly'. She was more reserved and composed in the nine years I knew her. The heavens listened too closely to her wish to escape from her battle with diabetes and depression. She was 33.

Mum did not know how singing instantly blasts Oxytocin, the love hormone, or how music-making fires up the entire brain, creates social connection, and cognitive stimulation. She named me 'Wing Han' solely because she wanted me to be intelligent, docile, and demure. 'Wing' actually stands for singing. 'Vocal' since infancy, I protested every formula-milk feeding because I was lactose intolerant. Having a dysfunctional G.I. tract and severe IBS, I fought her on every meal. She did what she could to raise a sweet 'swan', but I was a dozen 'dolphins' plus a white 'tiger' by nature. I roamed away from home at age three and idolized anything English at age four. In addition to getting my forehead stitched up twice and bruising my arms and legs playing with boys, I also gave myself the name Shirley at age 8. Despite taking on Mum's graceful yet weak physique, my toughness filled my childhood with adventures and hard-core skills to survive never-ending doctor's visits, pills and nasty Chinese medicinal soups.

The Dolphins caged

On one fateful night, the music of my childhood rhapsody took a sudden 'modulation'. During a pre-dinner shower, I had a vision of myself wearing a traditional, white mourning gown kneeling in a room. Mum admitted herself to the hospital a day prior for what appeared to be food poisoning. The hospital called during dinner. I did not tell anyone about my premonition. I did not know about its significance until years later when I had others.

Long story short, at the funeral home, I was forbidden to 'view' Mum's body for some superstitious reason. I did not listen. "I have every right to see the woman I called mother. I don't care if she is dead." So, I sneaked into the back room; I got my peek. An eerie voice in my head uttered in disbelief, "Life ends, just like this. My mother and my anchor are gone, just like that."

No matter how tough a child is, the impact of seeing a dead parent is beyond traumatic. Knowing I would never see her again, I was in shock. Yet, no one at home talked about loss, grief, change, or needing support. While physical care was uninterrupted, the habit or vocabulary to process loss was amiss. Indifference and emotional distance hurt. I concluded then my feelings were irrelevant. They did not matter.

My ability to smile, laugh, or rally my friends vanished; my happy memories gone. When insects crawled on the wall by my piano, I wondered if Mum returned to check on us. There were no dreams or tears about her. I began fantasizing and writing about dying young. A year later, when relatives visited and laughed, I would become enraged. "How dare they laugh; how could they?" I wanted to scream, but I did not.

My skin did it instead. My mother's manic-depressive nature started expressing itself fully in me after the funeral. Under a complete emotional void and the stress of disharmony, palm-sized patches of hives would itch, burn, and engulf my face, head, and any other parts of my body randomly. The embarrassment was aggravated whenever I had phys-ed, particularly during swimming lessons. I would pray to the heavens as I changed, "Please wait till I get home, please give me a day off."

Beethoven and Chopin to the rescue

Music became my Fairy Godmother. I was tempted by some bad influences but thanks to the grace of my Mum, the moral compass she instilled in me, steered me away from harm. Instead, I spent hours on the piano playing Beethoven's Pathetique and Chopin Preludes. 'If Beethoven and Chopin had suffered, it is alright for me to suffer too'.

In eighth and ninth grades, I began singing, coaching music and elocution, accompanying, conducting choirs, and organizing music contests. My rambunctious Tiger voice started to roar. I got 'noticed'. My music teachers, who gave me so many opportunities, found out about my loss. They started calling me at home to chit-chat every other day! Thanks to their emotional warmth, I resumed some faith. By 10th grade, I said yes to everything; I became a 'Prefect' and the chair-lady of the Music Club and other student bodies. As an accompanist, a pianist, and a soprano, I won awards. However, it was really being seen, heard, and valued by my friends that resuscitated my smiles and laughter. Dad helped, too. He found me a doctor who prescribed steroids to heal my skin. With good spirit and strong meds, seven years of torture finally ended.

I did very well academically both in high school and college. Overachievement is a great bandage for emotional wounds. Many awards and international performances later, I earned a full scholarship and teaching assistantship from the College-Conservatory of Music at Cincinnati to study the art of piano accompanying. I finished my Master of Music degree, and the promise of 'a bright future' was before me.

Instead of going after my career, I decided to marry the first boyfriend

I had in my life, the Texan I dated long-distance during my studies. Little did I know at age 24 that Emotional Dysregulation from my childhood would form an eight-year spiral of codependency, dissonance, and clinical depression.

The White Tiger muted

As Margot Booth, the therapist who saved my life, put it, "When one's drowning, one holds on to any floating device in sight." A man who was emotionally attached, supportive, intelligent, and faithful was unreal to me. My ex was one in a trillion.

"Your ex-husband finished what your mother left off..." Margot was right. By age 29, my ex helped heal some major emotional wounds. The woman in me emerged. I was no longer a little vulnerable Chinese girl on my ex's pedestal. From being guilt-laden whenever my opinions 'contradicted' my spouse's in public to undermining certain biological needs – to relinquishing a movie credit I earned in an independent movie to my spouse, I betrayed myself repeatedly.

I was so stubborn; I refused to listen to the anger, frustration, and resentment that were eating me alive. Hitting my fists and head against the walls, doubting my sexuality or crying all the time (even under the Eiffel Tower) was 'part of marriage' I thought. Then, I arrived at the exact age when my Mum died. At work, I might have been peaking, but at home, depression was pulling me into a deep abyss. I was prescribed antidepressants after I hatched plans to 'join my Mum' on two occasions. My weight dropped to 89 pounds. I was barely able to walk due to a severe infection. Both my GI tract and appetite gave out completely. The body does not lie.

The Inner Voice taking centre stage

One day, my heart-broken ex asked me for an honest answer, "Shirley, if you had a million dollars right now, would you still be married to me?"

My gut, my inner voice shouted, "You are at gunpoint, tell the truth." From a place of love, this voice sang its most daunting tune, "The truth is, even though breaking my vows is unimaginable, in giving you a chance to be loved as you deserve, and a chance for me to be loved as I deserve, I have to say NO, I will not be married to you anymore."

Sometime later, during a very explosive argument with my ex, this very voice forecasted to my entire body, "You are going to get very sick!" A full-body hive inferno consumed me within minutes. Twenty-four hours later, I was admitted to the ER at 2 am.

For the following decade, as I 'directed my own show', I held on to Margot's words, "Be your own mother; you deserve to be happy." After reading about Indian doctors healing patients with LAUGHTER, I began a daily regimen of Laugh Therapy at bedtime (comedy). Laughter quite literally giggled me out of clinical depression. Hyperarousal (a sign of PTSD), a poor work-life balance, stress, limiting beliefs about men, and an addiction to the past – still distorted my vibration with a lot of physical and emotional 'accidentals'. (A musical term for unexpected, derailing notes).

'When the student is ready, the teacher appears'. The catalysts of my rebirth appeared at the end of 2015 and 2016. A series of Mindset workshops, a stranger-than-fiction 'Streaming' session and a vision of my four-year-old self brought out the Phoenix in me. The Universe gave me a VIP pass to mentors, guardian angels, and endless materials on Energy, Vibrations, Conscious, and Subconscious Awakening, the Neuroscience of Music, Brain and Heart Coherence, and most profoundly, Emotional and Social Intelligence. I have been swimming in a sea of crucial life-learning that schools do not teach, and I feel like I grew wings.

The Inner Child always knows

Speaking of learning, children have superpowers. Back in 2007, the Universe guided me back to Hong Kong to help tens of thousands of children and amateurs sing, shine and succeed on stage. Singing, acting, and dance do wonders for young brains and minds. In developing an uncanny ability to instantly captivate and motivate hundreds of restless children in any rehearsal situations (welcomed by staff, teachers and mums), I began to connect with them on a gut level, particularly with kids who suffer from Psoriasis (stress), ADHD, anxiety, behavioural challenges, and bullying.

A new voice began to ring inside me after a mum came to me for help one day. Her ornery son had visions of his deceased father and became increasingly combative. She lost her husband to suicide, you see. I shared my story with the boy and asked for his permission to accept my help. He reciprocated; his behaviour improved. When his gorgeous voice was recognized, the support translated into increased mindfulness with which he used to address his emotions.

I saw the need to read, see, humour, respect and understand all children before I started serving them. The results? The excitement in their voices, sparks in their eyes and trust in their behavior said it all.

Fine Voices finding its voice

In 2016, the statistics of mental health decline, bullying, self-harm and suicides among children in Hong Kong and around the world came into my radar. The Tiger-Phoenix voice in me said, "NO! Something has to be done."

A light-bulb came on – "It all makes sense now."

While I knew in 2007 I wanted to use the performing arts for healing, the alchemy for real impact moulded for nine years. Although I was told my aspirations were lofty, the needs of these children inspired the creation of Fine Voices, a Performing Arts Society.

Promoting Emotional Intelligence, Social-Emotional Learning and Female Empowerment through the performing arts has now become my mission and my passion.

I produced two fundraising concerts The Magic of Dedication (2017) and The Wonder in Every Woman (2018), which brought awareness to emotional wellness and gender equality. The wonder of having incredibly generous musician friends donating their talents and time, and the public who supported us, convinces me that a bright future is possible when we embrace and embody 'Humanity' proactively.

Thank you Mum and Dad

'Mum, in the ceremony at the Women's Economic Forum in L.A., I received an Iconic Woman Award. My spirit flies high these days. I told everyone about my legal name change. You see how I incorporated the 'H' from 'Han' into 'Wing'? Bye-bye 'demure'. I will do 'beautiful' in my 'Whing' kind of way.'

'Are you singing along, Dad?
Thanks to you, Dad, my family and all my guardian angels!
I am 'Shirley' filling my life every day to the brim with
gorgeous roses, silly giggles, emotional wealth,
and the sweet music of serving children and women everywhere.'

IGNITE ACTION STEPS

I want to share with you my daily SWING routine. I have used it to great effect in vibrating on the frequencies of giddiness and gratitude. Living every moment in a state of confidence, courage, and compassion – that is the magic we can create every day.

Smile and Say Hello: Wake up with a smile. Say thank you or hello to the sun and to the day ahead in a friendly and excited tone.

Vocalize while Visualizing Intentions: In a calm yet confident voice, narrate your intention for a great day, in which your voice will be honoured and heard, "I'm looking forward to creating a day of vitality/motivation/cooperation/progress." This can be followed by a short meditation.

Dance: Turn on your favourite tune or compilation and get out of bed. Use music that is groovy or energetic to get your body shaking and jiving while you wash up, make breakfast, and get dressed. Tell yourself how you love and appreciate your body.

Sing (alone or with others): Sing to a tune that keeps your on your dancing feet, or to a song that uplifts, heals or inspires you with 'powerful' lyrics.

Listen In: Listen to your tone of voice throughout the day and see if it aligns with your intentions. Listen to different sounds - the birds, a giggle or laughter, the whisper of a breeze, or a minute of classical piano or guitar music. It is a great detox and sound 'massage' for the soul.

Laugh and Socialize: Chat with people or tell some jokes during breaks and meals. If you are alone, watch a funny clip or read a joke aloud from an app.

Compose: Notice your tones of positivity, delight, and motivation when you make delightful comments. Catch every negative and unfair comment you or others generate, acknowledge it, then rephrase it.

Learn, Thank and Smile again: At bedtime, point out how you have liked the day. Say thanks. Recap what you've learned if there were challenges and focus on the 'process of progress'. Smile - that is how every day ends beautifully!

Shirley Whing Chow, Soprano, Coach-pianist, Social-Emotional Wellness
Advocate & Founder of Fine Voices.
Shirley Whing @ Fine Voices. www.facebook.com/finevoices

Rosalyn Palmer

"All I need is already within me"

I share my story to encourage you to step out from behind any mask you might be wearing and follow a blueprint of proven, easy-to-follow steps for how to get through those life-threatening, soul-destroying moments. My wish is for you to emerge happier, stronger and with a sense of purpose. My story is hewn from the broken rock of my former self to show you how it is possible to reset your life, hopes, health, wealth and desires. Like a sculpture, you can emerge from that dark rock into something more beautiful, joyful, enlightened, transformed and true. I wish this for you.

From Disconnect to Reconnect:

Finding My Authentic Self

The most intense period of being born through fire took place over an 18-month period between 2003 and 2005. My life imploded, stripping away almost everything I knew, cherished, connected to and identified with. I went from a seemingly healthy and attractive 40 something who had made a million from her amazing PR career, living in a beachfront house in The Bahamas, to a single jobless mother in a rented house in England having cancer treatment and supporting my depressed father after burying my mother. This was my first major wake up call to 'let go' of what had gone before and reset my life for living at a higher level. I thought I had nailed it then, as the time I spent on the cancer journey was one of the most uplifting of my life. Yet it didn't hold.

The true transformation took a while longer. On the outside, I put the illness and losses behind me and looked okay. I found new and wonderful work, bought a house, made new friends, remarried and rebuilt a life.

Yet as I sat alone in a crowd at the Cardiff Millennium Stadium in Wales watching Madonna in concert, the pain overwhelmed me and I knew I could no longer pretend to be happy, whole or at one with myself.

I'd been a material girl, desperately seeking something in the '80s and '90s. With sheer hard work and determination, I rose from humble beginnings to be a success in the cut-throat world of PR in London. The material rewards and public accolades that went with it were many.

Perhaps I was growing old or growing up; but in that moment, I felt only messed up. Madge had sung "Hung Up" and I'd felt a bit better. Yet as I left, the lyrics to her song 'Nobody Knows Me' would not stop playing in my head – it went on repeat. "I've had so many lives/Since I was a child/And I realize/How many times I've died/Nobody, nobody knows me/Nobody knows me". That is how I felt in my life: Misunderstood. Lonely. Like I kept living the wrong life, an actress in a play I hadn't realized I'd auditioned for.

This pattern had been playing out for longer than I could remember. While struggling through depression after returning to the UK, using CBT (Cognitive Behavioural Therapy) to get off my meds, I realized I'd felt like that forever. I'd come through so many life events and losses that my therapist marveled at my ability to be merely depressed and disconnected, without going the whole hog and developing Dissociative Identity Disorder as a way of coping. My therapist wanted to use me as a case study. I wanted to feel happy. I wanted to feel alive. I wanted to sleep at night and have a sense of centeredness during the day that wasn't courtesy of prescription drugs.

I had many mantras for getting through. I'd drive myself on by saying: "I'm a Weeble: I wobble but I don't fall down" (this was advertising for the '70s 'Weebles' toys, which had weighted bottoms to keep them from falling over when punched). The trouble is that for most of my life, I'd look like I was bouncing back – and I would even do so, temporarily - but it was taking a huge internal emotional and physical toll.

Never more did I need an array of fixes to keep me from falling than when I ran my PR company in the '90s. Negative things such as alcohol, anger, sleeping tablets, or allowing my subconscious to take charge of my appearance and keep my body a size zero via bulimia. On the positive side, things such as acupuncture, massage, Ayurvedic medicine, psychotherapy, hypnotherapy, colonics, kinesiology, floatation tank therapy, and more kept me going. All the latter were like plasters holding me together. The former often just numbed the pain.

I launched my PR company with a £5k redundancy package, in my spare room, with my basset hound Rosie as the first member of staff. Three years later, its turnover was £250,000 and we were getting noticed. We had great staff, nice offices and were winning pretty much everything we pitched for, yet I was miserable. It all felt so burdensome. At night, I couldn't sleep. It felt like I had to keep spinning plates on poles. I was handling the UK PR for arguably the world's greatest motivational guru, Tony Robbins, and going through his premier live course - Mastery University. I was learning about my internal dialogue, digging deep for my values, tapping into my inner power. I then went on to represent Brandon Bayes and Robert Holden, so I embraced their teaching to heal many past wounds and develop a deeper understanding of myself. I felt happy some of the time.

For years, I tried without success to get pregnant. I tried every complementary therapy and medical procedure apart from the IVF I was offered, as by that point I was fed up with it all and not wanting the process. What I didn't realize at the time were two things: firstly, my mind was saying to my body: "Are you crazy? You can barely get through your 12-hour days, fueled by adrenalin and coffee. You don't even sleep at night due to worry — and you want to grow a healthy baby in this environment? You want to time the birth so you can be back at work in 48 hours? No deal!"

Secondly, my immune and hormonal system was highly compromised, having been depleted due to years of taking antibiotics as a child to counter nearly dying of whooping cough and German measles when I was 18 months old. I thought it normal to have constant tonsillitis, a tonsillectomy at 26, repeated glandular fever, no periods, psoriasis, IBS and shingles as I arrived in my 30s.

This compromised health came back to haunt me in The Bahamas. The PR company soared up to over a million pounds and we were winning a string of awards. We had been bought out and I thought I'd dodged a bullet by getting out of the rat race alive. I was a vegan. My size zero body was honed to perfection as I ran 5k every morning before hours at the gym. Then, I started to feel run down. I thought it was flu. I found a lump in my breast, following a mammogram that said I was fine. I thought it was a cyst.

My diagnosis came the day before Good Friday. I was 43 years old.

Given the type of breast cancer (invasive lobular carcinoma), and having young (adopted) children, I chose to go to the Moffitt Cancer Center

144 / ROSALYN PALMER

in Tampa, Florida not just for its outstanding reputation, but also because it's an independent clinic. I felt some of the other hospitals were in the pockets of the pharmaceutical companies and were bound to suggest a very oncological course of treatment.

Three weeks later, just before I was on the operating table, something spiritual and amazing happened. I had been advised to have a double mastectomy, chemotherapy, and radiation treatment after five further lumps were found on the Moffitt's MRI machine. Three days prior to the booked operation, we found a local church to go to. While the service was mid-way, I fainted.

I later found out that all the people in my home Community Church in The Bahamas had been praying for me at that very time. I came out of the church and had a feeling of total certainty that all the other lumps were not cancerous. Early Monday morning, I rang the hospital, spoke to my amazing surgeon, Dr. Cox and told him how I felt. He said to come straight in. After further discussions, he said that they would biopsy each new lump the following day, one after the other. He said that if all five showed up benign, then I would have defied all odds and proved all their advanced assessments of their new testing procedures wrong.

I did defy the odds. They did the five biopsies, one after the other. As each one was taken, it was sent to the lab. We waited and then the results came back. Negative. So on to the next one, and the next, and the next. By this time, I had so much lidocaine pumped into me that two interns were holding me down on the table for the last biopsy. I didn't care. It came back negative. Dr. Cox came to the room and told me that the Brits are made of strong stuff and gave me a hug. I had a lumpectomy; two weeks later I returned for brachytherapy radiation.

At the time, even this treatment knocked me for six. Thankfully, we had made another good choice: to allow time for nature to heal a body that science had saved.

Following a chance conversation at a party, shortly before all the treatment started, we discovered that a 10-acre farm was available to rent on an outer island of Eleuthera. What better place to recover than an organic farm that fronted one of the most beautiful pink sand beaches in the world?

We moved there. For two years we lived on the land and sea. I would haggle daily with the local fishermen for their catches, adding fish to my otherwise vegan diet. The farm was abundant with fruits. We grew mixed salad greens and watercress. I moved on to eggplant, courgettes, carrots and onions. I purchased bushels (large cardboard boxes) of amazing mangoes. I swapped homemade onion bread for tuna. I distilled Noni-juice.

I meditated, read, watched positive movies and walked the beach with my dogs. It was one of the most amazing and uplifting times of my life, and I recovered fully.

But the challenges continued. Will Polston's words became my mantra: "Strong trees do not grow with ease. The stronger the wind, the stronger the trees."

That's when it imploded. My father's stroke had preceded the cancer in me. Then, after our farm was destroyed by two hurricanes, doctors discovered my mother had terminal pancreatic cancer. My children had little stability as I spent the best part of two years in hospitals in America and the UK for myself, my father, and mother. Then I discovered that the bedrock, the financial safety I'd worked so hard for, was pretty much gone. Poor investments from a husband trying to hold it all together. The marriage didn't last after that. I had to go home and I returned with practically nothing.

It was a time of intense pain and overwhelm. Not only did I have to freeze what was left of our money in the bank, leaving with only what I could physically load onto a BA Flight out of Nassau with the kids, but I also found that I was not entitled to any support from UK Social services for six months upon my return. I had to sell my best and most treasured jewelry to support myself and the children. Now a single mother with no bank assets and two young children, my dear father gifted me a car and paid the rental on the small house I found.

Just as I watched my mother die from pancreatic cancer, my husband bought criminal charges against me. Three days after her funeral, I opened my door to face two police officers who entered the house and seized our passports. A bailiff arrived half an hour later and served me with a writ. I had to appear in the High Court of Justice in London to defend charges that I had abducted my own children from my country of permanent residence. I was reeling. I managed to pick my children up, bring them home for supper then to swimming class. I remember sitting at the side of that hot humid pool, shouts of fun and laughter echoing all around me, feeling utterly bereft and exhausted to my core. I couldn't eat or sleep; I could barely breathe. That night, I popped out three packets of sleeping pills. I sat in bed, staring at them scattered across the bedding, thinking how easy it would be to grab a handful, open the bottle of red wine and sink into oblivion to stop the pain.

Yet, I didn't. I couldn't check out and leave my children and my father. I felt there was love and hope and support somewhere, I just had to reconnect to it. My amazing father found a good lawyer. I fought the court case and won. My country of residence was and is the UK, so I set about making a new life here. It seemed like the perfect reset. I went back to work. My childhood sweetheart came back into my life and married me in a small 19th Century village chapel, on a windy, sunny day in May, in front of my family and friends.

I moved to be near my wonderful father and spent many years making up for lost time with him. I became Head of Marketing and Communications for The Leprosy Mission charity and spent times of pure privilege with some of the poorest and most marginalized people in the world. Hearing their stories and seeing their courage gave me my sense of self back. This period of challenges and upheavals came to a head watching Madonna that night in Cardiff. I found the inner strength to reset my life once more.

A second divorce and retraining to be a Rapid Transformational Hypnotherapist and Coach gave me the insight and perspective that finally healed me. Courses including LifeBook, and events such as A-fest, led to connections with spiritual, brave, heartfelt people. Eventually, I had the courage to understand that all of it had been for a reason. It awoke in me my spiritual calling. It ignited in me the wisdom, compassion, and empathy to share my story, help others, and save lives with my therapeutic training. It ignited in me a voice that is now shared via my books, columns and on the radio. All lead me back to myself, where I connect to my inner being and know my life promise with certainty.

For me, there have been many Ignite-moments that have changed my life, some more explosive than others. The most challenging and rewarding parts of my journey that got me where I am today is igniting the lives of others and sharing my losses and joys with you. Like a stubborn outdoor fire, it has taken several moments and much soulful kindling to finally ignite the fire in my heart, soul and life.

IGNITE ACTION STEPS

The wonderful way to check daily if you are living a whole and balanced life is to think of five fingers as your 5Fs: *Faith, **Fitness, ***Family, ****Friends, and *****Finance. It is like a compassionate To-Do list when you stretch out your hand each morning and check in against each category.

Doing this exercise across all the five categories will give you a values list that is true to you and moves you to want to live by these values or improve them. Keep your list handy and remind yourself of it daily.

Repeating this exercise each week lets you dig a little deeper. On a scale of 1 – 10 (with 10 being the absolute best place) rank each category in your life right now. Perhaps one category is a 6 or a 7, but you want that one to be a 10/10. Once you have your score for each, ask yourself, "What are my overarching goals in each?"

*Faith: Ask yourself: "What will I do today to build my faith in myself? What is there that is beyond me that holds me and all humanity together? What does God hold dear, and how can I fill my heart and soul and life with the pure love and guidance of this source?"

**Fitness and Health: Perhaps this would be something like, "If I were totally fit, I'd have more energy, feel better about my body, be sexier and love life better." This is getting to your 'why,' so now ask yourself "Why is it important for me to have better, uncompromised health?" The answers might be what you want, such as feeling sexy, and what you don't want, such as having to take sick time off work or being unable to enjoy walks as your back hurts too much. What actions will help you be fit in body and mind?

***Family: "How can I connect with my family today? Have I reached out to my family? Is there a family member, or someone I count as my family, who might need a call? Have I got everyone's birthday down? Am I remembering special occasions during the year? Do I make them feel they are in my thoughts by my everyday actions?"

****Friends: "Which friend shall I reach out to and make time for? Who are the five most important friends for challenging me and holding me accountable for my own growth in every way I wish to grow? Do I need to reconnect with any friends? Are there friends who are now just a number in my phone? Do I reach out to them, or do I accept we were together for a season and a reason, and let them go with my blessing?"

*****Finance: "What steps shall I take to attract and allow the energy that is money and reward flow to me? Do I need to work on my relationship with that energy? Do I need to take steps to change my career, or around the value that I put upon my services? Are there any blocks standing in my way? Who do I need to reach out to in order to remove those blocks? How can I benefit others from my good fortune and good finances? Do I remember to be altruistic and pay it forward?"

******Fun: How about adding a 6th finger - for fun! We are meant to do more than just endure life. This one is like the caviar. Remember to have fun in the process. Life is to be enjoyed! You deserve it.

Rosalyn Palmer, Rapid Transformational Hypnotherapist (RTT) & Coach.
Rosalyn Palmer Trust Transformation. rosalynpalmer.com

VIVIEN HUNT

"BEING is your brilliance."

My wish is that by reading my story you get curious about your own patterns and start to explore your life. Slow down, check in with yourself, notice where you are right now. Through awareness, new pathways appear and possibility opens. What I want for you are moments of joy through presence and the experience of being.

BACK TO BEING

I consider myself highly creative, intuitive and have a constant flow of ideas in my head. I can easily tap into and access this part of me. I love telling stories, and used to tell ghost stories before bed or around the campfire at night. I can visualise the story as I tell it, so that it becomes real. I see the images, and feel the energy. Even when I'm sleeping, my dreams can be likened to full length films, where details, words and people are remembered long afterwards.

When I started my work life, people would ask me 'from where was I getting all this stuff'. I'd be surprised as I thought we all had access to this steady stream of ideas, which I'm certain we all do. But perhaps like my own creativity, theirs slowly got pushed down, or pushed out.

Memoirs of a perfectionist.

It was my grade three school teacher, and yes I remember her name, I remember her very well. How she made me go home in the middle of the day, all by myself. I must have been only eight years old. Running and crying all the way across the school field, through the alley and down my crescent to collect my things at home and come straight back to share my unfinished work with the class. Shame and humiliation must have been a teaching method in those days, because the learning was long-lasting. With tears rolling down my cheeks, I handed over the cassette tape for all the room to hear the story I'd spent days creating. The now less than perfect version. A scary story I had recorded with clever sound effects; 'Creeeak' a door would open, craggy voices and expressions. A great story and ingenious use of technology for an eight year old, but not quite finished. Not yet good enough. I didn't want them to hear it like this, so I purposely didn't bring the cassette to class that day. But they heard it, and the teacher whose name I don't want to mention but still remember, was fully satisfied I'd learnt my lesson. While my classmates sat in silence, fearful with the realisation that at any time they could be next.

I would never miss a deadline after that. Even if it meant staying up all night. Actually, it was pretty normal at university, not to sleep for two or three nights, to write essays or prepare for exams. I thought everyone did that, didn't they? The trick was not to go to sleep at all, just work through your tiredness to find your second or third wind. I passed my courses, so it must have been a good strategy.

Long before university from an early age, I danced. I knew I always wanted to be a dancer but for ballet I was told I was too tall, too fat, my feet not flexible enough, my body not supple enough, just basically that I wasn't good enough. BUT I excelled at discipline, structure, routine and the perseverance of perfection, which kept me going to class almost every day for 24 years. It was dance that allowed me to tap into my dream side, my creativity and expression. Through dance I could tell my stories, without the need for words, told just for me, inside my head.

I quickly learnt it was impossible to survive in the dance world. There was no money in it, but worse was 'the look' I would get when people asked me what I did for a living. When I said I taught ballet, there was a strange response and the first thing they would say was, "why aren't you using your degree?"

I quickly noted that 'ballet teacher' was never going to be good enough, so the next logical step was… management consultant - the perfect job. As a consultant, I got recognition and paid for my great attention to detail, thoroughness, and on time delivery. Being a perfectionist was my strength.

Was I a good or bad perfectionist? I wasn't sure. According to Wikipedia, being a bad perfectionist can contribute to serious health problems, including depression, anxiety, eating disorders, low self-esteem, self-criticism and fatigue. Quite blindly, I made no connection and only reasoned that it must be good.

PERFECTIONISM, a positive trait that increases your chances of success AND can contribute to early mortality.

In my first consulting job, precision and detail were of the utmost importance, even recording my time had to be in 15-minute intervals. The new era of technology: email, internet, spreadsheets, Word and PowerPoint, unknowingly to me, was also the death of my Creativity.

The computer age sucked out my soul.

Fast forward 10 years, to one of the rare occasions when I made it to the yoga studio, an achievement in itself. "Ah, that's exactly what I need" as I glanced at a poster for a series of Friday evening workshops. I signed up right away. Not even knowing what it was about, I just knew I needed it!

I'd welcome any quick fix. No price was too much to pay, considering the pain I was in, my back and neck never quite easing up from all those hours of concentrated sitting. Sitting at my computer, in bad chairs, inadequate spaces, sometimes in basements with no windows. I'd built up my super team of therapists and healers to give me some temporary relief and keep me going; visiting regularly my acupuncturist, reiki healer, massage therapist, osteopath and chinese medicine doctor. My body (and mind) were always in pain. One month I even spent more than £1,000 on treatments just to 'feel better'.

STOP the world, I WANT TO GET OFF. That's what my Friday evening workshops were called and exactly what I was longing to do.

The first of four sessions was just about stopping. How hard could that be?

That was the moment I stopped flying on automatic. I wasn't even aware this was my pattern. I never knew another way. Numbed for so long, disconnected from myself, stopping and un-numbing was new territory for me. I was curious and willing but sensed by the serenity in the room this was going to be a tough and uncomfortable journey.

I recall we looked at a candle flame for what felt like hours. Even though it couldn't have been more than 10 minutes at a time, it was painful, my body hurt too much to sit still. There was too much chatter in my mind but yet I liked the silence of the room. There was another exercise sitting face to face, looking into my partner's eyes, just holding the gaze. I tried my best to hide my sadness, hoping to shield myself so she wouldn't see through me and touch my shame and worthlessness.

Deep, deep inside.

Each week I'd continue to peel back another layer of the numbing. Slowly moving closer to my discomfort, what was this feeling I couldn't be with? I noticed some tightness around my heart, agitation in my throat, but had no words for what I was feeling. Something was there inside my body not wanting to move.

I took it all in. I noticed what it felt like to be in a safe place. I experienced what it was not to be judged but supported. There was compassion in this room, not just for each other, but for myself. New territory. Each week I'd build on the exercises from the week before, trusting in my partner a tiny bit more. Trusting in myself a little bit more. Until I was the observer of myself, observing me watching my candle. Noticing me noticing. For the final exercise, I sat across from my partner this time holding her gaze in silence for 30 minutes. This time BEING WITH my discomfort, tears rolling down my face. Surrendering. She never looked away. Witnessing. Holding the space. All she had was love for me. She smiled. She could see me.

It's not like from that moment everything was better but the feeling that I couldn't be with, started to lose its power. The process to dissolve it had begun. My mind felt calmer.

Over the next months, feelings, emotion and information began to surface and flood my body. The body never lies, it is always the LAST place for pain to manifest, so I had work to do. This time I welcomed it.

In all this, what surprised me most was how I'd thought everybody who wanted to stop the world and get off, felt as bad as I did.

But, they didn't. They were there to pause, to get grounded, to connect. They were there to practice stillness, to get present and build resilience. This was self-care, restoring, and recharging. The workshops weren't a last resort for them, they were a first choice and intentionally how they designed their life to be. Something they did regularly for themselves; a good practice, a good routine, a good discipline.

That's what I really wanted. To feel that good.

What the workshops did, were to shift my self-perception and way of being. It was no longer a question of whether I was a good or bad perfectionist, both were self-defeating.

Which of my other behaviours and patterns were self-defeating?

My mantra used to be 'make more effort'. Now my mantra reads 'self-compassion and loving kindness'.

How otherwise could I make a difference to others and create positive impact if I wasn't showing love towards myself?

Setting off on a new journey of self-discovery, I made an intention to invite creativity back into my life and reconnect with my dancing!

Some weeks after my Friday night workshops, my yoga teacher, Louise, read a poem in class entitled Autobiography in Five Chapters. Wow, I thought, this is about me, this is my life story! I ran home, printed it out and stuck it on my fridge.

This poem became my guide. My roadmap.

The Five Chapters became an empowering way to check in with myself. The poem was a visible reminder of my journey and every time I went to the kitchen or opened the fridge it was there to nudge and encourage me.

I'd been living in chapters one and two of this poem for so long, stuck, but now that I knew about chapters three, four and five, I had something to move towards, somewhere to go. I still didn't know the how but the what was now clear. I needed to walk down another street.

You see, this poem is about a person who falls into a hole and continues to fall into the same hole until becoming aware of a pattern. Once self-aware, this person starts to make different choices and get different results. This simple poem was my guide to getting out of the hole, the hole I had created.

There is another way. I have choices. I hadn't always acknowledged my own choices, my role in creating my life and the possibility to change it.

This poem is still stuck on my fridge 12 years later. When friends or guests visit me, those who already know it tell me how much they love it. Almost everyone who reads it for the first time asks for a copy.

A workshop or poem is not the answer OR any quick-fix, it's about lifelong learning and practice. It took time to consciously embed practices and routines into my life and build awareness of which ones nourish me versus those that deplete me. I had to acknowledge all parts of me, good and bad. This meant lots of checking in with myself and the commitment to doing plenty of inner work.

Now I love being present, doing self-care, rest and restoration. Personal work is actually enjoyable for me as I discover new things about myself all of the time. What I know is, the clearer I got about how I wanted to be, the better I started to feel. Learning that, the better I feel, the more meaningful what I do can become.

Ignite Action Steps

Create your own practice to build self-awareness.

Once you know where you are, where you want to get to becomes much clearer. What's important is to stop and check in with yourself regularly.

Here's one thing I invite you to do:

Go to a quiet place, somewhere you will not be interrupted. A quiet cosy room or sitting in the park is often good for me. Turn your phone to AIR-PLANE MODE, you just need your timer.

Have some paper and pens with you and allocate one hour for this exercise.

Close your eyes and sit in silence. Set your timer for five minutes, to reflect: what in my life is no longer serving me?

When you open your eyes, on one side of your page, write down all the words and ideas that came to you. Take a full five minutes to brain dump ALL the things (e.g., behaviours, beliefs, relationships, circumstances, etc.) that are no longer serving you, i.e., things you have outgrown, keeping you stuck or holding you back.

Now look at each word one by one, and ask yourself the question, on a scale of one to ten (one being the lowest and ten the highest) - How much is this impacting my life right now? Be honest with yourself and write the number beside the word.

How will you know the number? Focus on the word, and ask for the number. Trust your intuition by taking the first number that pops into your head.

Circle your top three words to which you've allocated the highest numbers.

Look at your word with the **highest impact** of all three words, notice any feelings or emotions that come up for you. Notice without trying to analyse or judge. Now scan your body with your awareness. Where in your body do you notice this feeling or emotion? Scan for tightness, temperature, sensation. Where is your attention drawn to? What do you notice about your breathing?

On a new page write down everything you are noticing, take your time to do this, you are checking in and gathering information from the intelligence of your body.

Repeat for the other two words.

This is your baseline, you now have a starting point for your roadmap.

To close this exercise, journal on the following question for 15 minutes —What would my life look like without these three things?

Vivien Hunt, Leadership & Organisational Coach
with LeadSource Coaching. www.leadsourcecoaching.com

ANGELA LEGH

"Forgiveness is the seed that allows your soul
to blossom into wholeness."

It is my intention to help anyone experiencing an offense. There have been terrible things done in this world, and the truth is: no one escapes life unscathed. Tucking hurt away in our hearts does not serve us. Growing the seed in our hearts to forgive — both ourselves and the other person, is the way to true healing.

LEARNING STRENGTH THROUGH ADVERSITY

Adversity, via loss or illness, is bound to knock at everyone's door. But you don't expect it to all happen at once! That is what happened to me! - In less than 12 months, I experienced a natural disaster and I made the difficult decision to leave my toxic marriage of 33 years.

I am a two-time fire survivor. At age four, my family's house burned down. To say we were unsettled and displaced does not begin to touch the feelings I experienced. My sister and I were sent to live with distant friends whom only our parents knew. Though they were nice people, I felt insecure, unloved, tossed aside. My other lucky two sisters were shipped to our Aunt and Uncle, a known source of love, seen by us regularly at Sunday-night family dinners with my grandparents.

My mother and father spent the time searching for a rental house to accommodate a family of six. As a child, I didn't know how to understand, or deal with, the uncertainty that ruled our lives until we were reunited, months later. We all bore the scars of that separation in different ways. The hurt that sank deep into me was feeling unworthy of love.

Forty-nine years later, my house was completely destroyed by the Tubbs Fire, which devastated Santa Rosa, California, in October 2017. We received the evacuation call at 1:30 am. Opening the door to see what was happening, I heard an unworldly sound like a freight train coupled with a lion roaring. I slammed the door shut in fear. We gathered what we thought we needed. Fifteen minutes later, we were driving away, under an indescribable orange sky.

The fire torched over 5,000 homes and killed 24 people in a wind-whipped conflagration that stymied all attempts by firefighters to contain the inferno. Our house and everything inside, was transformed into a two-foot pile of ash in mere minutes. Witnesses told of the violence of the fire – windows exploded outward; glass shards reaching 40 feet into the street. Structures were fully engulfed in flames within five minutes, gone completely in ten. With metal and glass melting, a lifetime of stuff was instantaneously destroyed.

Though I have tried, the description of the fire on these pages cannot begin to express the hellish nightmare forced on my community. A wheelchair-bound neighbor was killed by the fire, as her father tried desperately to get her out. Other neighbors received no warning, had no time to escape, and were forced to jump in a swimming pool to survive, as they watched the inferno destroy everything around them.

While in our neighborhood, the fire skipped random houses. On our block, the fire destroyed 30-odd houses. A random few were left standing. Our Starbucks, a 15-minute walk, survived, but the entire subdivision across the street was annihilated. For the entire community life was unreal, with no ability to experience the familiar. Even our frequently-visited Starbucks, though still standing, wasn't open for two weeks.

The fire had a profound effect on both my husband and I. The morning after, many of us needed survival basics. I remember walking up an aisle in Walmart, with everyone in that store pushing carts full of necessities – toiletries, underwear, socks, shoes – the things we needed to start the day. All of us in shock, looking like zombies. The first few weeks we were sleepwalking through our lives as we tried to make sense of our situation. Maslow's Hierarchy of Needs became a living, breathing thing, as we were reduced to the most basic of necessities: finding shelter.

The fire pushed me out of my comfort zone. For five weeks, we took shelter at my mother-in-law's 1200-square foot house, four adults in a very toxic atmosphere. Sharing a single bed, there was no space to get away, a luxury no longer available in the ash pile that was left, of what had been my nearly 3000 square-foot house.

We crawled our way back to some semblance of regular life when we were offered the opportunity to rent a friend's 900 square-foot house. (Thank you, Linda Reed; I will never forget what you did!) Four months later, we were able to purchase a 4000 square-foot house; I needed space to 'get away'. Four months after that, I left.

It took a long time, but there came a point when I realized the fire was actually a blessing. For, without the fire, I wouldn't have been uprooted, forced into introspection. Without the fire, my life wouldn't have been reduced to the only 'thing' I had, my toxic relationship with my husband.

Leaving my marriage was a difficult choice. I loved my husband, but I could no longer live with what I perceived as negativity, frustration, psychological manipulations, and unfounded accusations being thrown my way. Our marriage was a mix of good and bad times; but even happy events, such as a vacation, seemed to me to be marred with outbursts of anger, exasperations, along with the usual negativities.

I knew I needed to leave him after I read a book which explained the pain and trouble I experienced in my marriage – it showed me how all of it fit neatly into a box called narcissistic behavior. Over the years of our marriage, I had set myself aside to tend to his and our children's needs. I lost myself. I didn't feel that I had a voice. I didn't feel like I could talk about what mattered to me either. Once I read there was little hope for improving the relationship, I knew I had to leave and regain ownership of my life.

A poster that frequently hangs in women's shelters states, "The first time he hits you, it's his fault. The second time he hits you, it's your fault." As harsh as that sounds, I can now see how the assessment applies equally well to emotional abuse. Those many years I spent feeling like I was a victim, I was proud to see myself as the innocent party in our relationship. I could have read countless books that would have supported, and even encouraged, my victimhood; squarely placing the blame for our problems on his behavior, not mine. But at some level, even when I did not admit it, I knew I held responsibility for our interactions.

Today, I acknowledge my role in our life's experiences. I was the woman who failed to establish boundaries. I allowed him to treat me the way he did, I let it go on for over 30 years. During the marriage, I indulged in narcissistic retaliation, trying to throw back at him some of the pain he tossed at me.

When we were out with friends, I was frequently told I was an angel for tolerating him. I used to laugh it off, but underneath, I sort of believed them. Friends had witnessed small glimpses of his behavior. But only I knew how deeply I felt wounded. However, what they didn't see, what they didn't know, was how I would retaliate against his behavior, with words or actions that would hurt him as deeply as he hurt me. I was no angel and he was not always the devil.

I now can see, without judgement, how I allowed him to play his role and how he allowed me to play mine. We both acted out our parts beautifully, right down to the end. If he had been kinder and if I had been nonreactive. If I had made the choice of establishing boundaries. If I had accepted myself as worthy of love, if I had held both of us to a base level of respectful behavior towards each other — perhaps he would have acted differently. But I did not practice any such behaviors. Instead, I played the role of a victim to the hilt.

I think that it took me leaving the marriage, to gain these insights. After I got far enough away from the daily drama, I could clearly see that I allowed myself to experience all of the negative interactions that brought this depth of pain and suffering into our lives. While in the marriage, I behaved as if I didn't have choices. I spent our married years blaming him for treating me poorly. 'Allowing' is a choice. 'Allowing' is like giving permission. I now see that I hold and accept the responsibility for allowing that pain.

As an empath, I was extremely distressed after I left him, knowing my departure hurt him greatly. By my leaving, it felt like I was inflicting more pain than he had ever experienced. For months, I struggled to rein in my empathic insights; to curb the inclination to run back to him, to be his savior. Ironically, in recognizing the same behaviour he used in our marriage, in the texts, emails and phone messages he sent, I found strength to continue my separate path.

The road back to my sanity started with securing appointments with a psychologist who specialized in domestic abuse, engaging a life transitions coach and seeking spiritual guidance. Church attendance became a regular event. I went to workshops and healing circles. I read every self-help book I could get my hands on. Books like *Reality Unveiled* and *Mind to Matter* made a huge difference in how I viewed the world. These books left a profound mark on me – the subject matter included spiritual growth and physics, energy medicine and the effects of emotions on healing. I read about the behaviors of atomic particles, the energy fields in and around our bodies, the amazing ability to heal through energy medicine, and the purpose we have on this earth. The conclusion that I eventually came to is best summed up by this quote:

"We are not human beings having a spiritual experience; we are spiritual beings having a human experience." - Pierre Teilhard de Chardin

I learned we all have a Soul, some call our higher selves, that stands with us through our lives' journeys, observing and, at times, assisting us to complete our lessons. Each soul existed before this life and will continue to exist after this earthly physical existence ends. Our Souls are our containers, filled with unconditional love and forgiveness, peace and harmony They are our connection with the divine. I believe that our Souls go through many lives, each time learning a little more about how to become closer to the light of God. As spirits in heaven, we raise our hands and say "Pick me" to learn a lesson on earth, things that cannot be learned in heaven.

Seven months into our separation, I no longer blamed my ex-husband. I reached the point where I thanked him for every harsh word, every controlling act, rage and accusation. This is not a shallow "I forgive you"; I genuinely thank him. I know that when we were spirits together, he agreed to play a role, as did I, that led us both to learn and grow from sharing this experience in this earthly realm. It could have easily been the other way around, with me as the leading toxic individual and him as the victim. As spirits, we choose our roles, knowing the end goal is to help each other learn deep truths and travel farther along on the path of spiritual growth. I know he chose the most difficult role. I am in awe of the strength of his spirit, agreeing to accept a life of hardship so I could learn. I thank him for all he has done to teach me the lessons my soul yearned to learn.

However, even with my progress from blaming to forgiving him, I still had not truly reached what I call "Quantum Forgiveness." At first, I chose to forgive the past, but I still blamed him for current behavior. I saw him as someone whom I still should fear, and therefore avoided meeting with him. I was very afraid of experiencing the negative behavior again. I felt raw and vulnerable, I sensed that the risk of being exposed to his pain was too great, if I spent any time in his presence. However, in order to be able to work through our marital settlement, I needed to change the way I saw him.

A concept taught in neuro-linguistic programming is 'people are doing the best they can with the tools they have'. Intellectually, I could apply this to my ex-husband, but emotionally, I still carried fear. Although he has sought help, and he is working to change, I strongly believe the life path that allows my soul to blossom, would not fully open if I had returned to the marriage. For me to be fully me, I must release him, and send him off with love and respect.

Healing began with the Hawaiian meditation Ho'oponopono; I would repeat, "I'm sorry, please forgive me, thank you, I love you," for up to twenty minutes at a time.

Of all of the practices I have done to recover, I believe that Ho'oponopono has done the most to heal me. I cite the words while I drive; I think the words while I stand in line; I go to bed thinking the words, and I wake up thinking the words. It is only through the continuing and consistent practice of Ho'oponopono that I can now easily, seven months after I left, see him as a good man, without adding qualifiers. Ho'oponopono also aided me to see myself as a woman who has grown. A woman stronger than before. A woman working to heal my wounds so I can experience the best life has to offer. Remarkably, I now comfortably reside in a 500-square-foot house. During my practice, I grew to understand our situation was my creation. Ho'oponopono said with the intention to heal oneself is the true spirit of aloha. It is one path to true healing.

IGNITE ACTION STEPS

"Forgive others, not because they deserve forgiveness, but because you deserve peace." - Jonathon Lockwood Huie

You too can benefit from the Hawaiian meditation, Ho'oponopono. Simply repeat, "I'm sorry, please forgive me, thank you, I love you." Repeat these simple phrases for fifteen to twenty minutes at a time. (These are the same words I repeated, while I thought of my ex-husband.)

Ho'oponopono is an ancient Huna ritual, a way of life that started in Hawaii at about 650 BC. The word means 'to make right' and it refers to correcting the wrongs in people's lives, all the way back to your ancestors.

The concept of Ho'Oponopono means that I take full responsibility for everything in my life. I am the creator of everything in my world, I am responsible for everything in my life. By using Ho'Oponopono to heal the part of myself that created the marital situation I was in, I was able to fully embrace my responsibility for creating everything around me.

During my practice, I grew to understand our situation was my creation. Ho'oponopono said with the intention to heal oneself is the true spirit of aloha. It is one path, out of many, to true healing.

Ho'oponopono is related to the concept of Aloha, a greeting, a farewell, a way of being. Hawaiians are taught that the spirit of Aloha is a part of all, and all being a part of me. When there is pain — it is my pain. When there is joy — it is also mine. I respect all that is, as part of the Creator and part of me. I will not willfully harm anyone or anything. When food is needed, I will take only my need and explain why it is being taken. The earth, the sky, the sea are mine to care for, to cherish and to protect. This is Hawaiian - this is Aloha!

Angela Legh, Inspirational Leader at Reveal Change.
www.revealchange.com

MARNIE TARZIA

"It is never too late to live the life you want."

I hope my story inspires you to go after the life you want. To find the courage to be true to yourself. To take steps each day that lead you to your best self and your best life. I encourage every woman to value herself enough to be the author of her own story and to go after the life she wants with passion and perseverance.

MIDLIFE REVIEW AND RESET

By the age of 45, I had acquired everything we women are taught we need to obtain in order to be considered successful. How could it be that I had attained all of those success markers and still longed for something different, for something more?

I had come to a place in my life where I appreciated what I had in my life and yet I was longing for something more professional. I was celebrating my 20th wedding anniversary, our beautiful daughter was flourishing and I had reached the top of my career ladder. I had worked very hard for twenty years. I felt financially secure. My husband and I had built our dream home, I drove a brand-new car and we had just spent spring break on a wonderful family vacation cruising around the Caribbean.

I had acquired a Master of Arts Degree in Leadership Studies and been promoted to the leader of Children's Services for my district and managed a $12.5 million budget. Reaping the associated rewards, meant

I had the privileged executive office, with a beautiful glass window and a wonderful view.

I had actively participated in creating every portion of my career and professional life. Wondering why I no longer saw myself in it, took me into uncharted thoughts and feelings: I wanted a more flexible work schedule. I wanted a more compassionate boss. I wanted more autonomy over my workload. I wanted a job that spoke to my heart.

Was I being realistic or was I asking for too much? Is it possible that I was acting like one of those high-maintenance employees that management would classify as a "BMW" in the workplace? BMW is the code word for a spoiled employee that always 'bickers, moans and whines'. If anyone had heard my inner chatter lately, undoubtedly, they would tell me that I needed to get some cheese with my wine or was it whine? I laughed at myself and just kept going.

Then came the Friday before I started my summer vacation. I had just exited a very stressful work meeting with the Director of our division. I had worked long enough to know that this was the type of professional partnership that could no longer be salvaged. My boss had a tendency to lead with either a carrot or a stick. She had the attitude that you pass or you fail. You do well or you don't. It was evident that we had very different values. In the early days of our working together, we had a cohesive, collaborative working relationship and then suddenly and without warning everything changed. While I couldn't pinpoint what led to this, I did know it was no longer healthy for me to stay where my own frustrations were toxic to my inner purpose.

Intuitively, I knew that I needed to do something; I just didn't know what that was yet. I would keep my internal antennae pointed out to the universe, hoping for answers.

That Friday was a beautiful, sunny afternoon. Returning to my office after lunch, I was startled by a middle-aged man on a ladder, peering inside the room from the outside as he cleaned my window. His positive energy was palpable. He had wireless headphones on, smiling as he bopped and sang along to the music on his phone.

I remember thinking, "I want whatever he has. I want that energy. I want that enthusiasm." How could it be that my window washer was happier cleaning bird poop off my window, than I was in a position that I had spent my entire career striving to obtain?

I sat down in awe of this window washer who was outdoors enjoying the summer sun. It was just him and his music. By contrast, I felt restricted to the indoors. I felt the weight of the department and district on my shoulders. I had to scan in and out of our office. My entry and exit times could be tracked like teenagers working at McDonalds. I felt jailed.

Not that I had anything to hide, but I resented it when employees were not trusted to regulate their own time. The window washer was free. He had the autonomy to do his job in any way that he saw as fit. The disparity struck deep! I had to follow the rules of bureaucracy where proper process came first and people came second. He had the freedom to do his work any way he liked! While I on the other hand was shackled to the vision of an organization that valued progress and money over people and altruism.

Have you ever felt like you have everything and nothing at all at the same time? That's exactly how I felt about my work that day! This was the first time I told myself the truth about the preceding four years of my career. I felt like I had everything. My ego had me believing that outer riches equals success: net-worth, a big home, fancy car or social status.

As I much as I was appreciative of all of the blessings in my life, I was cognizant of the fact that I felt a lingering sense of inner poverty related to my work. I no longer felt that my job supported my purpose and passion. I was experiencing a lack of fulfilment. I wanted to feel purposeful and passionate about my career again.

As I watched that man working from his ladder that day, it occurred to me that I had spent 22 years working to get to the top of my career ladder and at that moment I realized that my ladder was up against the wrong wall. The paradox of my success was that I had acquired everything I thought I wanted but, in the end, I could see that it was nothing I really needed.

That realization was jolting. Now that I had told myself the truth, what was I going to do about it? Sometimes the hardest conversations we have are with ourselves.

I needed to get out, but I couldn't physically leave the building. I felt 'jailed' for the remainder of the day with my lunch and afternoon breaks finished. I decided to move my body. I walked out of my office, and down the hall to mail-box. Oddly, when I saw other employees walking around the office free from their cubicles, it reminded me of inmates freed from the confines of their cells.

I found an envelope addressed to me in my mailbox. The letter identified some changes I was being asked to make, which would add to my already full-time commitments. As I read the words, it sucked the life right out of me. Walking back into my office, I felt deflated and completely robbed of my energy and self-esteem. Looking around for the window washer, I saw he was gone, but the window was clean. That clean window was a metaphor for the clarity I suddenly felt. I had stayed in my job for far too long. I was ready to take the leap and leave. I could only hope the net would appear.

I picked up the phone and called over to our community college and asked the Dean if he had any work that he could give me. I love teaching. I am a lifelong learner and it brings me ultimate satisfaction to present research in a way that is informative, inspiring and entertaining. As a result, I am well suited to the role of Professor. The thought of being in a college classroom excited me. The Dean requested I send my resume and scheduled a meeting for the following week. He hired me on the spot as a contract faculty member. This contract guaranteed work for three full semesters.

Most people looking out for me (including the Dean) queried: was it was wise for me to relinquish a full-time, permanent, prominent position for a teaching contract? Despite the fact that my decision seemed unreasonable to anyone using logic to quantify a decision, my intuition told me that teaching would be bringing me closer to my goal and point me to the gateway of success. I could not be swayed.

I believed then as I believe now — that if the goal is to stay true to oneself, then the question is always: "If I were not afraid, what would I do?" For me, the answer was if I was fearless, I would pursue a career with teaching in the hopes that it would morph into a career where I would publish a book and start my own business as a motivational speaker, trainer and coach. It was very liberating to quit that prominent position to return to a role that called to my heart.

During my tenure at the college, I discovered the Science of Well Being and Flourishing referred to as Positive Psychology by Dr Martin Sielgman. I was so inspired by this new science that I signed up for an online course to learn more. Studying this modality was a life-altering experience. The knowledge I've acquired in this science combined with leadership studies has helped me to acquire the tools I need to be the CEO of my own life.

In studying the research on Midlife I discovered that it is a complicated time in the life cycle. We women conduct a midlife review. This means we reflect on where we are in our lives. It is a time where we compare where we are in relation to where we would have hoped to be. We are usually kind caregivers to children, spouse then house and often in that order. It is common for women in their 40s and 50s to feel that "there is nothing left for me."

When I reflect back on my previous professional life, I can see now that it was a time of significant stress. It occurs to me now that I was a little like the circus juggler trying to keep of all the balls up in the air simultaneously while the audience looks on with bated breath to see if any of the balls get dropped. That resonates with me as I was juggling too many jobs throughout that period of my life.

In retrospect, I can see that in taking on less work, and in taking on work that I love, I am able to do less things well. I am also healthier and happier which benefits my family.

In the final analysis, I recognize that eliminating the workload I had, allowed me to pursue and focus on doing work that I love. I ended up spending less time working, which equates to more time for family and other activities I enjoy. It also means I have more energy to devote to what I am good at and do it well.

Working hard for what we love feeds our passion and keeps us motivated, while working hard for what we don't love has us feeling stressed. Consistent tension left unchecked, leads to inner corrosion which can manifest in illness or a crisis of the spirit. I'm thrilled I avoided such adversity, by listening to my inner wisdom and taking swift action.

Now three years later, my life is exactly as I dreamed it. I have taken on a day-job with the provincial government, acting in a leadership capacity, doing a job I love, with people I adore.

I appeared in a best-selling book entitled Awaken Your Inner Hero where my daughter wrote her heroine story and named me as her supporter. The book requested mentors to participate, so I wrote on my positive approach to parenting.

The best news is that through my work in writing, coaching and speaking I've worked to empower women to live their lives with purpose, passion and perseverance.

I do this through motivational speaking, training sessions and coaching. I love supporting women to chart their own course and to help women define which goals will fit for their lives, values and dreams. I have never been happier.

I am living my dream life now. I have a sense of freedom that I never experienced in my old job. I wake up each day excited to go to work as I have a sense of purpose, passion, autonomy and fulfilment that I didn't experience in my prior role.

Ignite Action Steps

I would advise all women who are feeling stuck and who want to get traction in reaching their dreams to:

- Identify your goals and create an action plan for executing these.
- It's important to note that some goals can be achieved immediately while other goals require long term planning and commitment.

It is important to develop hard goals and hold yourself accountable for achieving them. As the old saying goes: "What gets measured, gets done."

It was a helpful exercise for me to write about a time in my life when I was thriving and had accomplished an important goal.

- Identify a time in your when you were flourishing and accomplished an important goal.
- Make note of the environment, conditions and the type of support you had around you when you were thriving.
- Examine the conditions you had created in your life when you were successful in achieving your goal.
- This exercise will allow you to observe the conditions you require in order to make your dreams come true.

It was highly beneficial for me to design a vision board of my goals, using pictures to illustrate where I wanted to be in all aspects of my life: mind, body, heart and spirit. Ambiguity is the enemy of success. Put in your order because the universe delivers.

Create a vision board to clear about your goals:

- Pick up a low-cost poster board at a dollar store.
- Organize your materials: scissors and glue, magazines, flyers, pictures.
- Let your creative genius take over in creating a collage of pictures that illustrates your hopes and dreams for yourself.
- Finally, once your vision board is created, visualize yourself in this new life where you feel a sense of purpose and passion.

Join or start a mastermind group.

• Be among like-minded, positive people who are dedicated to creating a supportive environment where action orientated people gather to achieve their goals.

• Add accountability: have your group hold you responsible for following through with the action steps associated with obtaining your goal.

Having this circle of support is valuable as it is a mechanism to share ideas and resources. I would also advise to ensure that you are surrounding yourself with people that want you to succeed. We cannot be around negative people on a chronic and consistent basis and expect to succeed. Just like we aspire to eat clean and take in healthy organic food and avoid toxins we too must be careful not to allow toxic people into our inner circle who will work to derail our dreams. Be intentional and thoughtful about the people you surround yourself with.

In the final analysis, I can see that I was conducting a midlife review, where I was simply taking stock of where I was in my life as compared to where I had hoped I would be. I then began working to identify what my gifts were as a person while endeavouring to identify where those gifts would be best served. I understand now that I prefer to work, fulfilling my highest purpose. That time of tension and turmoil in my professional life was simply a springboard that catapulted me into the life I always dreamed of. Although it felt like a burden at the time, I can see it was my greatest professional blessing.

All of our experiences shape the evolution of our growth as long as we remain open to learning the lesson. Have you ever felt that something larger than yourself has got your back and won't give you anything that you can't handle? I can honestly say, I have felt that way for as long as I can remember.

For any woman reading this right now that may be feeling helpless and hopeless in their life, please hold on. Hold on to your power. Hold on to your purpose. Hold on to pride in what you do and to passion in what you believe. Wake up with a positive mindset each day and persevere in advancing forward in the direction of your dreams. Always remember that if you aren't where you want to be, then you just aren't there yet. Remember. You have a choice. Your life belongs to you. The window washer reminded me: When we feel powerless in our self-imposed prison – we also hold the key.

Marnie Tarzia, Author, Speaker, Leader, and Educator.

ALEX JARVIS

"The beauty of life is to love and be loved - let LOVE in."

My story is centered around the Rose. I want you to be inspired and encouraged to believe in the ultimate gifts we hold within us. My intention is to introduce and invite the high vibration of the rose to join you on your journey of love. To look less outward for answers, but trust your intuition looking inward for the true inner guidance.

WHAT'S LOVE GOT TO WITH IT?

It took me half a century, living in fear of a violent female stalker and being diagnosed with cancer of the right breast, to be STILL; to stop and smell the roses, and be open to receive LOVE.

From a very young age, I felt things. I felt the pain, stress, and the isolation of others. My mother unexpectedly conceived her third and last child, my only sister Nichola. This should have been a time of joy and happiness, except confusion set in.

I felt unloved. With the weight of the world on my shoulders, I asked myself: Why?

Why had things changed? Why had my mother switched off? I felt her pain, her total disconnection, as she abandoned me, the whole family, and herself.

As a child of three, I did not know we were living in a country plagued with unrest, the start of a civil war, politicide, mass murder, and genocide. It was the early 1960s. A year before, we had travelled six weeks by boat to

Indonesia. My father, a petroleum technologist, was on a 'fast track' working for Shell, a UK/Dutch oil company. Destination: Pladju, South Sumatra - his placement for the next five years. A 'hairy, disorganized country,' my parents explained, where they were under 'Marshall Law.' The family had to be extremely careful outside of the refinery and had to abide by curfews that were random. Any local authority, junior or senior, might have the power to deport someone — or even to have people shot. It was impossible to know which rule to follow, and when, or even what the ever-changing laws were.

After witnessing things a child should never have to witness, seeing, smelling, breathing in the fear surrounding me, a voice started screaming in my head: "I must save the world. I must save my mother. I must save my father. I must save my family. I must make everyone happy again."

I carried this belief throughout my childhood and into my adulthood, always trying to make people feel happy. Unfortunately, this was totally unachievable in the most important area of my life: my parents. My father, with my mother's encouragement, broke his contract with Shell Oil to return to the United Kingdom for the safety of his three children under five. A Cambridge University graduate destined for acceleration, he was now blacklisted and held back for his insubordinate action. My father always seemed very sad to me. For some reason, I felt responsible for my parents' pain. My mother told me years later my father cried with boredom and frustration, feeling forced to stay in a position that did not challenge him. Yet, Daddy stayed with Shell Oil all his working life.

I realize now, during this time I put everyone before myself. I never really understood or appreciated the importance of self-care and self-love. My life was filled with many failed relationships, trust issues, self-loathing, anger, and a 'hurt' that was so deep I was afraid that if I tried to look inward, I would open a can of worms. I looked outward for all my answers and compared myself to everyone around. Nothing was good enough.

Many years later, when I reached the glorious age of 50, I started to look inward and realized we actually have input on how we create our own dreams, how we view things, and how we react. Don't get me wrong, to this day I have strong reactions to certain situations. Only now, I tend to be the observer and watch what comes up. I will feel into what is unfolding, asking myself 'Is this mine?' 'Is this reality?' and even asking my intuition to please show me more.

I expressed my bafflement to a friend about how I might suffer sleepless nights and worry myself silly, to the point of anxiety, over some issue that could actually dissipate even if it hadn't been resolved.

She said to me, "It's not the situation but how you react to it."

I believe that all things can be taken away from us but one thing: our freedom for how we feel, see, and believe. Choosing our attitude towards any situation is always present, if we pay attention.

Time to pay attention was in short supply throughout my career as I flew around the world in private jet planes, working long hours as CEO for a large corporation in Australia, reporting directly to the company president in America. Moving in these high-powered circles, attending all-night parties, I thought I was loving every minute of it. My days were so full, I didn't have time to think … I avoided all emotional attachments, building a protective wall around myself. I chose to engage in relationships that were geographically impossible, attracting partners that were unattainable and emotionally unavailable — just as I was to myself. The one thing I definitely managed to do right and to love was being a single parent to my beautiful daughter, Katelin.

My body screamed at me by starting to function incorrectly for ignoring the balance...

I needed between my feminine and masculine energies. After twelve surgeries in nine years, all had a common theme: the right side of my body, right breast, right shoulder, and right ankle. Metaphysically, the right side of the body is often regarded as the masculine side; the giving side, where you express. It represents, among other things, the father. The left side of the body is often regarded as the feminine side, the receiving side, where you take in. It represents the mother.

From this, I gathered that I needed balance in all areas of my life. I was always ignoring my feminine side — the receiving side. Strangely enough, at first, I felt euphoric over being able to move in a different direction. I stopped running corporations. It was such a relief to have people caring for me, rather than having 200 people reporting to me.

Initially, all these ailments and surgeries felt like a punch in my stomach. When I went through times of sickness, adversity and hardship, I felt laughed at, disbelieved and like I had no voice. The feminine nurturing side was missing in my life. The disconnect of my childhood taught me to keep my feelings inside: to say what I thought people wanted to hear; to be liked, not to rock boats or rattle cages.

I wasn't successful all the time. In no way could I appease the female stalker. Remember her? At one point, my house was boarded up after each window had been broken every week for several weeks. Her daughter was in the same school, same class as my daughter. This woman threatened my daughter's life, hounded me day and night, calling over 300 times a week ... That's when I really tuned in.

I continued to have my windows fixed, only to go through the same process again and again. Not feeling safe, I was staying in hotels, sleeping in my car with my daughter Katelin, not feeling supported or protected. I felt totally abandoned and started to repeat a pattern originating from my childhood. Years of practiced shutdown and self-sabotage took over.

The surgeries and broken bones slowed me down enough to hear my inner voice, faint as it was in the beginning. That weak little voice I now call my intuition, led me to have a rose reading. After this reading, I decided to study and become a Rose Alchemist. The rose is known to be the highest vibrational flower. It held space for me in my times of need, embracing me, lifting my thoughts and vibration. I surrounded myself with roses in my house and work environment.

Rose Alchemy showed up in my life in even bigger ways. I started to read books on the history of the rose, which heightened my interest. The mystery of the Rose is steeped in many cultures. It shows up in numerous traditions, religions, wars, peace, songs, poems, literature and predominantly, love. The Rose is pure LOVE.

I love 'The Way of the Rose' and its pathway. It consciously healed and transformed all that inhibited my ability to fully embody beauty, truth and love in every step of my journey through life. It then helped me to live and manifest from that higher vibration. When I aligned what is above with what is below, it brought balance to my left and right, to my yin and yang. I felt the rose of my heart fully bloom. I entered a unified field of presence, in which I believe all things are possible.

Looking back, I realized my journey with the Rose had been constant from a very young age. All my life, I had been surrounded by roses in one form or another. My family home in the UK had a huge garden full of rambling roses.

At age 50, I was unaware I was to about to embark on an even deeper journey of self-discovery which was mildly inconvenienced by a cancer diagnosis. Roses continued to show up. For each and every surgery, roses were delivered to my hospital bedside. Instantly, I felt at peace. People came in and out of my room, bringing their guests to smell the sweet scent of the large, pale-pink roses. Gaining confidence on my new path, I rose above the pain in my past. I am still working on banishing the belief that I need to pay in hard dollars to receive any form of support.

Once I open up, it all shows up — the unconditional love of my daughter

Katelin, my parents and my friends. I only need to practice awareness, gratitude and forgiveness. Stopping, observing and daily walks connecting with nature; taking in, embracing the beauty, color, smell and movement of my surroundings all helped build my awareness. Feeling, seeing and hearing with an intensity like never before. Swimming, meditation, massages, being by the ocean and daily walking of a nearby labyrinth – laying roses in the center.

With labyrinths, the same way in is the way out, so the path is circuitous. It took me into the center of myself and then out again, giving me a more profound knowledge of who I am. The inner circle of the labyrinth is also connected with the Rose. It is a six petalled rose-shaped area, known as the rosette, and a place to rest. By peeling the petals back, I uncovered different parts of myself. It has been said the rosette, also known as the rose window, is a jewel symbolizing heaven. All of this was my path to forgive others, which turned the key and unlocked the gate to forgiving myself. The Rose essence was present in my heart, walking the journey with me.

In the process of forgiving, my question is, why do we always want a happy ending? How about a happy existence? Sometimes what we believe are our failures actually bring us happiness over time. We have the choice. It is a choice to be happy. Our opinion is the only one that matters. Life is truly about the journey, not the destination.

I believe the pure love of the Rose was calling me to remember my true path to being fully me, so I can work doing my part to make this world a better place. Embracing the Rose's gift allowed me to gracefully and easily remember to awaken my power and purpose. Once I willingly surrendered to walking the path of awakening, embarking on my inner journey, I found everything changed. I saw the beauty in my ability to be present, to look less outward for the answers and trust my intuition, looking inward for my guidance and observing all that showed up in my everyday life. I connected with the stillness, the inner truth and tapped into my intuition.

Now I embrace the unknown, enjoying the process, being patient, recognizing the bliss in the waiting and chaos. To be in the very moment and to expect the unexpected. To have the strength, knowing and courage to navigate through adversity. Creating a pathway to lasting inner peace, connection, joy and abundance. The sudden realization hit me: The answers are within and always have been there for me.

Most of my adult life, I have looked outwards for my answers. My ability to navigate through the process of looking at my life has let it unfold naturally. I feel that each of us on the planet contributes to the ever-evolving journey by engaging, motivating, and inspiring each other. It is a blessing that allows us to feel totally at ease, continually growing. Our expansion to this connection is so powerful and extremely effective, yet subtle. When you open to the beauty of the Rose and the journey it offers, be prepared for synchronicity, joy and unconditional love. The more resolved we are with our own past story and life issues, the more open we are to positivity, wellbeing and LOVE in our life.

On my own sweet journey of the Rose over the last few years, I have been naturally guided to many destinations all over the world and, as if by magic, the essence of the Rose has shown up. In Dubrovnik, Croatia, I stumbled upon a secluded monastery from the 15th century, with gardens full of Roses and an old-fashioned pharmacy that produced and sold Rose water, Rose essence and Rose creams. Not only did I pack my suitcase beyond capacity, I had to buy extra luggage to take home 67 kilograms of treasured items. Later, my daughter retraced my footsteps and brought home an additional load of Rose items.

At first, I was surprised by the Rose, by the beauty of seeing her in full bloom or in a tight bud and how she appeared in the most unexpected places. From ancient Rose water to Rose gardens; to a country's history where the Rose was respected, honored and played a big part in traditions. To the name of a person, road, drink or consumable, the connections kept showing up. There was an unspoken language.

It has been no surprise to me that when we open our hearts to the Rose, she supports and guides us, enabling us to be in our joy and spread love around the world.

Rose vibration is magnetic, dynamic, and multi-dimensional.

Over the last nine years, the synchronicity, appearances and stories that unfolded became more and more common. I realized as I travelled the globe that I was in the right place at the right time. It was no accident that I had such a strong pull by the sheer energy, vibration and essence of the Rose. I was being called, to sing and be sung to. As the Rose slowly unfolds her delicate petals, she embraces and holds a high frequency space for each and every one of us, singing sweetly to facilitate the awakening and expansion of us all. The gentle, powerful, serene rose will ignite and inspire, inviting our own petals to unfold — and from a bud, start to bloom. The Rose and its essence activates an inner knowing and guides us towards the inner journey to create heaven on earth.

It took me a half century to see the Rose in me. I needed to learn to trust the waiting, to embrace all the ambiguity and unknown of my future, to unfold over time. Only then, in this absolute acceptance, did I find that anything, truly anything, was possible.

IGNITE ACTION STEPS

• Surround yourself with roses in your garden or a beautiful vase, or find an elegant print depicting roses you can hang on the wall or share on social media. Once you start looking, the Roses you need will appear.

• Stop. Be still. Take nature photographs when you walk. Start a photo journal.

• Walk a nearby labyrinth or purchase a fabric labyrinth to walk at home. Another option is a finger labyrinth to trace your finger around (they're magical in their rose connections). The labyrinth is all about flow and acceptance. A labyrinth is an ancient symbol that relates to wholeness. It combines the imagery of the circle and the spiral into a meandering but purposeful path.

There's really no right way or wrong way to walk a labyrinth, but generally speaking there are three phases:

• Releasing on the way in — letting go of what no longer serves.

• Receiving a sense of peace and calm — as you pause in the center.

• Resolving to engage with the world in a new way, as you follow the same path back out.

Some general guidelines for walking a labyrinth are:

• Focus: To prepare, sit quietly and reflect before walking the labyrinth. Some people come with questions, others to slow down. Some come to find strength to take the next step during times of grief and loss. Its winding path becomes a metaphor for our journey and where we find ourselves on our path. Pause and wait at the entrance. Become quiet and centered. Give acknowledgment through a bow, nod, or other gesture, then enter.

• Experience: Walk purposefully. Observe the process. When you reach the center, stay there and focus for several moments. Leave when it seems appropriate. Be attentive on the way out.

• Exit: Turn and face the entrance. Give an acknowledgement or gesture.

• Reflect: After walking the labyrinth, if you wish, use journaling or drawing to capture your experience.

Alex Jarvis, Rose Alchemist, Speaker Author CEO.
Vanillaesthetics / JARVIS Interiors. www.jarvisinteriors.com.au

Jeanette
Shine brightly
always
All [the] best
Love A. Phyll

PHYLLIS ROBERTO

"Give the gift of light. Shine a little brighter every day."

While reading this one small story, in the life of an incredible woman, I hope you see your own strength, your own beauty, your own zest for life. Know that all you need is within you. Be inspired to live every moment to the fullest, ever curious, ever interested, always the participant rather than the observer in your own life — to the very last breath.

TABLES TURN

It was typical chaos of unwrapping gifts, children underfoot and the kitchen overrun, as Christmas brunch got underway. That made it easy to ignore the ringing phone. Christmas greetings with whoever it was would have to be shared later.

How awful I felt when I discovered my oldest sister Pat was spending Christmas alone at her daughter Jeanette's while they were away – and I had ignored her call.

I discovered she was at Jeanette's because of a stalker. She felt vulnerable in her ground floor apartment. Also, her back had been bothering her, she was physically hurting and no longer feeling safe, Pat had decided to change her living arrangements. With Jeanette's house full, she needed a place while her condo went up for sale.

"Come stay with me." I offered. It was easy for me to say come here, as she had done numerous times over the last few years. Sometimes I had been home - others she had been my house-sitter while I worked away. It was Pat's 'home-away-from-home'. She had come and gone as she pleased.

Not this time. "I don't want to come if you aren't going to be around," was the plea rather than a statement. I replied that I wasn't working, which didn't look to be changing any time soon. The downstairs suite was empty. I'd be delighted to have her stay.

On the other end of the phone, Pat burst into tears, crying out, "I think I will come home." Then laughed at her own desperation as she called me 'Mommy.' My heart broke. For reasons still not completely known to me, my big sister was at the end of her rope.

Waiting at the baggage carousel, I was shocked to see her being wheeled in by an airport attendant. I soon noticed her laughing and flirting with the young man as he grinned and teased her back. Ahh, the wheelchair was only for convenience I thought. I was excited and delighted to see her. Her eyes lit up as she saw me. My heart expanded.

I thought Pat would be wanting to leave our prairie winter to return to the cherry blossoms in a couple months. She talked of making her stay a six-month retreat, until after the 50th-anniversary party in July. Although fine with me, I was a bit surprised.

Her November checkup had revealed osteoporosis and arthritis causing her back pain, making it more comfortable sitting than laying. An anti-gravity chair along with the bed for sleeping downstairs and another anti-gravity chair in the dining room upstairs with lots of pillows was required. In no time, her upstairs nest was arranged with books and papers and all the little necessities for daytime. We created a routine to enable both of us private space and time. Pat took care of her own morning coffee and regular routine in the suite downstairs. I had the upstairs to myself until noon, when we shared lunch.

I bought tickets for a play or two for date nights and planned the menu for my annual 'senior's' supper. It was always fun where Pat was, so hosting neighbours and friends and extended family was a given.

None of these took place. Brief visits were all that could be managed. Pat did not have the energy and the pain was too great to visit for long. She did, however, take daily pleasure in being outside. It was a miracle the winter was mild.

Reluctant trips to the chiropractor didn't alleviate any pain. Reiki, gentle massage, EFT tapping, meditation, journaling, and daily walks gave only momentary relief. We made trips to the health food store for supplements and the doctor for blood tests and X-rays, along with prescriptions for painkillers. There was desperation in the search for something, anything to relieve the pain. Often I could hear Pat moaning during the night. "Oh, God. Oh, God." I lay awake helpless, tears welling and heart aching. There seemed nothing I could do. Nothing was helping long term.

Toward the end of the month, a Touch for Health practitioner gave Pat some relief. Just enough that we got our hopes up and believed recovery was imminent. Quickly our excitement faded as the pain returned a few days later. Pat's daughters, Vivian and Charlotte, came to visit bringing meals and loving care. They were shocked to see how bent over their mother was. She spoke reluctantly about this possibly becoming her new normal.

To get her strength up, Pat walked outdoors daily. The distance became shorter instead of longer. By the end of January, three weeks after her arrival - there was no improvement. Pat was becoming less and less mobile. We believed muscle spasms, osteoporosis, and arthritis were the enemies.

Early one afternoon, Pat had managed her way slowly up the stairs. As she crossed the kitchen, our eyes locked. At that moment, I felt the intensity of her pain, her vulnerability, and her desperation. In two steps I reached her and took her in my arms. Holding her close, I was dismayed to feel how small she was, how fragile she had become. My heart ached as she sank into the comfort of my soft strength and whimpered 'Mommy'. My bigger-than-life sister was no longer the powerhouse I had known all my life. Somehow it had become my turn to offer strength and guidance. I felt unprepared even if willing.

A few days later, I was alarmed to discover Pat had not been taking her medication properly, afraid she couldn't afford pills not covered by health insurance. Age-old fears of having to scrimp still dictated. At least here I could reassure her. Money was not to be worried about.

I was now responsible for dispensing medication and accompanying her to doctor appointments. Fresh-air walking had become fresh-air sitting in the early afternoon sun. It now took a couple of hours for her morning routine before making it upstairs to the main living area. Thinking she wanted some independence, I did not offer help. In retrospect, she probably did not want to upset my schedule.

I continued some of my routines but stopped going out evenings. Pat seemed even more vulnerable at night. Watching TV together gave a momentary distraction from the now constant pain. I heard the bath running numerous times throughout the night, her only other relief. Childhood comfort foods, sweet currant scones smothered in butter, baked macaroni and cheese heavy on the cheese, rice pudding and apple crisp with thick brown sugar topping barely tempted her feeble appetite. Instead, I gained unwanted pounds while Pat continued to lose.

I did not see the improvement we were led to expect. Talk of apartment choices now leaned toward shared accommodation and assisted living.

February X-ray results revealed significant differences from the November ones taken instigating a CT scan. The sun shone brightly in the clear blue winter sky as diamonds sparkled across the expanse of pristine white snow. A perfect day for the 45-minute drive. After the appointment, I was about to suggest continuing to the national park and the Rocky Mountains. I turned to my passenger seat but said nothing. Pat looked exhausted.

Two days later results were in. We were told to come to the clinic first thing the next morning.

February 26, 2016, Dr. Lisa took Pat's hand "The results are back, and it is not good. It shows cancer in the right breast and three places in the spine. We aren't talking about a cure but we will arrange treatment for pain relief, comfort and quality of life."

Both Pat and I are reeling – we had been under the impression that cancer had been ruled out. Feigning calm Pat asked, "How long do I have? Tell me straight."

Dr. Lisa's eyes misted over, "Possibly a few months to a few years."

"How many is a few?"

"Maybe two years, maybe five years but not longer than that."

"Thank you," was all she said.

We sat in silence, tears welling up in three pairs of eyes. Dr. Lisa easily detected the cancerous lump, although the same test was clear three months earlier. The doctor left the room and Pat turned to me, "I guess I won't be celebrating my 90th birthday." I held her in my arms. We both cried. Another 10 years was not to be.

Our grandmother lived to 104, longevity was the expectation in our family. How pleased I had been just a few months earlier. Teresa, Pat's oldest daughter, helping Pat apply for her passport had asked, "Do you want the five-year or ten-year?" Without hesitation Pat declared, "Might as well make it ten." I loved Pat's attitude.

Only last year she had driven a 2000-kilometre trek. She had no fear of travelling alone, stopping as she pleased, to visit or see the sights. Pat was still sought after as a mentor and teacher of Enneagram. How could this be – she was a vital, vibrant woman with so much still to offer?

My mind spun back a mere five months ago; I had been racking my brain thinking how to get Pat to the local community hall for her surprise 80th birthday party. Much to my delight, she had come to me. "Phyll, can you take me to town?" Perfect - the timing was right, I would swing by the hall after her errand.

When Pat went into the store, I texted the party planners, "We are on our way." Pat came out with a bag of nachos, not at all what she had needed. That item was out-of-stock, and she didn't want to come out empty handed. We laughed at the silliness.

The beautiful day made a good excuse to suggest taking the long route home, passing by the hall. Pat agreed. As we approached the hall, with its full parking lot she said, "You might as well pull in here."

My heart sank as I thought, "Ahh she must have guessed about her party."

We walked in – to friends, family and neighbours hollering "SURPRISE!" As I moved Pat to the front to take her bows – she stepped back presenting me to the crowd. Everyone was having a great laugh. Finally, Charlotte came over and pointed out the sign. A Book-End birthday party – for me, the youngest at 60 and Pat, the oldest at 80. They kept the surprise by telling me it was for Pat and telling Pat the party was for me. Her supposed needed trip to town was a ruse. Nachos indeed! Well done everyone!

Three days and nights of partying. Eating, drinking, singing and dancing, with storytelling around the campfire. Not getting to bed before 3:00 am. Pat was the last one down. Only five months ago and now a death sentence. How could this be?

We were sent to an emergency appointment with Dr. Chu at the Cross Cancer Hospital. Dr. Lisa could give no details; she had no information. We didn't know whether we were going for a few hours or a few days. Everything was unknown.

I made a hurried lunch, packed overnight bags and we headed out. Although uncomfortable for the two-hour drive, Pat walked unassisted into the hospital. To decrease pain and prevent paralysis, radiation on the spine had already been arranged. Both of us unnerved and scared, with no time to think, or see any options to weigh. New to this, neither of us questioned. If the pain could be reduced, it may be worth it.

Finally, with concrete information, I contacted the family. Excited adult children and grandchildren gathered. Mama was in for a visit. Struggling and choking back tears, Pat bravely repeated her diagnosis, "I spent the day at the Cross Cancer." She said, "It does not look good." Faces dropped, the excitement of Pat's visit crushed as tears flowed. No one had expected this.

A slippery slope downhill, radiation appeared to cause more problems not less. The anticipated short stay turned into a hospital bed and recliner chair at Teresa's. Soon round the clock care, Pat's daughters and sisters providing overnight assistance. More family and friends gathered.

Before we could blink, Pat was admitted to the Grey Nuns Hospital for palliative care.

I'm told, many slip away, alone, in the solitude of the night.

Not my sister Pat. Her moment in the limelight was not to be denied. In a hoarse whisper, she demanded her brothers and sisters gather around her. We laughed. We teased. I fed her ice cream and rhubarb. She smacked her lips. Her children and grandchildren, nieces and nephews crowded in, overflowing into the hallway. Pat insisted her son, Tony, to lead everyone in song. All voices were raised, singing You Are My Sunshine, Take a Load Off Fanny, 100 Miles and other favourites. Smiling she waved her hands, conducting the choir. Patients, visitors and staff alike lingered by the doorway and joined in. As always, Pat attracted the attention of young and old.

I stepped out of the room to make space for the doctor to step in. Moments later, March 24, 2016, less than a month after the diagnosis she was gone. Passing on wings of music and laughter, surrounded and uplifted by love, she was gone, off to her next great adventure.

What a gift she has been all my life and oh how I miss her.

Living and dying, giving and receiving. Embracing both equal, although opposite sides of the coin is a clue to living our fullest life. Giving comes easily to most women. Receiving – truly receiving – not so much. It took a crisis for Pat to reach out. What a beautiful gift to myself and others who loved her. Surely, we can learn to ask for help, for what we need, for what we want, consciously, living our life to the fullest...

IGNITE ACTION STEPS

Try this 30-Day Experiment. (If 30 days is daunting, start with 5).

Notice throughout each day

* When you could use a helping hand but don't ask.
* When you do ask and receive help.
* When you are asked or your offer of help is accepted.

Ask yourself

* When do I feel grateful?
* When do I feel appreciated?
* When do I feel valued?

Each day, journal what you notice.

It feels good to be needed and to contribute. Be a giver so others may receive. It takes courage to ask for help. Be brave. Be a receiver so others may give.

Phyllis Roberto, Personal Development Facilitator and Coach, Speaker, and Author. Prairie Rose Wellness.
www.prairierosewellness.com

TRISH MRAKAWA

*"Forgiving yourself and forgiving others creates
new possibilities for your future."*

I am sharing my story to help you. To empower you and inspire you. My story centres around one of the most defining moments in my life, and one of the greatest lessons I needed to learn from and continue to learn from to this day. My wish for you is to practise the power of forgiveness so you can move mountains, celebrate all that you are, where you have come from and live your life unlimited.

FORGIVENESS IS MY POWER MOVE

It was time. I'd fought against it for so long. And I had no idea it was coming.

It was exactly one month after my fifty-eighth birthday. I innocently boarded a flight to Phoenix for a women's retreat where thirteen women would come together around the concept of the Phoenix rising. The Phoenix is a powerful spiritual totem, the ultimate symbol of strength and renewal. How did I know a lesson would be presented to me before the weekend even began?

As I nestled into my seat on the airplane, I pulled out a book to read, as I had done so many times before. The book for this trip was Vishen Lakhiani's Code of the Extraordinary Mind. A fitting choice for a transformational weekend as it talks about redefining your life and succeeding on your own terms.

I flipped to Chapter Four, which contained a story called Advice From A Monk In A Hot Tub. In this chapter, Vishen recalls a meeting he had with a monk on a retreat in Fiji. The Monk said to Vishen, "Do you know what your problem is? You have low self-esteem." Of course, Vishen could not believe what he was hearing. "I don't think so. I think I'm pretty confident. I run a business. I'm thrilled with my life."

The story continues through Vishen's struggle with this concept and boiled down to a buried belief that he, himself, was not enough. And in this sudden realization, he felt he was not worthy.

As I read those words 'not worthy' a vivid memory leapt into my mind. Those were my mother's words. You are not worthy. You don't deserve this. You will never be good enough!

I burst into tears. Sobbing loudly for all to hear. I tried to stifle the uncontrollable crying. In an effort to calm myself I reached into my bag and pulled out my journal I had tucked away to use later in the flight.

I recalled the exact place in my own home that my mother stood and said these words: "You are selfish. Spoiled. You don't deserve to have anything you've gotten in your life! You'll never succeed. You'll never be good enough! You will never be loved." Equalling 'not worthy'.

I recalled the rapid beating in my chest as the person I look up to the most, broke my heart into pieces. How could she say these things? I was twenty-five years old. An accomplished equestrian rider and coach with my own business and had found a way to buy my own home and riding facility. I was proud of myself for all I had accomplished. Why wasn't she?

I was left standing alone in my living room shocked at what had happened. Broken by her words. Dropping to my knees I cried out loud. As the tears dried up, I curled up into a little ball wanting the world to go away. In a flash I was four years old again. I was dressed in my favourite red velvet dress with my blond ringlets cascading down my back. I hug the curtains tightly at the window watching my father leave, sobbing loudly as my Mother's voice echoed in the background, "See, he is leaving because of you. You will never be loved. You are selfish. You don't deserve a family. You are not worth his time. You made him go!!" I remembered feeling the rough pile of the carpeting on my face as I lay there. Curled up in a ball on the living room rug.

My mother was a prisoner of her mind. She suffered from bipolar disease. Every day I would enter a room and not know who I would meet.

The happy, loving mother with breakfast laid out for me. The weeping form curled up in her chair. Or the angry woman who lashed out at anyone who was there. My father took the brunt of this. What a patient man. He never left his family. He loved my mom so deeply. He was always so calm and patient. I learned those valuable lessons from him.

That night after my mother stood yelling at me in my own home, I slept long and hard. Exhausted from the emotions running through me. I robotically went through the motions of my life that week. Taking care of business and pushing thoughts away.

As the week progressed, I found a new energy. The sadness grew into anger. How could she say these things to me? I had heard that when someone hurts you, write them a letter but don't send it. The action of writing the letter will help release the emotions. I wrote a letter that day that was never delivered. I was supposed to burn it to help with the feelings of hurt and anger. I don't know if omitting the burning-part was responsible, but those emotions got buried deep inside me.

As I scribbled furiously in my journal on the plane, I felt those emotions start to percolate to the surface. The hurt, anger, resentment and deep sadness had been buried for so long. Why was this showing up now? I sunk into my seat as my rapid breathing slowed back down to normal. I closed my eyes and slept for the rest of the flight wondering if this is what I was destined to face during this weekend of strength and renewal?

The next morning I awoke early to a beautiful sunny Arizona morning. The sun was shining, and I vibrated with excitement about what the day would bring. I was going to meet and form new relationships on a journey with a group of dynamic women I had not met yet.

Part of my morning routine is to listen to inspirational people. One of my favourites is Matt Gil who does an amazing body of work called Mornings with Matt. I listened to Matt talk about forgiveness and how forgiving yourself and forgiving others can help you move forward in your life. When Matt asked, "Who is one person who you know you can forgive?" I knew at that moment it was my mother.

Matt challenged his audience to take a bold step. Write a letter to them in a way of an appreciation exercise. What I appreciate about you is... Then move into writing, what I forgive you for...

This took me back to March 2018 when I started a journey with Lisa Nichols and her Speak and Inspire Quest through Mindvalley. It was there that I first learned of the Mirror Exercise. This exercise was so valuable to me, it helped me take off the layers of myself that were holding me back.

For a month, I stood in front of the mirror each day, said my name and stated seven points of what I was proud of myself for, what I forgave myself for and what I committed myself to.

My answers to each surprised me, as did how connected to myself I've felt since I began reciting them. It's a bit creepy to talk to yourself in the mirror but it has started to feel like I'm honouring myself in doing so. Looking in the mirror every day required me to take off the layers of who I've been in the world. It required me to take off the cloak of protection. That everything was okay.

So, reflecting on the impact of the mirror exercise and the challenge of the letter writing from Matt, I decided to combine both powerful techniques.

I wrote that letter to my mother.

It read:

Mom, I appreciate all the love that you gave to your family.

Mom, I appreciate how you allowed a cat and eventually a dog into the house even though you were afraid of animals.

Mom, I appreciate you for all the times you spent with me at the horse shows.

Mom, I appreciate you for fighting to keep your family together when you felt like leaving us.

Mom, I appreciate you for the Sunday dinners with friends and family.

Mom, I appreciate you for sharing your love of travel with me.

Mom, I appreciate you opened your house and home to everyone with no judgement.

My stomach churned. My head was pounding. My hands shook. I could barely write. Never before had I been able to bring up memories of my mother in a positive loving light. I had buried not only the hurt that my mother caused but also the beautiful things she did for me, my sister, and my dad. The table was always set with the most exquisite china for our Sunday roast-beef family dinners. The garden she planted in the middle of the city so we could experience the wonder of growing something ourselves and the taste of fresh vegetables. The bedtime stories she told as a child that continued as stories around the campfire as a teenager. There were so many good things.

Having acknowledged these new feelings, I continued through the exercise:

Mom, I forgive you for all the times you told me to shhh, that my voice didn't matter.

Mom, I forgive you for being sick.

Mom, I forgive you for the dark times when you told me I was not enough.

Mom, I forgive you for not being able to control your illness and being a prisoner in your own mind.

Mom, I forgive you for being so kind to other people and so evil to me.

Mom, I forgive you for not having the deep, meaningful conversations with me that could have steered my life.

Mom, I forgive you for all the fights that you had with my kind, gentle father.

These words did not come easily. Tears streamed down my face. Cleansing tears. It was an emotional release like I had never felt before. A sense of calm came over me as I realized that yes, she was sick. She was not in control of her mind.

Just writing those words of forgiveness shifted my perspective. Then I gathered the strength to write the next statements:

Mom, I commit to you that I will stand in my greatness and when the negative chatter kicks in, I will just press pause.

Mom, I commit to you that I will use my voice unapologetically to serve and add value to the world.

Mom, I commit to you that I will live in authenticity and embrace all that has come before me that has shaped me to this person today.

Mom, I commit to you I will live without judgment of others and open my home and heart to everyone.

Mom, I commit to you that I will appreciate each and every moment throughout the day.

Mom, I commit to you that everyday I will sing and dance in joy, love, silliness, passion and peace of mind.

I commit to you, my courageous Mom, that I will receive the energy, strength and vitality you send to me from the other side, so I may live my legacy.

As I committed these words to my mother, my heart seemed to become warm and beat more slowly. I found myself standing up taller. I puffed my chest out and a smile came to my face. A smile that had not been there for a long time.

Never before had I been able to bring up memories of my mother in a positive loving light. I actually didn't reflect on her at all. I had blocked good memories with the bad. Those feelings of sadness. Those thoughts being small. That I was no longer impacted by that moment in time with my mother that dropped me and rocked me to my core. The 'aha' that buried things alive never die.

I felt like I had already learned the lesson I was brought to the Phoenix Rising retreat to learn. The event had not started yet and I felt as if I could go home. There was already a powerful transformation that had already taken place within me.

But there was more to come. At the end of the first day the thirteen women sat in a circle and were guided through a powerful meditation focusing on our power as women.

The emotions ran high for me and tears streamed down my face as I cleansed more of the past. The words were spoken, "If there are any women in your ancestry that you want to come in now, invite them."

I took a deep cleansing breath and suddenly my Mother, my Grandmother and my Sister all appeared. I felt surrounded by a loving light and the warmth radiating through my body. My fingers tingled and my heart beat rapidly in my chest. I knew I was loved and protected. I felt like I had come home again.

Now I celebrate all the times I had with my mother. The precious family vacations to Idaho where we skied during the day and sang songs and played music long into the night. I value and celebrate the time she spent with my horses. She even learned how to pull a horse trailer behind her station wagon. I celebrate her strength with her battle with bipolar disease. I celebrate how hard she fought to keep the family together.

Now I celebrate how I found the strength through forgiveness. I am still the independent strong woman my mother raised. I am now more open in my heart. I can speak my truth. I can live my true authentic self. Now I live a life unlimited.

Forgiveness does not excuse the behaviour. It doesn't condone the behaviour. Forgiveness creates space for new possibilities and moving forward. Being who we are designed to be.

IGNITE ACTION STEPS

I invite you to look at the power of forgiveness. Ask these questions daily, and repeat this exercise as often as you need until you release the shackles of fear, resentment, and guilt.

The Mirror Exercise:

- State your name, I am proud that you... (state seven points of pride).
- State your name, I forgive you for... (state seven points for forgiveness).
- State your name, I commit to you that... (state seven commitments).

Be sure to track in a journal what you realized about yourself during this exercise.

Now I propose that you use this exercise to forgive someone else:

- State the person's name and seven statements of what you appreciate them for.
- State the person's name and seven statements of what you forgive them for.
- State the person's name and seven statements of what you commit to them.

I have found it valuable to track in a journal what I realized about myself during this exercise and any emotions that come up for me.

I trust, believe and know that forgiveness will work for you.

Trish Mrakawa, High Performance Coach. Trish Mrakawa Coaching.
www.trishmrakawa.com

ASTUTI
MARTOSUDIRDJO

"Beliefs are the seeds of life. They grow to become gardens.
Planting uplifting beliefs in life's garden, blossoms inner peace."

My story shows you how burnout can truly catapult your growth. I invite you to redefine your priorities so you too can evolve and discover what matters most in the present and what is your natural state. Fill your life with everything that uplifts you and you'll soon find out that the Universe has your back!

UPLIFT!

A JOURNEY FROM BURNOUT TO INNER PEACE

I'm sure I met all the ghosts in my office building.

How could I not? For one full year, I worked close to 100 hours per week, including weekends. Every night after 11 pm, I heard loud footsteps when every office in the building was pitch-black, apart from mine. I checked. Of course, I did.

Since I arrived at the office by 7 am, a taxi would pick me up at 1 am almost daily to take me home at night. I memorized how to exit the reception area in the dark, without bumping into anything on the way and make it to the car waiting outside.

This was my routine until one early afternoon in December 2008 when I couldn't get up from my desk in my spacious office. My body refused to move. I felt like my battery was drained... Shocked yet, ironically, not surprised, I sat there...

Let me take you back to the beginning...

In January 2008, I started working for one of the major banks in Switzerland. It was about to embark on a global overhaul of their recruitment function, starting in Zurich. They needed someone who had worked for banking and executive search industries, with change-management experience to play a big role. This task was to build a new team with additional capabilities for the Bank. Steep learning curve indeed. Truthfully, I was addicted to challenging goals. I said, "Yes," excitedly.

Born in the UK to Indonesian parents, I'm no stranger to changes and transition. By the age of 28, I'd already lived in five countries in Asia, Europe, and North America. My mind had been trained to adapt to different cultures and establish myself in diverse groups. Over the years, I've come to accept that what I've enjoyed most is building something up from scratch. The opportunity to create something innovative, different, or ahead of its time – strongly appealed to me.

This project was high profile in scope and size, with ambitious timelines. The second day on the job, I had the most important meeting, to choose the external consultants. That accomplished, meeting schedules and deadlines were queued up by the end of the first week. We kicked the project off a week after that. My mind was focused. I was clear what I was there to do and what success looked like. I hit the ground running.

I had two teams to manage: (1.) the existing team and (2.) the project team. Each had two distinctly different focusses. I also played the role of (3.) subject-matter expert for the new capabilities to be built on, which means I rolled up my sleeves, sorted out the details of stepping into three (in-one) full-time jobs.

I met my existing team in the mornings and at the end of the day. In between, I attended back-to-back meetings: gaining approvals, designing structures, calculating what was needed to run the new department, etc. After everyone left the office around 6 pm, I continued working in the much-needed silence to finish the day's agendas. This was how my days rolled. In my mind, I had a great structure. I wouldn't drop anything. True, except recharge-time, exercise, social, me-time and rest were not parts of the structure.

During the first month in this mode, my HR Manager asked me what

I thought was a strange question, "How do you feel?" I remember saying, "I don't feel. I just get on with things." Three times she asked and received the same answer from me. I was convinced this was the best strategy for the situation. My Boss had the same question. She, out of many people around me, was the most concerned. I assured her all was under control. Every time I heard such a question, my mind automatically narrowed it down to my work. My health and well-being were irrelevant! So bizarre, considering I was thinking of everyone else's well-being in this transition, except mine. What a blind spot. In hindsight, being unconsciously inconsiderate of my own wellbeing was the biggest clue to the root causes of the burnout.

Six months into this project, the Bank had a crisis. Its share price dropped drastically overnight. It impacted not only the company but also the country. One out of four people you met on the street were clients. There was a period where many were paralyzed by the fear of the uncertain future. I caught some colleagues staring at the computer looking at the low share price. This motivated me further to show up differently at work, to help to ease the situation in any way that I could. "I must help my colleagues."

Growing up in Indonesia from the 70s till the 90s, I experienced stability as a luxury. Turbulence and changes were inevitable. I could see the Bank's crisis impacted many people, yet I was emotionally detached from it. I made a choice to be there for my colleagues. I lent my ears, mind and heart to them. I proposed ideas that might help. Consequently, I took on supporting others, without even blinking. Deep inside, I was overwhelmed. I juggled too many things. Time and energy ran out fast. I talked myself into work every day, "Keep going, you can do it." The decision to avoid feeling seemed helpful. So I thought.

To build more time for work, I added more unhealthy habits of skipping breakfast and often dinner. Having a sandwich over a lunch meeting happened almost daily. Eating while talking was not for me, so the sandwich was often untouched. No exercise. Not drinking enough water. A lot of coffee. I was sleep deprived. The most sleep I got was five hours but more likely it was less most nights. My mind was so busy that it was hard to fall asleep and stay asleep. The quality of my sleep was questionable.

Yet, I kept going this way. I felt like I did not have the energy to think of other ways to be and do in the situation. I felt too tired to change the structures I'd put in place. Many things started to feel too much. I became more easily irritable and frustrated. My aura of composure was thinning week by week. I noticed my usual sharp mind forgot names, even of the person having a conversation with me. I often lost my train of thought and it took a while to get back to it. I used to be praised as a fast thinker. Progressively, this changed for the worse. I was scared yet I did not know what to do nor did I stop.

The exhaustion level dipped as soon as I reached home. I often woke up feeling more tired than before going to bed. Because of this, I became reclusive, hiding away from everyone including my parents and siblings, whom I used to be in touch with regularly. I avoided them because I didn't want to answer any questions. I was simply too tired. In fact, I thought if I didn't call them; they wouldn't know how I was (or wasn't).

I showed up only to select invitations from close friends. They could tell that I was only physically there, not emotionally. They knew I was exhausted. I felt grateful they didn't give up on me; for continuously inviting me out even when they knew I'd often say 'no'.

It was a lonely and draining journey. I experienced a diminishing ability to connect with people as if there was nothing left of me to share while at the same time, I couldn't even feel the love coming from anywhere. I felt disconnected from myself and others. Feeling numb, I wondered whether *dying while being alive* felt like this.

Then, that afternoon happened. A colleague came to invite me to have lunch together. When I realised my limbs were not responding to my brain's commands, I just sat there... She had to help me up out of my chair. It was a pivotal moment. Extreme exhaustion took over. I had nothing left. I no longer could deny I was in deep trouble. Living like a zombie was not an option. I quietly vowed to myself: I'd do anything, however uncomfortable, to get better.

I informed my boss of my situation. After two days off I sought the help of the Counsellor (psychologist) on staff. "I'm just really tired!" To impress on me how serious my condition was, he said, "No one will miss you if you die on the job." He expressed disbelief that I had functioned at the pace I set for myself for as long as I did. An entire year.

Professional diagnosis – approaching the end-stage of complete burnout. He had already sent 11 cohorts to a clinic specializing in burn-out recovery. "Thankfully, you admitted it now, stopped before you ended up in a hole and couldn't get out. You will have to be very disciplined to recover. DO all recommended therapies: for the body, for the emotions and the mind. You need to RE-THINK how you approach work."

I did just as he said: I did it all. For eighteen months. Starting with Shiatsu…

My colleague gave me the therapist's number. I phoned immediately. She had a cancellation. I could barely talk when I got there, "I'm so tired. Please fix me." She never spoke anything till the end of the session. She assigned some exercises to do at home. I went every day for two weeks. (Later, I added Grinberg Therapy to relearn to understand what my body communicated, so I could do something about it. I also did Pilates the whole 18 months, and beyond.)

At home, everything sank in. I sat on my bed, staring straight at the wall imagining the worst scenarios. "What if I couldn't get better? What if I could never return to work? Will I end up on the street? what if…? what if…? what if…?" One after another, fear after fear after fear, came up. I felt like I was being sucked down by quicksand. The only way to survive was to stay still until help arrived – new thoughts! After a while, I breathed in and out. I calmed down. I focused on what I was told: "Thankfully the burnout hasn't quite reached the end stage, where you are at the bottom of a well and there's no way to get yourself back up. With discipline and adequate help, you will get out of this." The discussion with the Counsellor struck home: I was a human being, not a robot.

I had me to blame for this. I proactively added more work on an already steep learning curve in a very short period of time. Why did I do this to myself? Why did I not even care for my own wellbeing? Why did I ignore everyone else showing how they cared?

With the help of my therapist, I learned the relationship between the conscious and the subconscious minds. This made me realize that the irrational decisions I made stemmed from limiting beliefs I had about myself and life.

Through a series of sessions, I discovered the dominant limiting beliefs at play during this period: 'I must exceed any expectation in order to be loved.' 'I need to always be strong.' 'My role as a leader is to nurture, educate, and protect others first; I come second.' 'Achieve more and more at any cost.' Looking back, I named myself an 'achievement addict'.

These beliefs, formed in my childhood, were running my life unconsciously. Until this job, such unconscious beliefs helped me to be successful, to move ahead swiftly on my career trajectory. This time, they pushed me too far and my body fought back.

The most ironic part of this was that my actions were driven to get more love, yet in the process, I abandoned myself, without even realizing it. I didn't treat myself with kindness and affection. I couldn't celebrate the joy of achievement. To get the acceptance and love, I had to achieve again and again. Deliver more and more. My boss and colleagues loved me. I was the one who didn't love me. It was me that didn't appreciate me.

Realizing this lack of self-love brought me face-to-face with the deepest grief of my life. A cocktail of emotions: sadness, guilt, shame came up because I abandoned my mind, body and spirit, while also neglecting people I cared for very much. I betrayed myself.

As I took the necessary steps to restore my body to health again, I worked with therapists to reprogram my subconscious mind, to heal and uplift my beliefs, letting go of those internal ghosts. Forgiving myself was the key to deep healing, and it was the hardest to do. It was worth everything though. As I healed deeply, my life transformed.

With more love and energy in me, I redefined what success meant to me. I revised my definition of what 'strong' looked like. I updated my lifestyle to accommodate new thought patterns using them to oust any former limiting beliefs lingering like those previous ghosts. I refused to lose more time. I was committed to showing up in my own life, feeling safe and enough just as I was.

Self-love is the main focus in my life now. I make conscious decisions every moment to fuel my life with mostly love. I choose to trust that asking for help is a way of loving, as much as giving help. It is a foundation for a deep and intimate connection with others that will carry me far in life, feeling safe and loved.

It took me an intensive 18 months to get back to a fit body, with renewed mindsets about myself. After a five-week leave, I returned to work on lighter duties with a supportive and competent team, overseeing the scope of the work that I was passionate about.

My new uplifting beliefs became the seeds of my new life. Planting healthy seeds make lush gardens. I chose to integrate them into my life to fuel me to answer my current calling. Five years after my recovery, I took a leap of faith to change my career. I left my corporate and executive recruitment path to become a Life Coach and Subconscious Mind Reprogrammer. I help both Achievement Addicts (like I was) and Procrastinators to become Uplifted Go-getters - ones who remain focused, present, at peace and energized as they deliver an even bigger and deeper impact. This mini death – the burnout I had – awakened me profoundly. It brought me to the path of my uplifted life. To the world, I declare: "I am here, I am home and I am showing up!"

IGNITE ACTION STEPS

Two tips to help you either prevent or recover from a burnout:

1. Improve your physical wellness.

• Unblock the energy blockages in your body. I recommend the non-invasive Japanese therapeutic bodywork, Shiatsu, that uses kneading, pressing, soothing, tapping and stretching techniques to reduce physical and emotional stresses.

• Spend 20 minutes everyday dancing to your favorite music. Move and breathe.

• Improve your nutrients. Get adequate intake of vitamin D ideally from being out in the sun. Healthy fats, including omega 3, are important. This supports your immune systems and regulates mood (wards off depression).

• Sleep well and enough. It's needed for the body to repair and detox everyday.

• Prioritize and plan your evening accordingly. Eliminate activities, food or drinks that disturb it. Create a sleeping ritual to get your body ready to sleep: 20 minutes before bedtime, stretch your body and listen to a meditative recording to slow down the frequency of your brain.

2. Uplift your beliefs in your subconscious mind.

• Your body, mind and soul work as an inseparable unit. They're designed to self-heal and self-regulate through your advanced intelligence unit, also known as the subconscious mind, which runs that three-part unit.

• The subconscious mind is a part of our mind (accounting for 95% of the mind's capacity) that serves as a database of our beliefs-based (automatic) programs and habits, which has adults operating in autopilot mode everyday.

• Beliefs are assumptions we have about ourselves, others, and life. We often are unaware of them because they were mostly formed in our childhood, between the last trimesters of pregnancy through the first six years of life.

• It's important that your subconscious mind works for you, not against you. In subconscious-mind-reprogramming, speed and depth matter most. Rapid Transformational Therapy (RTT), a hypnosis-based method does just that. It gets to the limiting beliefs that cause self-sabotaging behaviours, heals the emotional traumas that created these beliefs, replacing them with uplifting beliefs, rapidly, permanently.

Astuti Martosudirdjo, Uplift My Life Today. www.upliftmylife.today

JENNIFER MONAGHAN

"Have no fear, step to the edge with love and hope in your heart.
When you jump, you will find your wings."

I wish to bring more awareness to chronic disease and illness so that people know where they can find and access support on their journey. My own experiences often left me alone and I further self-isolated. I wish for anyone experiencing pain and dis-ease to find the support to triumph through it! My deepest hope is that chronic pain can soon be a thing of the past.

THE PAIN GAME WHERE I WIN!

Many of life's journeys often start with a very defined beginning, then have a distinguished and easily recognizable ending. Not so when you live in chronic pain and every day feels like death and anguish. One keeps trying to believe pain-free moments can happen and make life worth living again. My chronic disease and pain journey swallowed over a decade of my life.

To understand the full story, I need to start at the beginning.

When the chronic pain started in my pelvis, it was a sharp, stabbing, unbearable pain. Previously, I had suffered a tubal pregnancy with a similar sensation. This new pain started below my belly button, travelled straight down the right side of my pelvis and into my leg. It was non-stop, excruciating, stabbing pain.

During the day, the pain scale was an eleven out of ten. At nighttime, the pain went off the scale. Often the only way to make it through the night was to hold my body, rock and talk encouragingly to myself. At times, I would just cry and pray. Eventually I'd drift off to sleep, briefly. In the first couple of weeks, I thought it would disappear.

I went to emergency and a kind doctor offered to do a surgery for endometriosis and cysts. I was hoping that this was all it was, and I would again experience relief. After the operations, I felt good on morphine in the hospital, so I thought the first surgery worked! I thought it was handled. At home, the medication wore off and the pain returned.

I went to my doctor. She informed me that surgeries often do not address chronic pain. I went home with anti-inflammatory drugs and relaxants for pain management.

Throughout that first month and the following years, my life was full of exploratory surgeries, emergency operations and tests. Tests for everything. I was filled with confusion and jam-packed with questions. Seeing one doctor led to a referral to another doctor, another referral and so on. I would see specialist after specialist for my uterus, then bladder, then bowel. I was seeing the best of the best in the medical field. No answers. Nothing helped.

The pain didn't stop. It was becoming crystal clear that this anguish in my body had no plans on departing. I remember the moment when the thought crossed my mind: What if this lasts forever? The thought of this possibility shook the foundation of my whole world. I found out later, it is common to have such thoughts and feelings in the beginning of the chronic pain game.

My emotional life came to a grinding halt. My brain went into overdrive. I spent countless painful hours and sleepless nights interacting with Dr. Google, searching for explanations as to why the pain was not letting up. The hours wore on. The days and weeks added up to months that, in the end, lasted almost 17 years.

I'd already experienced waiting endlessly on a diagnosis. Unexplained symptoms that started after summer vacation when I was 13 weren't diagnosed til I was 22 years old. Narcolepsy with cataplexy were the culprits. I was just coming to terms with living life with narcolepsy while caring for three children full-time, including my infant son and his 6-year-old step-sibling twins. Already exhausted.

Did the chronic pain stem from a physical or medical issue? Was it emotional or even spiritual, perhaps? What did I need to do to fix me? Could

I be fixed? I was scared. I had no idea that the agony would test me mentally, emotionally, physically and spiritually. Yet, it became the source of my greatest growth over the next 17 years. Learning about patience was just one of the gifts. Perseverance was another.

When every door shut before me, I learned a lot. Acute pain comes and goes with life's bumps and bruises, serving to alert us to possible injuries. However, chronic pain (defined as pain lasting longer than 12 weeks) affects 1.5 billion people on this planet. Likely, someone you know has chronic pain. It is more prevalent now than ever before, a symptom, perhaps, of a great uneasiness spreading throughout the world today.

The first five years were an endless, epic quest for medications, magic juices, surgery, needles and acupuncture. The Chronic Pain Center offered courses on managing pain. I tried working with a physical therapist, even did talk therapy for the mind. In the midst of all this searching and alternative medicine, combined with whatever western medicine offered, my brain started to send other painful sensations everywhere.

During these years, I lost five pregnancies. Two were tubal, then a surgical mistake tragically stole my fertility at 28. I struggled privately, telling only my closest friends.

In addition, between the ages of 22 and 28, I was a passenger in three car accidents. All of them were rear-end collisions, adding whiplash recovery to my struggles. Looking back, I remember thinking it could have been worse.

It was a light bulb moment when I realized not being the most positive mindset was creating my reality. How could I manifest the best-case scenarios, if I was expecting the worst to happen? With this awareness, I started thinking more positively, expecting the best outcomes. I attended all appointments at the Pain clinic and with my doctors at the Sleep Institute. I was choosing to beat this pain,

I said, 'yes' to botox injections in my pelvis; and to Lupron, a drug to put me into menopause to prevent the monthly adhesions from endometriosis. The pain caused such bone deep fatigue that the sleep I did get never really felt like true rest and rejuvenation. In addition, the narcolepsy could make me feel like I was drunk and ready to pass out. Progressive, slow atrophy of my core muscles was causing loss of mobility. Standing and bladder control are all part of a strong core which I no longer had, due to all the bed rest.

Also, the narcolepsy made the pain game different for me. The constant drowsiness meant I really never felt awake. Imagine not sleeping for three days and wanting to now go live life. Impossible!

I worked outside the home, turning business into a major coping mechanism. I made a habit of staying in constant motion to keep my mind off the pain. All that did was create an even deeper sense of exhaustion. When did try to sleep, the pain kept me tossing and turning with few periods of actual sleep.

In addition to conducting readings as an intuitive medium, I worked mornings at the airport. I rushed home for my son after school, then worked a late-night bartending shift. Busy and happy helping people, I was also planning my upcoming marriage. In the midst of all this frenetic activity, desperate to hide the pain, I declined get-togethers and outings. I often canceled plans with my girlfriends or went home early.

Desperate for answers and a change, was it time to move? Maybe the cure is in leaving the city! I needed to see if there was a natural way to deal with this. I left all my clients, both jobs, and quit working. I would not work for the next two years.

I moved to the Slocan Valley (AKA the Kootenays), in British Columbia, Canada. Maybe the rural wise women knew a way? I had heard stories about natural healing - another path to go down. I found colonics, lost weight and felt it effectively eliminated toxins from my body and helped with pain. It was my first sign of hope.

I was sent to a nearby neurologist for nerve conduction tests. Result? My nerves were not the problem. Every doctor's appointment I felt hopeful; and this confirmation, like others before, showed no concrete reason for my pain. I was crushed. The only thing that seemed to have alleviated my pain was colon hydrotherapy. I studied for two years to earn my degree. Where I lived was a great place to launch my alternative practice and gratitude flowed through me for it also being a safe place for my whole family!

Our quirky neighbour provided an 'Aha' moment. One day he fell off the deck of his cabin and broke his collarbone. He was pedaling his stationary bike so fast, he flew forward over the railing and the bike fell on top of him. What happened next was nothing short of mind blowing. He sat in silence for 22 hours a day, meditating and mentally moving the broken bone slowly back in place. He never went to the hospital. He rejected any attempts for help. Within three weeks, he could put the same amount of pressure on both sides. I was blown away! Proof to my weary heart that true healing can be attained through the power of the mind. Could anyone do this? Could I?

Then another move. My marriage was breaking apart. Caregiver stress wore down my husband. Our relationship plummeted, and I had to leave immediately. Time to vacate our enchanting home. I felt I hit a wall and moved to a nearby city. Embarrassed, we were in the women's shelter for a total of 22 days.

I found a basement suite by a middle school where I enrolled my son in grade seven. This is where my life shrinks, turns shades of dark grey and slips into darkness. A fog fell over my brain. My waistline bloated almost making me look pregnant. I was literally plugged up. I could barely move. My metabolic rate slowed to a crawl.

I do believe, as an empath, with so much pain trapped in my body, weight became my attempt to shield myself from the world. I deeply grieved my failed marriage. Daily, the pain spread throughout my whole body, sending sharp, shocking vibrations. Odd burning sensations, pins and needles, feelings of frigid-water-like pain, spreading all over my skin and deeper. I became very depressed, anxious and began again to self-isolate. Every day, my physical body grew increasingly sensitive. I kept going, adding life in where I could. Sometimes simply standing in a grocery line would hurt so much, I'd abandon the items in the cart. Out of options, I was feeling raw and hopeless. Whenever possible, I retreated into the safety of bed and a desired dream state. Haphazard sleep was my only escape and comfort.

By 2017, I struggled to get out of my wheelchair to take pictures with my twin and our parents. I just wanted to give up. I still had my young son at home. He needed me and he became my one 'why'. I would say things in my head like, "If I were better, what would I do?" Then I would focus love and happiness in my heart. I'd feel my smile, with my eyes closed. I day-dreamed a different ending; nothing even remotely close to the suffering in my reality: dancing, visiting family and friends. One thing I repeated every day: "If I ever get better, I'll take the stairs for the rest of my journey."

In May 2018, I had a family member tragically pass away, and my daughter was ill in ICU. My heart was heavy, with death all around me, was it my time as well? It had now been 16-plus years of constant pain. For the first time, I felt there was no plan for the next doctor's appointment. I tried not to show it, but this was it. I had no moves left on the chessboard of chronic pain and dis-ease. My spirit was officially exhausted and I felt like I was on the edge of breaking.

So many symptoms were travelling through my body, I couldn't keep track. My world felt officially over. I was alone and without hope. My GP made an appointment to see yet another neurologist. I agreed – one last doctor's appointment. I wasn't excited. I'd had so many disappointments. It was hopeless. I told this new specialist I felt like I was dying.

The neurologist gave me a definitive diagnosis. Missed by the first neurologist many years back. There WAS an explanation for all the pain.

Small Fiber Sensory Neuropathy (SFSN), is when your brain is confused and sends the wrong signal to the wrong body part. The electrical, burning, stinging, cold ice or feeling water pouring on my leg was explainable. I was overwhelmed! A diagnosis — finally! I had no idea that this was to be the beginning of my own miracle. I was happy beyond all measure!

Heading home, I prayed. Amethyst in hand, my heart full of love and excitement. The diagnosis fit and answered years of questions. I felt in my being that I had just been granted a miracle. I finally had an answer! I could get my life back and carry on.

Before leaving for Burnaby, my sleep specialist, who also wanted to help me achieve a pain-free life, expressed concern about mental and physical health. Hearing me sobbing for a solution, or even a plan, he knew I was exhausted; almost completely out of gas in my tank. He suggested I try high-dose amitriptyline. I wasn't very trusting at this point, but I promised him I would give it a shot. It was time to give this burden away, so I stepped out of my own way and took the 150 mg dose. It felt like the biggest risk of my life, as it's a very strong drug. Stats stated a 30% success rate. I worried if I took that high a dose, I may never wake up! Nervously, I took the first tablet.

Nothing changed, at first. What a joke, I thought. Then, after about three weeks, it happened.

I remember the very day I was oddly out of pain. I could barely walk, but that morning I felt different. It was almost foreign, but I wasn't in pain! I wanted to go outside. I could move. I could walk again. I wasn't tired. I was full of an internal energy and free from the gripping chronic pain! I was happy. Life came flooding back in now that I had awareness and the space to feel it. My mind felt clear, my emotions lifted. I took my first step toward a new life and a new me.

My heart goes out to anyone who has lived with chronic pain and suffering. It is emotionally and spiritually debilitating, as well as physically. It robs the person of the life they desire to live. Now I support others in dealing with this difficult issue and talk to whoever will listen, about being your own best advocate and working hard to understand all your diagnoses. Your life is yours to live. Take care of it, so you can live.

Ignite Action Steps

The consistency of a sleep routine and waking up at the same time every day produces a magic I only knew after I experienced it. After waking, the first thing I choose to do routinely is get out of bed in the morning, without my phone, and stretch. Our whole family stretches together before we begin our day.

Then I do 20 minutes of dancing, make a good breakfast, and THEN I can pick up my phone. I strongly advise you to find a routine that works for you and discover your own flow.

Next I did meal planning, removing gluten and dairy. I made sure we had purified water without chemicals. At sunrise and sunset, I do breathing exercises to ground myself. My showers at the end of the day remove the drudgery from my skin and spirit. They have become an integral part of my routine. Another daily habit is finding my groove. I start with everyone's favourite music in our home; we made a group playlist.

Here's the one I designed for myself:
Morning Routine: Design or choose a stretching routine
- Twenty minutes of dancing
- Make a nutritious breakfast
- Electronics, only after the morning routine

Daily Grounding Exercises:
- Sunrise: breathing exercises
- Play your favourite music (include family members in creating a playlist)
- Sunset: breathing exercises
- Day's End: A meditative, cleansing shower
- A consistent sleep routine: Go to bed and rise at the same time every day.

Spiritual Connection:
- Breathe, rest, and release
- Find the joy in everything
- Live full-out

Having control over your emotions, managing them through breathing, resting, and releasing, will lead to finding the joy in life.

The best part of the whole experience is I learned how to live full-out. I am soon to be a grandparent of two sweet babes. I have lost 115 lbs. (Super happy about that.) I love that I can stay awake all day and enjoy all the miracle moments the day has to offer.

And, I always take the stairs.

Jennifer Monaghan, Life Coach / Medical Medium / Inspirational Speaker
www.jenspaingame.com

GEORGIA VANDERVILLE

"The door that opens with love stays open."

I intend to share some tools to help you move instantly through tough moments and experience the place above the turbulence and clouds... where the sun shines and we soar peacefully through blue sky. We will reside in that space, where our Inner Echo speaks and resonates within.

MY INNER ECHO

Where was I? What was I just doing? What do I like? Dislike? Where do I keep the salt and pepper? What was happening?

I was 33 years old and I'd forgotten how to drive my car. In fact, I couldn't remember anything!

It was 5:30 Saturday morning. With my husband and 2 & 3-year-old boys asleep, I had an hour to interview a potential employee in our mini warehouse (aka garage). Due to the recession, or rather our acceptance of it, we allowed our company to dwindle from eight to zero employees. My world was crumbling. Our candle company was swallowing my soul, my family was a chore, food was a necessity, and pleasing others was a requirement. Then, there was me - with a burning question: "This is who I came into the world to be?"

This interview is going smoothly; she'll be an awesome employee. My two hours of sleep is normal; I can make it! I'll sleep tonight, tomorrow, later, when I'm all caught up. I'll survive. But then…it happened: My brain twisted. It somersaulted in my head. My vision blurred. It hurt and fear set in. I was terrified! It felt like a gargantuan roller coaster ride, deja vu that had no beginning or end.

I sat there staring at this woman, not sure if I was twitching or standing on my head. Approximately 120 seconds later my brain became still. Internally terrified, I abruptly ended the interview. She didn't seem to notice and wasn't fazed, but I sure was! Something had just happened. I had no idea what it was. I went and laid down with my husband, Nick, and fell asleep in his arms. It would be okay; I'd sleep it off.

A few hours later, I found myself feeling a bit lost while in the kitchen. I, unexpectedly, had no appetite, but my boys did. Breakfast time with two toddlers is fun! I'll make eggs. Wait…how do I make eggs? What a dumb question, why would I even need to ask that! Wait…salt and pepper…you put in salt and pepper, but where do I keep the salt and pepper? The entire day continued like this. Just relax. Sleep it off.

Sunday - this day would be the best! I woke up that morning feeling rejuvenated, it must have just been lack of sleep! Phew…much better now! Only, the morning became a laborious chore as we slowly figured out how to prepare for church. We diligently dressed, packed and made it to the car. Every Sunday, I interpreted for my deaf friend at church. I love sign language. When I was 12, my friend and I created our own 'sign language' so we could talk to one another during church. (It worked until her grandma realized and started sitting between us, holding our hands still to keep us 'quiet'.) This precious time encouraged me to become fluent in American Sign Language. I had been interpreting since my oldest was in-utero; same church, four years later, nothing had changed. I got this!

At 15 years old, I learned how to drive a stick shift. For the subsequent 18 years it was clutch in, shift, clutch out. Now, I had no idea how to operate this vehicle! I had gears grinding. The car was stuttering and jumping, the engine was on the verge of implosion, but I figured it out. By golly, I had this! I started driving and realized I had no idea how to exit my own neighborhood, let alone where the church was. I asked my phone for support, and 20 minutes later we arrived.

We made it to the building, and like the last four years, made the way to our seats; only today, I'm feeling confused. I'm seated in front of my friend and I'm ready to interpret. Ok…let's start! Only nothing came out. Nothing computed! I only remembered one sign, "Sorry." I sat there for two hours in terrified tears.

By Monday afternoon the chilling truth set in. Something was massively wrong and sleep wasn't going to fix it. Neither was pretending everything was okay. Apprehensively, I caved and asked Nick to take me to the Emergency Room.

As the weeks passed, life improved. These events are like turbulence on an airplane. Once you get above the clouds you find peace and sunshine… you just have to get through the takeoff, wind, rain, lightning, thunder and darkness to find the sunshine above. One day at a time.

Tests and doctor visits persisted. I remained strong for my family. A friend told me about a free family event hosted at our University, UNR, that we call the Watermelon Concerts. It was us on the grass, filled with music, kids, families, laughter and watermelon. This became our happy place. We started searching for more playgrounds, parks and peace. We connected with nature and things started to brighten.

I told one good friend about what was happening. She ended our conversation and I never heard from her again. Shocked, I decided this was my business. I would do this alone. I didn't want others to judge, doubt, leave, or feel sorry for me.

Nick and I were continually searching for answers. The MRIs, CT scans, blood and urine tests, and a sleep-deprivation test all gave little direction. We tried a study where I wore an electrode contraption on my head for 72 long, embarrassing hours. It was like having an octopus stuck to your dirty scalp for days, all while trying to be part of society. Not able to find what they were looking for, the doctors did one last test: lumbar puncture.

This test gave doctors the results they wanted, but it left me in the most excruciating pain I have ever experienced — and I am someone who gave birth to two boys with no pain medication! After having what felt like a meat thermometer-sized needle inserted into my spine to steal my spinal fluid, I was left with the most powerful back, neck and head pain known to mankind. I lay, incapacitated, on my back on the living room floor for three days as my two toddlers scrambled across my chest. I bravely wiped my tears as they gushed down over my temples, into my ears, while my boys asked, "Why can't you play with us? Why are you crying, mommy? What's wrong? Please get up!"

"I love you," was all I could reply. Confusion and fear resided in us all.

Once the pain subsided, I was back at work. Through our business I had become very close friends with some of our customers. One friend was a professor at UNR. Three years prior, she was diagnosed with Lou Gehrig's Disease (ALS). I watched her regress from a strong, intelligent, professional role model to only being able to move one finger, with her sweet forehead strapped to a wheelchair because her neck no longer supported her head. She died shortly after our last visit.

This looming future terrified me! I had an amazing husband, two wonderful boys, a business and many other things I still needed to do here on earth. I refused to let misery be my path!

As summer was in full swing, I was connecting broken dots. Memories were surfacing. One evening, while at our Watermelon Concert my cell phone rang. It was the dreaded news. "Georgia, you have MS." My life had just ended! I was going to have my head strapped to a wheelchair. Mistakenly, I had connected MS with ALS. My life was imploding. The solution: medicine. Or so I was told. I jumped on board, soon to find myself sicker than I was before from the side effects of the medication. I unnaturally gained weight, had abdominal pain and would profusely sweat for no reason. The sudden and prolonged burning and reddening in my face, scalp, neck and chest were alarmingly apparent and caused concern for those around me. I stayed at home to keep others from being uncomfortable. I felt like a lone coyote, running aimlessly, trying to find answers. My doctor felt like she was the only one on my side, so I wasn't completely solo; until one afternoon she called and told me she had just been fired because the hospital administration wanted her to push certain medications on patients. Morally, she couldn't do it anymore...so they fired her. I was alone again.

Who would fight with me? On this solitary journey, I realized I would have to be the one to fight for me. I took an interest in Georgia. It was difficult to take time for me, to spend money on myself, but I did it. To respect myself and honestly put Georgia and her Inner Growth before my business, husband, kids, friends and family was an adventure. Once I started, the time and money showed up. Employees showed up. Teachers and lessons showed up. And a shift began. The less I invested in others, the more I evolved. I was compelled to grow. It was like I was in a cavern overflowing with stalactites and stalagmites that were all lessons I could break off and ingest — all I had to do was reach out for them.

Meditation appeared and I embraced it. Through this, I saw someone I didn't recognize. I loved her and wanted to transform into her. She was ME! I was headed in her direction. She was healthy, happy, vibrant, positive, loving, a leader, teammate, daughter, wife and mom.

While on vacation, due to another large deja vu, I ended up at UCSF hospital in San Francisco. I met with three multiple sclerosis research doctors. They all said to continue with the medicine even after being asked for other options. On discharge, the student doctor suggested to cut out gluten. I immediately ended 100% contact and ingestion of any gluten, and my head started to clear up.

A few months later, while chatting with a barista about deja vu, I mentioned that I was never hungry afterwards. I would not eat for a day or two. The idea of food was not entertaining, especially sugar. I had absolutely no desire for sugar. He blew my mind when he simply said "That's your body's way of communicating with you and clearing out what it doesn't want. Listen to your body." I dropped sugar as well. Like magic, this fog that I didn't even realize was there...lifted!

After a year and a half of taking this painful medication, I attended a drug-company sponsored dinner and everything I dreaded was before me, like a buffet. Wheelchairs, oxygen tanks, unhappiness, hopelessness. I immediately left them, forever. This was not my future! They could keep their poison!

Previous beliefs no longer served me; they suffocated me. The blinders no longer covered my eyes. I saw my truths. I learned how to uninstall those beliefs and install new ones. My lessons and beliefs were like being in a checkout line at the grocery store. They were on a conveyor belt for me to decide what I wanted to pick up and keep or let cruise on past into the void. I could also discard the past 'spoiled lemon' lessons to be carried away, forever. Health came, family, happiness, employees, love, kindness, initiatives, money. It all came without force, just acceptance.

Through our candle company, I became very close friends with an extremely famous woman in Hollywood. We spoke every day. She was a highly influential public speaker, an author who appeared on Oprah and Saturday Night Live, the list goes on. I had a tremendous amount of respect for her and she for me. We had many profound and uplifting conversations. One day I was brave enough to tell her about this burning desire in my heart: I wanted to be a public speaker, to help others grow and evolve. I wanted to share, heal, teach and connect. I wanted to help clean up the earth, and to inspire others to do the same. I was excited for her encouragement, direction and support.

Instead, she protectively and lovingly informed me, "Oh honey, you can't do that! It's tough, and you can't get into this industry unless you're already in it or linked to it. You're good at candles. Stick to what you're good at. You can't be a public speaker." Like any good young lady, I accepted the limitation. I put my faith in her words. I buried my Inner Guidance for a while; but while doing some inner excavating, it resurfaced. No matter what was said, I had to follow my feelings. I had to trust Georgia.

Continuing my growth, one day while visiting an Ashram I found an uphill path. These 2,000-pound stones led me to my future. On top of this hill I sat down and went into meditation...this one was deep! I had studied forgiveness and this was the moment to activate that knowledge. I watched, as past memories drifted before me. I was grateful for the lessons attached and I forgave the people, including myself, who were now floating by. Release! I finally agreed to let go, forgive and be free; free from all boundaries. An hour later, drenched in tears, I was a different woman! I was Georgia Vanderville.

Unsure what the future now held, I had to help others experience this new freedom. I had to teach, love and share. I wasn't a teacher or a speaker. I was a candle maker. How could I share? This new energy went into our team, products and customers — and we flourished. We soared above the clouds. Still, I felt there was something more.

It all came to fruition: The most divergent confirmation and opportunity. At a conference, I bared my soul, my experiences and growth. No more hiding. The gift of sharing my story on stage in front of 860 people was presented to me and I said, "No problem." I nailed it! As I proudly walked off that stage, it hit me: I can be ANYTHING I choose to be! I learned to trust myself, no matter what. I stepped into my own power.

You have a voice inside of you. I call it your Inner Echo. Find it. Nurture it. Let's find your past, current and future Echo and make it strong and prominent!

Now, this is who I came into the world to be!

IGNITE ACTION STEPS

Most of us love lists. They help me organize thoughts. Try this – it will be powerful. Start by writing down strong thoughts and feelings about life around you. Once you pay attention, you'll notice ideas in your head that really aren't true. Ideas like, "I have to work incredibly hard and personify perfection to be acceptable and worthwhile." Look at the unkind words people said to you when you were younger. Make your list of beliefs and unkind statements. Also, write down a few you DO want to hang on to, yet know you shouldn't. Beliefs like "You can't do it. You're no good at that. That won't be successful."

Keep a list of the good things you've done… to balance out the negative. Keep it positive.

The key? Be selfish! It might be hard for others to accept, because it means adjusting themselves. They will understand and benefit from it later. Take time for yourself, whether that's an extra ten minutes in the car once you drop the kids at school or setting your alarm for 25 minutes before anyone else wakes. Create your 'me' time. Respect yourself!

Meditation has taken me to amazing places. You can simply use your imagination. Close your eyes and relax. Feel your breathing and connection with yourself. Imagine there is a space rocket sitting next to you. Consider your written beliefs and new ones that pop into your head as you relax. Start small, work on just a few beliefs at a time. Pay attention and you will feel them in your body. Once you've identified the feeling and its location, take your hands to the spot (eyes closed) and pull that feeling out of you. Place that energy, feeling and belief into the rocket. Now close the lid and hit launch! Hear the engine roar and feel the energy as it leaves. Observe it shrinking smaller and smaller. When it's almost 100 percent gone, watch the brief spherical burst of energy as it explodes; those beliefs now gone forever!

Forgive yourself and others, for events small to large. Feel others forgive you. Simply place the hurt onto your conveyor belt or into your rocket ship and let go.

Like everyone, I had opinions and ideas that I carried with me for many years. Sometimes these beliefs keep us safe. Often, it's that we feel connected and identify ourselves through them. Identifying an idea that no longer serves you can be painful, yet freeing. It hurts when you feel the belief is still serving you or that you could have changed it but haven't. It's been with you for so long. It's hard to let go and release.

Now is the time. Flip your viewpoint. Realize you can look at each belief differently and say goodbye to what does not truthfully serve you. Break down your own barriers. Throw off that safety net of self-doubt and replace it with self-worth, direction and trust in yourself!

To step forward towards change, you may have to step backwards first. But once you do, the sky's the limit.

Georgia Vanderville, Leader & Public Speaker. Shortie's Candle Company.
www.shortiescandles.com

VIRGINIA L LEHAY

"What we talk about heals; in the telling/retelling of our stories, we make compassionate discoveries that lead home to self."

My wish for you, in writing my story – is to encourage you to put your story into words, using: poems/prose; diaries/journals; memoirs; letters… to see your history laid out in Genogram… that you too, in the unraveling of hidden truths, feel the healing – in ending silences, breaking cycles, transforming energy and creating a new story going forward.

MY COMPASSIONATE DISCOVERIES

We shared a New Year's drink, to celebrate the arrival of 2005. My mother and me. Maybe it was the spirit of the evening or the spirits in our shot glasses - that led to her talking openly. (*I'll never know. Four months later, she was gone.*) For me, the truth she admitted that night was welcomed. It ended 46 years of waiting…

This is my Hansel and Gretel story. To mark my way out of the deep, dark woods, I too dropped breadcrumbs that got eaten up by the birds. In my case, the breadcrumbs were pivotal memories and the birds had two names, 'Silence' and 'Repression'.

I know exactly when I was carried off into the *deep, dark woods*:

The morning I met the fascinating, red-headed bundle of life that was my baby sister, *was when it happened*. I ran to my parents' bed, snuggled between them, drinking in every part of her precious newness. Mom got up to care for motherly rituals. It was still early on a cool April morning, so I snuggled down under the covers.

When my mother returned, these words were scorched into my memory: "Virginia, get out of that bed!" I felt instantly 'bad' – like it was my fault. Was she mad at me? It would be 50-plus years before I'd understand the significance of her use of my given name, 'Virginia', rather than the nickname affectionately assigned to me early on, 'Gini-Lou". It was an accusatory message directed at my father, not me.

In that same month, during my grade three class recess, on a day I was wearing a pink dress made for me by my adoring aunt, the principal (Mr. McC) requested I bring my math scribbler to the teacher's desk. As he was pointing out my math mistakes with his left hand, his right-hand slid under my dress... I froze. My homeroom teacher, Mr. S returned, surprised to see Mr. McC, acknowledged him and abruptly exited. How could he just leave? Doesn't he see what is happening? He looked right at Mr. McC. Isn't he going to stop it? Isn't he going to say something? Anything... That year, I lost trust in authority figures. I was unsafe and unprotected at home, and at school. To have my mother and Mr. S. leave so much unspoken, messed with my mind and left me spinning.

Over that summer, whenever Mom was patching our clothes, I stood by the sewing machine, waiting... waiting for the breaking of the silence that followed the 'Virginia-command'. It never came. Gardens were planted, berries picked and canned. Haying time began.

I fall off the back of the hayrack. My father was furious that I'd climbed up despite his warning. My brothers, newbies at driving a tractor, let out the clutch of the old John Deere with such a jerk it loosened my grip. I fell flat on my back from 12 feet up. Angry, my father instructed me to walk to his Chevy pickup and wait for him there.

My hobbled-crawling gait signalled how injured I was. Dad fetched the truck to pick me up, called my faster-running brother (*the replacement for a phone*) and drove us home. The pain was so intense, I was soon vomiting. It wasn't long before my mother sent my brother running to fetch Dad from the field to take me to the doctor. No visible injuries. We were sent home with instructions to return if I vomited again.

My parents didn't wait that long. They were friends with a chiropractor neighbour; we stopped at his acreage-office on the way home. Every adjustment he made on my body, brought relief that was as immense as the pain had been intense. I recall the words of his assessment. "All her internal organs are jarred out of place." He was talking about my physical insides, but for me, those words were *acknowledgment* of the agonizing, emotional turmoil that I felt within me.

I didn't know where I stood: With Mom? With God? *Was "Virginia" bad?* There was so much I couldn't comprehend. My mother *not talking*, didn't make sense. She talked about *everything*. She was a *lay-psychologist*, when it came to marriage problems, child-raising and issues in general. It seemed, after every family visit, she went into an endless litany of observations, conclusions and/or judgments. Yet, she left me questioning endlessly day after day. The torment deepened into an anguish too heavy to bear, for the little girl that I was... I couldn't handle it alone or wait any longer; I took things into my own hands.

On my 10th birthday, instead of making a wish while blowing out my candles, I said a prayer. "Show me your will and teach me how to do it." Although that prayer sounds like it's about the lofty idea of serving God, its underlying theme was personal need. It's what a 10-yr-old knew, had been taught to say. The feelings behind the words were my true prayer. Somehow, the silence had to end...

Since nobody was speaking up for me or talking to me, I talked to God. It helped that God lived next-door. The church property bordered the east edge of our farm. Churches weren't locked back then. I would go sit with God anytime.

That winter, I snuck the five-inch-thick medical textbook down off the top of the wardrobe and read all about male/female organs and functions, studying the pictures intently. When summer returned, I spread a blanket on the lawn, pulled it over my head, hiding the *True Story* magazines I *borrowed* from my mother's collection. From stories submitted by real people about teen crushes and love affairs, I learned about the bodily sensations that accompanied sexual touch, information the textbook didn't mention. Now, I had some answers! They weren't enough, but they gave some explanation. From this reading, I learned to trust my own research - my own learning. This competency gave me enough to make it into my teen years and eventually to stand up to my Dad.

My father wouldn't let me date. *Spring of '67 we'd had a row.* Indignant about his rules, I pushed a limit he'd set, without crossing it. He had a different view. He accosted me in the hallway when I was on my way to bed. Accused me of disobeying him. I protested. He slapped my face. That slap sunk righteous indignation to the core of me. How dare he? Where was his accountability? More questions roiled within me.

I considered quitting school, and leaving home, but I loved my academic studies. Yet, I *needed* more independence. Once again, I took the situation in my own hands, applied for bursaries and was accepted at the Banff School of Fine Arts.

That summer, ecstatic to get away from home, I experienced the freedom of living in a dorm with a dozen girls my age. I loved the Creative Writing courses. What I loved as much, was taking luxurious, hot baths, shaving my legs for the first time and *dating*.

I came home strengthened by my summer's freedoms and independence. I decided to push the issue. The opportunity presented itself in late September, on a drive to a Legion Ladies Auxiliary catering event; again I asked for permission to date. He finally confessed his fatherly fears, saying boys only wanted one thing, which brought in a new element, *an actual father-daughter interchange*. What a paradox! He was worried about me dating teenage boys, for 'that' reason, when he was the one visiting my room at night...

My father's heart condition flared up that evening and he was taken to the hospital. A month later, he was dead. Even though the sexual abuse was finally over, I felt another heavy weight settle over me. Did my forcing that conversation bring on his death? I was torn between relief and guilt. Grieving was nowhere in sight. The internal conflict was back with a vengeance. I buried myself in schoolwork and applied to attend Creative Writing courses again the next summer.

One more year of school to go, my conflicts with my mother went underground. Silence on key issues was still her method of control. She did allow me to date, but I felt great pressure from her to not do anything that would make her lose face as the Lutheran church organist. In her talking about everything but what needed to be talked about, there was still no real talking. NO resolution. I couldn't wait to graduate.

I left home with so much unresolved, I was an energetic ball of incompletes. I attracted my first husband. He was a great listener. The floodgates opened. I told him everything, almost... We married, had three children, separated and divorced. I married again, gained a step-son, and had two more children. Still full of unexplainable angst and black holes of pain, I had plenty to pin it on. Relationship hurts and everyday life issues, serve excellently for repression. My parents modeled it. I'd learned it. Now I was doing it.

Even in the worst of my dysfunction and repression times, I was never silent like my mother. I was approachable; available to talk about the hard things, hidden things, always lobbying for openness. I stood tall for family communication. I hadn't learned it in my family of origin, so once again, it was up to me. More conversations with God. Mountains of books for bibliotherapy. Page after page of journaling about *everything*... Not knowing what I was trying to unravel, I was looking anywhere and everywhere, but never finding the peace of mind I was seeking.

My awakening came when my daughter was sexually abused by a cousin, during a summer visit to my mother's house. When she came home, her behavior was different and I recognized the 'acting-out' was pain speaking. When I was alone, I screamed and cried, "Why her?" in another conversation with God... and then got to work. I made the space and created the safety for her to open up about what had happened. Got her into counselling; then my older boys and lastly myself. Finally, I woke up to the need to address my own past. The more I unraveled, the more my heart and mind pieced the bits and pieces together and filled in the blanks, the more I understood.

Looking back, talking to God when I was ten, was the way I found to break the silence and end the waiting. After that, I found other creative ways. One avenue that opened to me, came when I was given a five-year diary. I loved how creative writing let me incorporate my life events and write my voice into characters in stories. I wrote one such poem in my grade twelve year and the teacher requested to use it for interpretation in our English class. Which was amusing to me, as even I was guessing at its meaning. (I wrote a poem about that poem when I was 35, when I did understand what it meant.) In welcoming new kids into our school, being a supportive listener, I made the space for them to voice their pain. A more direct means of breaking *silence*. I also composed lyrics, set them to music and performed them. My mother never argued with the words I put in a song, so in that way, she heard me; I knew I was sending her covert messages. For three years, I wrote our local news column for the county newspaper. In other words, I became very accomplished at busyness in service of coping and repression.

In my adulthood, I journaled: several notebooks per year. When I was upset, I wrote letters. Doing the writing brought resolution, so most were never sent. However, none of these activities, explored the reality and/ or healed the impact of what I went through when I was nine. Decades of repression had blocked event-recall, leaving me with a morass of feelings no longer connected to memories. The energy of unresolved childhood traumas, perpetuated cycles in my family, affecting and hurting my children. Facing this reality, made me press ahead. I had to 'heal my past' to break the cycle.

I repressed so completely, that I needed help, but I had little trust for authorities of any sort. However, still trusting my own learning, I read a LOT of books. Though I found nuggets of truth and wisdom in my volumes of reading, two books were pivotal: Robert Wegner's 'White Bears and Other Unwanted Thoughts; Suppression, Obsession, and the Psychology of Mental Control' and 'Genogram In Family Assessment', by Monica McGoldrick and Randy Gerson. I didn't just read White Bears and Genogram. I studied them. I taught myself to map out genograms for myself, and eventually for others. I designed repression diagrams, to make sense of what I had done to cope, and to retrace my steps. Essentially, I became the first volunteer of my own research project. I was able to use my own Genogram, along with using Wegner's studies to design tools for myself to reconstruct lost memories and come to resolution. Applying genogram to my life, and later, my coaching practice, I taught myself and others, "We stop passing patterns down the generations, when we process up the generations."

In 1990, I saw a Psych Nurse in private counselling practice. I was so ready for the experience. We started by going over my mailed-in pre-session assignments and then talked. Near the end, she asked me, "Do you know how long we've been talking?" I thought a couple of hours, maybe. I was shocked to hear her say, "Seven hours". Every moment had been productive, testament to how much of my own work I had already done, how ready I was to pull it all together, to deal with everything. She closed with two exercises, that revealed what was next. First, I was to visualize a gift-wrapped box, followed by two questions: "to whom are you presenting the gift? what is the gift?" Instantly, I saw myself giving the box to my daughters. However, upon opening the box, I saw it was empty. The legacy I wanted to gift them – was not yet accomplished. In writing this chapter, new insights came up into my heart, answers to questions my daughters are asking. It's a story I'll write for them. My mother finally ending the silence New Years' Eve 2005, is part of that narrative.

Next, she directed me to take any book down from her shelf, open it and read the first passage my gaze fell upon. The words stimulated both fear and longing: it spoke of following one's calling and mentioned counselling. My heart plummeted; how would I get from farm-wife to counsellor? My heart sang: it was the desire of my heart, to help others as I had helped myself.

Within a year, I was on my path to becoming a Life Skills Coach and OEC (Operant Effectual Counselling) practitioner, the beginning of a career path that is still my passion. My private practice, Discoveries for Compassionate Living, came into being.

My hope is that you can find your own path to bring healing to the silent areas of your past – rewrite your 'herstory' – and pass on new legacies...

IGNITE ACTION STEPS

Silence and repression can make original events inaccessible by just recall. It is possible to sleuth them out, bringing closure and transformation.

Five Reasons to Own a Journal and Write in it...

• **Closure:** Research demonstrates the use of words/language when we write or speak, engages more brain functions, providing a more complete closure than other activities, such as dance, music, art, drama, etc., which can also have a cathartic effect.

• **Ends or Stops Repression, before it Starts:** Journaling brings thoughts and feelings into our conscious, where they can be processed, transforming the energy. Cleaning our 'mental house' has great benefits.

• **Brain Limitations:** Our brain can hold up to 8/9 details easily. Writing those down frees us to connect with the deeper thoughts and feelings that need to be examined.

• **Release:** When we accurately name our feelings, we release them.

• **Health:** When we name and release feelings, our bodies are freed from having to express for us – through minor or major maladies.

A Journaling Process: If you want to make sense of feelings and/or any event: **1:** While writing, do not censor or edit, Do not worry about sentence structure, grammar, punctuation or neatness, sequencing or even making sense. **2:** Let go, and touch the deepest parts of yourself. Feelings are stored in the body. **3:** Write about what happened, how you felt it then. How you feel about it now. **4:** Notice what quietly seeps into your mind, as you are writing. **5:** Trust the process, and shift to writing about that.

Genogram: Mapping out Your Family History: If you are drawn to Genogram, there is a reason. Trust your inner urgings and find the way. Engage the services of a Genogram therapist or coach. They can diagram your Genogram with you, help you see the macro and micro patterns/cycles.

Put it up on your wall for your children to see their ancestral picture at a glance. Do the opposite of 'silence' – talk about it freely. Give your children the legacy of knowing their history, so they have the information to understand 'your roots', which are also 'their roots'. Awareness prevents getting caught up in repetitive hidden-cycles and patterns. With your open sharing, your children can choose the legacies they embrace and pass on to their own children – Give them the gift of freedom.

Virginia L Lehay. www.compassionate-discoveries.ca.
www.facebook.com/genogramcoach

DEEPANJALI SAPKOTA

"I love you unconditionally - free of any conditions."

My intention for you is to experience unconditional love, not only towards yourself, but to your children and others in any tense situations. Out of a genuine desire to help myself and others suffer less, I invite you to try the unconditional-love magic-potion. It makes for a peaceful, joyful and happy life. The unconditional-love magic-potion works even if the love of your life stops loving you.

LIFE THROUGH THE LENS OF UNCONDITIONAL LOVE

Our son was less than two years old, when my husband said, "We need to talk. This is not working. I'm not in love with you anymore."

I only asked two questions, "Are you sure? Is this what you want?"

We were in a park with our son. I remained calm. I didn't cry or shout. I simply sat there in shock.

We had been married for six years when we got pregnant. I was happy with our marriage and growing our family. At times, I knew something was off, but I couldn't pinpoint anything. I thought it might be his work. If I asked him about it, he would say, "It has nothing to do with you."

We both loved our child but staying in the marriage just because we were married or had a son made no sense to me. So I told my husband to go, figure himself out, and be happy.

Later, I understood he was trying to figure it out for himself before he said anything to me. He told me our apartment was small. Since he had often said he needed space, I saw nothing wrong with him getting an apartment for himself. I didn't think we needed to live in the same house. I had trust. In the preceding month, I helped make it ready and even cleaned his place.

The hardest part!? He came. He took his clothes. He left. It was like an emotional vacuum.

I didn't realize till then. When the door closed, it was the end of everything we had. That was it. End of chapter. SO incredibly painful!

This was not discussed. He informed me, but I had no say. I felt betrayed. Let down. All sorts of emotions. Hurt. Angry. Abandoned. But I didn't have time to feel.

We had our child. I had to pick up and keep moving. I also saw it was difficult for him as well. He felt guilty. We always said we would be honest, so I could not be angry with him for telling the truth. Because I loved him so much, I wanted to make sure he was okay. Because I focused on him, I forgot I needed to give the same to myself.

Given I had said throughout our relationship that I loved him unconditionally, this was now a test for me. Did I? Could I? What did that look like now?

First question: What did 'unconditional love' mean to me in separation? It's easy when you're in love, when everything is going fine. Unconditional love means no conditions. So the answer was obvious: I needed to love him unconditionally in this situation as well.

Other thoughts interfered: Now he's told me he doesn't love me anymore. Do I cry about it? That's when I really began to understand the deeper and fuller meaning of unconditional love.

We often used to wonder how people go from being in love to having such difficulty going through separation or divorce in a civilized, peaceful, calm way. How can adults forget to put their kids first? Now I was finding out how hard it was, and how easy it was to give in to the emotional compulsions. So tempting to say "F-off! Why did you do this to me?"

I continuously expected myself to put unconditional love into practice. Every time I felt angry or caught myself bashing my ex-husband, I would remind myself, "If I love him unconditionally, how do I behave? What do I say? How do I interact?"

I also understood he was suffering. That made two humans suffering and deserving of compassion. In the process of experimenting with unconditional love, I learned to take responsibilities for my actions and inactions as well, admitting I did cause him pain knowingly or unknowingly. Yes, I was angry; however, practicing an unconditional love mantra showed me that his taking the step to say, "This is not working," was an act of love. I told myself that, if I love him, I must learn to let him go.

At that time, I felt if our child grew up in the context of parents under the same roof, it might be more difficult. When he was a baby, he did not have the capacity to judge his parents for good or bad love. He did have the capacity to feel love. The only important thing was for us both to love him, regardless of where we lived or what direction our individual lives might take us.

My son was less than two years old when we separated. Now 14 years old, he is calm, happy, balanced — and has an amazing sense of humor. Staying together for the sake of our child would have been 'pretend-love'. He would have been exposed to our fights and discontent, thereby modelling for him a relationship that was NOT a union of two hearts. It simply means not bringing our marriage/separation/divorce story, our discontent, our fights where it did not belong — onto our child's heart. When I struggled, I turned to teachings of others to guide me.

I remembered my grandmother's wisdom and tied her common sense in with my interpretations of Kahlil Gibran. My grandmother taught me that the only job you are born to do is to know who you are. She taught me to contemplate meaning, whether in a textbook or the Bible or the Koran. Spend time pondering what words of wisdom mean to you. Kahlil Gibran helped me form the basis of my unconditional love beliefs. I borrowed concepts from his stories and made the beliefs mine. I wanted to BE unconditional love.

I had to come up with my own recipe for unconditional love and learn what worked for me. It may work for you, or you may need to focus on another concept such as peace. If, like me, you are going through a separation, hold the concept of peace in your heart and mind. Implement unconditional love or focus on separating peacefully, whichever works for you. Unconditional love carried me through my own tough spots.

When we find we lack any principles, it is up to us to learn and put into practice new ways of living in balance, starting at home and then outwards. If living and being guided by unconditional love is what you want from the deepest part of yourself, it is possible. Guided by my son's pain, I found it became possible for me, once I moved past my own self-pity.

It wasn't easy during those first stages of separation. I often felt sorry for myself over losing this person I loved the most. I realized that every time his father left, our son would cry. Then, I felt so bad that I would hold him and cry too, telling him "oh baby your father left us..." etc.

Ding! My inner being slapped my head, "What the hell are you going on about? One moment you want to practice unconditional love, and the very next second you give in to victimhood. Is this how you want your child to grow up?" I did not want him to learn how to feel sorry for himself because I behaved like he was losing out. I had to make it a natural thing for his father to leave for work and going to his own place instead of being home with us.

That was a hell of a wake-up call. Immediately, I changed that whole dynamic from me, the poor-victim, to "I want my child to be happy." I made the whole experience of every day parting more fun, turning it into a game of hide and seek. It no longer took a toll on me or my child.

A few things that helped deal with the separation were how we agreed to put our child first. A reminder of this commitment eased our ways when phases of anger would erupt. This was probably easier because we were on the same page. Communicating clearly what we both wanted, trusting we both knew we were good people who wanted each other to be happy. That was the basis of our transition from a marriage relationship to a separated and divorced relationship.

I know it can be difficult to put into practice this thing called 'unconditional love,' but it only takes one of the two struggling people in a relationship to start. Once started, both can take a role in helping each other find their way back to their center.

I had started my self-awareness work in my career before this all happened. Prior to my current job, I jumped ship every time there was a conflict until I realized I was the common denominator in every failed dynamic. I learned I had to change myself. Now, I have stayed in the same job for over 11 years because I managed to work on myself. If not for my own on-the-job experience, I wouldn't have had the tools to deal with my separation. I would have been a very emotional, anger-driven person.

Being this way took a lot of educating and practicing. I needed to practice what I preached in my mind, by putting it into reality with myself first. Translating my vision of how I wanted my separation and relationship with my ex-husband to my parents, family and those around me was another angle of using unconditional love. I was the first to get divorced in my immediate circle/family/culture. Divorce was not at all common in Nepal. Now it is more accepted; and sadly, bitterness and strife are a common state in divorce situations.

People were surprised. They asked me, "How can you talk beautifully about your ex-husband?" I would find myself telling them naturally answering their confused stares with "I love this man unconditionally. That means I love his soul, not what he did or didn't do. The soul is beautiful. It is true that I can never speak poorly about him. Things didn't work between us, but he's the father of our child. He's the best father. I would never ask for any other father." As I encountered this line of questioning over and over, I would also say, "It's the Being in him. The real person inside all of us deserves unconditional love."

I had to learn and relearn my path. It was all about doing what's right for me, even when it did not make sense to others.

When my son was small, he often asked questions about why we separated, if it was his fault. Was it because he was born? Children naturally feel at fault. I had to reassure him that it was not, and that we would both always be there for him. Children don't fully understand, but they feel. As long as the child feels the love, whether we are together or not. We keep doing this naturally. Our values are aligned.

Today we call it positive psychology, though it was natural for me to educate my son that having divorced parents had its perks. He had two homes, two vacations. He gets the best of us both. Most precious is the 100 percent presence with both the parents. We always loved each other; now, it is just in different ways.

Whatever I said to my son, I followed up with actions. I think this is key in building this level of relationship. Words without action have no value. I continue to see his paternal family, and we share beautiful moments. What we have created today is how I envisaged my future after separation — sharing moments of our son's life, a meal, birthday celebrations, a good laugh.

I learned so much during this whole process. Believe me, it took years to master this skill of mindful-living, and I must say that every second was priceless. I gained personal experience of how to truly love unconditionally. I learned about my many qualities which I had no clue existed. I understood myself better, my communication skills became more impactful, relationships and finances improved. I was at peace.

My desire to continue to learn and educate myself on the human capacity to love; to cultivate deeper levels of human values such as kindness and compassion, led me to discover my passion in life.

Remember how I left every scenario or conflict until I learned I was the common denominator? I brought the same principles first to the workplace. It was here I experimented, extending mindfulness in every corner of my life. I practiced it both at work and at home. The workplace gave me a playground full of people with their own wounds and lifetimes of confusion to really hone my loving, no matter what and make it a movement in my current career.

In 2012, our organization had a huge restructure; the whole process was fraught with difficulties. People suffered. With a colleague, I started a group to help us all deal with the situation by practicing mindfulness. It greatly helped people to navigate the crazy and lengthy restructuring process.

I am convinced that in humanitarian organizations such as ours, people are passionate about the causes they stand for – and it is also vital that we take care of each other. So, I kept going.

Luckily, the human resources department gave me a full green light to do some grassroot works. The group-work continued, and after one short year a mindfulness program was embedded as part of the organization's wellness program: 150 staff went through it. People have been benefiting from it in the 11 years I've been here.

Find and simmer your own magic potion of mindfulness, unconditional love, peaceful interactions and joyful living – all the things that make your days flow with ease. You know what they are for you. Unconditional love was my key to a new path in life.

IGNITE ACTION STEPS

When I first started learning about unconditional love, I began by loving myself. I honored, valued and empowered myself first, giving me the ability to recognize others and offer them the same gift in return.

Unconditional love is about doing things and acting with love without expecting the same in return. For example, when I go I to another person's house, I always take things like flowers or treats. I do so without any expectation or wanting something in return.

During tense interactions, involving my ex-husband or a colleague, I would do my best to have compassion and listen first. I always keep in my mind that the other person is also going through difficulties. If they didn't say the right word or do the right things, they too might be struggling. Seeing someone this way and looking at what is happening for them helps me maintain my calmness. I refrain from judging them in that moment, just because they didn't do or say the right thing according to what I perceive as right.

If someone is challenging you, first be silent. Take a deep breath. Understand your own emotions first and what is going on in you. I manage my own emotions before any kind of reaction. I let go of all the reasons I feel they should be a certain way. I choose my actions. I have stopped being reactive, and that empowers me. When we can maintain a respectful and understanding state, we retain our power and hold our dignity. This makes it possible for the other person to retain their dignity, as well.

Unconditional love has made me a better person. It has made me a kind and more understanding person, and I am proud of that today. I love and understand myself better. By being this person, I see the impact I want to create around me. When I offer that kind of love, much more love and appreciation grows, and I can be the person I truly want to be.

Practicing unconditional love has changed my life. I know it can change yours.

P.S. Stop talking sometimes and just offer a hug. We all need hugs. They manifest more unconditional love – immediately. A hug is a gift to the soul.

Deepanjali Sapkota, Officer

SUSANNE RODRIGUEZ

"Everything you choose, you choose consciously. Decide and create to live a life in peace. Align your vibration to your wants."

If you are an over-giver like I was, my hope is you will find the way in to honour yourself, put yourself first so you can truly be there for others, nourish self-care; and most importantly, give from a place of peace. What you give, you always get back. When you honor yourself, you honor everyone.

CHOOSE YOUR PEACE, BE YOUR CHOICE!

Mermaids, a symbol of feminine power, are often depicted as rescuing those at risk of drowning, though it meant breaking the rules themselves. They also symbolize women's hearts and passion, ignoring the analytical mind and what was proper. Growing up, I never knew how to access my own power or modulate the giving energy of my own treasured heart. Connecting with the earth's waters, and the mythical home to the mermaids, I found and honored my own limits. I saw where I could expand many limitations and help others; help more, help endlessly, but also help too much.

After years of unlimited giving, there came a hard stop in my life. It was after decades of loving and over-loving others and always abandoning myself. I remember being curled in a fetal position crying uncontrollably in my $5,000,000 dollar home. My life appeared complete with a private airplane for our travels. I was volunteering for 120 homeless children, then adopting and helping to raise five beautiful young teens of my own, while spending endless hours providing a comfortable life for my family by having everything catered to them 24/7 – through me.

The pressure had become too great. I, Mrs. Loving, was endlessly giving to others, yet feeling lonely and sad inside. I got up from my curled ball in my luxurious surroundings and walked straight outside to my car. I felt I had to move away from this spot in my life – be somewhere else, anywhere else. As soon as I closed the car door, I started praying and asking God to please take my last breath – just finish it. Just end the agony I felt. I actually held my breath and truly believed with the power of my mind, my breath would just stop, and the pain would be finished. I could end this suffering by asking. God would mercifully open his gates.

Instead, I felt a beautiful warm feeling I can only describe as utter love and idyllic peace all over and throughout my body. Like the comforting feeling of the ocean and the tranquility of a mermaid floating, I was claimed. I felt God speak gently but firmly, like a father does. "Sweet child, you are not finished here on this planet. Remember why you came here! Remember who you are."

As soon as I heard His word and felt His love around my heart, I knew I was unwilling to give up. I shifted my emotions instantly and walked back to the house. I knew I had to move out of that situation but didn't know exactly how, at that point. Instead, I focused on aligning with my feelings and moving forward to create a new state of being for myself. I welcomed His new direction and embraced what I needed to do. God had not spoken lightly, and I was determined to listen.

My first major encounter with God happened in my early 20s. I was in a motor vehicle accident while vacationing in Greece. The driver, knowing the curve ahead was impossible to maneuver, jumped out of the vehicle, saving himself. The car, with me and my three friends inside, flipped and rolled off a mountain. We went careening 250 feet over the rocky hillside cliffs to the canyon below.

On my way down, I was holding on to my seat and the roof at the same time, hoping to save myself. I felt God looked at me, through my right window, to take me to the other side. Everything stopped in the chaos, and despite the falling and the panic, I chose to have a bit of an argument with God in that moment. I was not willing to leave this planet just then. My biggest dream was to be a mother and to have my first baby be a boy. I felt I had a life to live and things to do. I wasn't ready to go with Him.

I remember being in God's caring arms one moment and then the next thing I remember was finding myself unharmed, with some minor bruises, not one broken bone and very few cuts from all the smashed windows that landed all over my body. I crawled out of the car from the front seat floor, through a tiny opening in my window, since the roof was crushed all the way down on my seat. The vehicle had tumbled down and crash-landed in the middle of nowhere, in the darkness of night, off a mountain, in a foreign country.

My friends had been thrown out of the car and splattered all over the rocks. They were dead and dying around me. Amidst their screams and anguish, I went to find help. I walked myself back to the top of the mountain on the darkest, most horrifying night of my life.

It took me years to comprehend what had happened and the second chance I was given. It definitely shaped me into a more conscious, grateful, and God-loving woman. I remember to always say to myself when things get rough, "You, my girl have no reason to complain. This is your God-given second chance. Go shake it off and be grateful to still be here, living this life and dreaming of being a mother."

Having met God in this way, I enjoyed teaching His word. I raised my two beautiful boys and assisted many families in raising many other children. There was so much joy in my own heart, despite what happened. I felt connected to my soul and purpose; but somewhere along the line, I got lost.

Where and when did I lose my alignment? How did I forget to feed my soul all these years? How come no one seemed to care about my well-being or watch my back? I had to admit, trying to keep it all together for everyone by acting like God or Mother Teresa was a colossal mistake on my part.

How did I get from crawling out of that car wreck to this moment, 20 years later, sobbing in my Lexus parked in front of my mansion? How did I go from arguing with God to let me live – to asking God to now finally finish me off? I shook myself from these thoughts and decided to walk to the beach behind the house. Instinctively I sat down near this massive pine tree, a gift from Mother Earth. It was the biggest tree on the beach, and it called to me to crawl into the root system, where I cried for hours. I never thought it was possible to cry so much. I cried for all the generations of women who been given so much to raise and hold their families together, no matter what they needed themselves. I cried for the woman I had become. Feeling connected to the warmth of the sand and the solid foundation of the tree roots, I continued to sob. I imagined my tears, flowing out to the ocean. Surrendering to the wisdom of mermaid. Letting go. Drop by drop I detoxified all that no longer served me.

I stayed there for as long as it took to let go of my beliefs that this life was no longer worth living. I recognized that nobody understood my heart and saw MY need to be loved, but that didn't mean I was willing to give up or pack it in. I wanted to be treated with unconditional love. I needed care and compassion. I consciously decided to look at myself – to give myself the love I needed. I decided I would guard, maintain, and nurture my own inner peace. I would discover how to create my own deep joy, conscious flow, and love for life. Regardless of where I was right now, I wanted to walk in my own light and then be a light tower for others.

Since this was my second chance, I firmly believed God did exist, and that I could talk and negotiate with Him. Call it your Higher Self, God, Angels, or the Universe. You can converse with It too! When we are conscious and in the moment our purpose will be revealed. Your willingness to ask and align to your highest vibration can happen. You have to be gentle and calm and surrender to being in the best hands possible, no matter what. God is LOVE, and that is the vibration in all important, life-altering conversations.

Coming back from the beach after this amazing cleansing and awakening, my skin was blazing with the worst sunburn ever. The pain I felt externally was nothing compared to the pain I felt in my reality. Everyone around me: My kids, husband, mother, in-laws, church, volunteer groups – none were willing or ready to let go of their easy ride – provided courtesy of Susanne. I had always put everyone in front of my own needs. I believed this might bring me the love I wanted to receive. Was this conscious? Was this planned? Did I know what I was doing?

My "breakdown" in the car and on the beach taught me I had been trying to control being loved and appreciated by doing everything for everyone. I thought if I unconditionally loved them, they would give the same in return; except, that wasn't happening.

I started to speak to each of them. I began by creating a family meeting with my two boys and the love of my life, my husband. I communicated the change of purpose and vibrations I planned to create from that point forward. I explained I wanted to stay being their loving mother, but I needed to first look after myself by creating peace in my heart and soul. I further explained that, if they saw me changed, it was because of my new journey which they could join, but never hold me back from. I would never again be disconnected from the most loving part of my heart. I was no longer willing to give the peace in my heart away. For the first time, I took care of myself and loved myself first.

When speaking to all my loved ones and colleagues in conscious meetings, I always combined a cup of tea or cacao with a long hug at the end. I then began to create a new road map for myself, putting my needs on the top of my daily routine. It felt like going on a road trip, a journey through my soul. The difference from any of my past trips or walks, is now, I take my backpack full of love for myself! Hallelujah! I felt so good and aligned to continue to walk in the light of my life purpose.

I started first with the conscious breath when I woke up in the mornings. I practiced gratitude to all my organs and grew the love I felt in my heart. Always setting my vibration to the highest level to be aligned with my amazing purpose was the most important part of my self-care. This was big! I had never done the day like that before. I expanded to waking up, then after the bathroom, wandered into my kitchen to create my morning drink with 1 tbsp of apple cider, a teaspoon of turmeric, a pinch of pepper and manuka honey in a warm cup of water!

Sitting in my favourite spot in the house, leaning against the softest cushions, I would listen to my breathing and relax. Enjoying my elixir and awakening all my senses I practiced creating an internal smile and manifesting joy throughout the day. I continually told myself today is a day of peace, love, and creating the most beautiful memories. I quickly felt my purpose of going deeper to assist others in the journey as a healer-coach, and to share vibrational light from our universal God.

Flow throughout the day was the gift I created that keeps on giving. A life of flow felt super happy, peaceful and aligned with my purpose! Every afternoon, I set aside time again to meditate, to tap into and stay in my vibration, walking in my light and living in my purpose. With time, through a deep breath anywhere I was or went, I could visit that place I created: The pond of peace, where I could tap into and balance the mermaid's powers, such as untamed personal sensuality, perception, and love.

Despite feeling such a range of disconnect and a loss from needing so much from others, I found my way. Now when I come into contact with my family, I always hug them and allow them to be in the moment, in the Now with me, just as I am. I no longer must do things to obtain their love. I just have to be love, and more love filters in.

Now I travel the world, healing and teaching people how to create the most abundant lives filled with love and harmony. In my journeys, I have learned powerful tools from amazing doctors, healers, and cutting-edge coaches. They have shown me that we all can stop ourselves from falling, from feeling lost. That by connecting with nature, listening to ourselves, and speaking up for our purpose, we will radiate love. In all that I do, I aim to find the PEACE and the joy, so I can offer that to others. I do it not to get love in return, but to grow it bigger. Bigger in me means helping others be bigger in themselves, which ultimately benefits everyone.

Like the mermaid who swims through the cool wave and floats in the calm sea, I honor the flow that we each need to find. The moving waves lift offers. There are high tides followed by low tides, that then rise again. We all can learn from the mermaid; her zest for life, mischievousness, and even doing what looks wrong to others but feels so right within. The next time you find yourself giving more of yourself to others, or sacrificing your own needs, seek to love yourself without any boundaries. See that love can radiate in – long before it has to radiate out. That is the peace I wish for you!

Ignite Action Steps

I have learned and practiced much of how to live consciously in the past three years by traveling with a shaman and coaches from Costa Rica and Australia. I currently teach in Bali, Europe, Costa Rica, and in the USA at our retreats. Most of what I have learned is now an essential part of my life.

Any one of the 21 pillars of consciousness living can become part of your daily practice: Conscious breathing, eating, hydrating, exercising, sleeping, meditating, intentions, relationships, grounding, sun-gazing, being present, observing of yourself, setting intentions, gratitude, holistic-detoxing, being in nature, healing the relationship with yourself, awakening your inner child, volunteering, surrendering, sound healing, natural medicine and being present in the NOW works wonders to expand the consciousness of you.

Please, after you read this, close your eyes:

See the most beautiful place you have ever witnessed in the jungle or forest. See yourself walking toward a pond in all the lush green that surrounds you. Listen to a waterfall running gently into the pond. See the birds watching you walk toward your peaceful pond. As soon as you enter, you are surrounded by this blessed one-of-a-kind precious water, and you realize you can swim like a mermaid. You swim, dive, and splash like a wild, free, beautiful mermaid. Now stop. Find a place to relax, float, and look around – feel all of this peace inside yourself – deep in your heart and soul. Your self-created peace is in the 'Now'.

Feel that peace, smell the surroundings, feel absolute abundance and joy all over, and throughout your body. That is the peace and vibration you can hold on to and take into your day. Feel this peace you created.

Now see your partner, child, or someone you love come closer to your pond. Invite them with a heart full of love – share how you feel at peace. With loving boundaries in place, invite them into your pond, see them respect your space, respect your peace.

Guide them to gently walk toward you – always consciously choose the words you speak. Always honor your pond with kind words; gentle, fun, playful movements, bringing only these positive images and interactions to your safe waters.

This is your pond, your meditation – you, setting your intentions for the day. Your interactions are up to you when you leave your meditation space! This peace is yours in any storms or hurricanes that life might swirl around you. Take a deep breath and go back to the vibration you created, and feel that peace in your pond! Breathe deeply and slowly, knowing you have created your place of inner peace.

Be in the *Now* in your body; see all things around you from an eagle's view. If things become tense, walk away. Explain you are choosing to honor kind energy. Strive only to create a conscious, loving, joyful, peaceful life for everyone around you.

Now you are awoken! You are renewed and powerful! You are the divine light! You are tapped into the Mermaid's infinite energy! Welcome to living in your purpose now, driven by a desire to respect and love your peace.

Hold on to peace for all your days.

Susanne Rodriguez, Certified in Medical Massage & Physical Therapy, Shamanic Yoga RYT 300, and facilitation of Conscious Retreats. Abundancenow.love

TARANUM KHAN

"Follow your heart always but with your mind in it!
Passion plus strategy equals success!"

I have lived many of my dreams. Don't be fooled, it has come with a fair share of blood, sweat and tears by evolving repeatedly. I wish to inspire and infuse hope. Life is a journey. Take action to pursue your dreams. Failure fuels my fever to get creative and I believe accomplishment is sweet. Either way the outcome is positive. Are you living your dream?

IN MAKING NEW ROOTS

A few untold glimpses of my 'Immigrant' life reveals a story of hope, invisible hardship, living dreams and inspiration for continuing to strive with all my might.

A scholar of Canadian Literature, I arrived to Canada loaded with education and ten years of trailblazing Higher Education Management experience. I am known to have broken many norms in my personal and professional life. Being a nonconformist, I earned a long list of firsts under my belt before moving.

Appointed as the first female administrator in my homeland at the University of Jammu, J&K India, I made history. I was young, from a minority community and the only woman to win one of three interviews out of 300 applicants. For a female to opt for such an exacting position was unheard of. Many, including the selection committee were baffled with my choice.

During my time as a young female officer at the university. I encountered resistance, adversity and challenges. Some colleagues were quick to show their ugly face outright; others hid and played dirty games from behind the scenes. Nevertheless, I was also lucky to have supervisors who recognised my potential and nurtured my skills along with colleagues who backed me. My biggest achievement was the trust I built in my relationships. Had I let negativity take over and impact my choices I would not be the proud woman telling this story.

I have my parents to thank. Growing up, they showered me with love. I was raised as their only CHILD and far more than a son or a daughter. We were not a traditional family. My parents gave me space and confidence; relatives considered me wild, almost spoilt as I fearlessly spoke my mind but at the same time they were in awe. Teachers doted on me and friends loved me for my unassuming nature and guts to stand up for anyone in need.

Altaf, my childhood sweetheart, love and husband has been my number one self-appointed fan. When we got married he understood and knew that, unlike most brides, I wasn't leaving my parents' home. Contradictory to the societal norm, we chose to live with my parents. Eventually, the birth of our two sons completed us and they were my parents' newfound joy. We have always lived together, as one family unit.

While life was blooming for my family and me, unrest due to the situation in the state of Jammu and Kashmir, India worsened by the day. I was well aware of the heightening tensions and religious divide amongst the population with militancy on the rise. The charged environment, with frequent clashes between religious sects, which led to violence and imposed curfews left me convinced that this place was no longer an ideal fit to raise a young family.

In my university years, I built my reputation with sheer grit as the most resourceful and sought after officer in the university by taking on challenging assignments. In pursuit of innovative experiences, I even managed to earn two opportunities to visit Canada during that time. First in the capacity of a Research Scholar and second to represent my University as a Panel Expert on Public Relations at the Global Conference in Toronto.

My fascination with Canada started even earlier, as a child, when my first cousin immigrated to Canada with his family in the '80s. I imagined living in the fairytale land. I was especially enraptured with a box of crayons my cousin brought back. My crayon box had 12. That pack was filled with 64 shades! The way Canada established its identity as a place full of prospects, boggled my teen mind. Crayons – so many different shades, symbolic of an inclusive multicultural space – a magical land beckoning me. During my cousin's visits, we heard mesmerizing stories of clean, green, naturally beautiful spaces. These stories and later my own professional visits were instrumental in cementing my decision to relocate.

When we decided to immigrate, there was no question, my parents would move along with my husband and our two sons. In fact, my parents consenting to come and live in Canada was a determining factor for us to relocate.

On my earlier visits, I had found Canadians to be well mannered, generous and welcoming. What I loved about the people I came across in Canada is their strength to stand up for tougher things in life. They are not shy of difficult conversations, accept fault and embrace change. I value the progressive, community focused mindset and effort of most people to make things better around them. This experience further guided my decision to relocate. Especially as I wanted my two sons to live in a country that would provide them with unlimited opportunities to grow up with love in their hearts. I wanted to give them a chance to be all they envisioned and choose their own paths and create their own legacies.

Decorated with recommendations and awards in innovative management, I left behind my hard-won accomplishments. I was a well respected, dependable and sought after professional responsible for a role that involved direct supervision of 75 employees, catering to 36 Post Graduate Departments,157 affiliated Colleges with an annual turn over of one hundred thousand students.

Legacy does not pack in an immigrant's suitcase or cross international borders. Eight years after landing in Canada I am now well recognised as an outstanding consultant. Leading the Canadian Career Strategy Sector, I am known for resourcefulness and connections, an exceptional educator with contributions to numerous books, podcasts, interviews and recognition as an optimisation influencer. Not many know what it took to turn the FOB (Fresh off the Boat) life around. In Canada being an immigrant, I had to learn to advocate for myself. It was and at times still is hard to talk about myself. The struggle with it is real, but I do my best.

So I proudly wore the "feathers of my achievements in my hat" and heard mixed messages, such as, 'over qualified' and 'no Canadian experience'. My qualifications were accredited for Canadian equivalence and accepted at par but the reality of acceptance was far from its surface value. A big piece of the puzzle was the cultural disconnect. As a newcomer, I also faced the confusion of where to begin! Life is a journey in pursuit of our respective dreams; taking action results in one of two possible scenarios. First and more important failure – which in my case fueled my fever to try harder and get creative – is also as an opportunity to learn 'what doesn't work'. Second, as you might guess, is accomplishment, which, after putting in the work, is as sweet as honey. Either way is a win!

Learning from failure and my drive to succeed spurred me on even when the push-back hurt. My FOB status was in complete contrast of the reality that I had carefully crafted. Being recognised was my normal, therefore an initial shock here was: Nobody knew me!

To make matters worse, I felt at a loss for words; I spoke fluent English but my vocabulary was different. Communication styles were conflicting. Sometimes I did not make sense; at other times people did not make enough sense to me. Extra effort went into listening to non-verbal cues. My culture teaches me to stay humble, so talking about oneself equals to what Canadians call "tooting my own horn". One of the things not favourably looked upon in part of the world where I came from. In contrast, I learned it was an important skill to have for being successful in business here.

On the surface it might seem trivial but the process of immigration has deep consequences on one's self esteem, mental, emotional and physical wellbeing. I am a very grounded and confident individual, yet my insecurities showed up in the form of several health conditions. Relocation for me turned into an extremely solitary endeavour on many levels despite being blessedly surrounded by a circle of loving family and friends. Thoughts questioning my decision to uproot and move, judging myself for jeopardizing my stable career and family's socio-economic security are by no means foreign. Though being successful now, makes it easier to talk about.

When people learn about the life I lead, they are surprised and often ask, "Why did you come here?" No kidding; my home was full of amenities and luxury. Nine helpers worked in our home on a daily basis: cooks, cleaners, gardeners, chauffeurs down to the housekeeping. Call me crazy, but I left physical, financial and mental comfort for a struggle to build from scratch.

Repeatedly, I have used my passion for life to strategically turn things around. This was no different. I dug in my heels, put on my researcher hat and went nuts. Within two months, I recognised the gap that I as a newcomer faced, while navigating into the Canadian workforce. I made it my aim to help internationally-educated professionals who were experiencing barriers similar to mine. I made a conscious choice of finding work in the nonprofit sector instead of going after my niche in the field of post secondary education. Turning my career full circle wasn't easy, and I am thankful to many who were supportive and have been a part of the uphill journey.

Despite my parents' well-founded leeriness of my decision to move here, recognizing I would have to start all over again, they were always supportive. They said, "You have a year to give that country a try and if things don't go as planned, you must come back to pick up where you left off."

I reassured them, saying, "That won't be necessary." Within a few months of landing, things started to work out; we found accommodation in a family-friendly neighborhood, my husband and I found jobs and the kids started school. At that moment, I was so focused on making every aspect of life work at par with what was left behind that I lost sight of the bigger picture, including self-care. I guess certain things come to you with age and experience; in my determination to succeed, I did not see what my parents did!

My parents arrived with us, but only as visitors on visas. After six months, it was time for them to exit the country and that is when insecurity and severe anxiety hit me for the first time. The uncertainty of applying for the visa and waiting for a positive outcome time after time eventually took a toll on my physical and mental health. I put up a brave front, internalizing everything till my parents boarded the plane to go back home, but broke down right after their departure.

After they left, I turned into a zombie; my days were a cycle of repetitive tasks. I did what I needed to get done like going to work and daily chores. All day I would wait for the time to call my parents, factoring the eight and half hours time difference. That would be the highlight, my happy time. Putting the phone down brought a deep sense of loneliness which usually ended in bawling my eyes out till I fell asleep. Looking back, I feel so sorry for my husband and boys as they were at the receiving end of my breakdown. Losing my daily face-to-face contact with my parents, felt like my heart had been ripped out of my chest.

Anxiety and stress can do weird things and might be related to the scariest episode of my Canadian life. One night driving home, my mind went completely blank. I did not know where I was or how to get home. I was alone on a road, black open space, feeling hopeless, with no clue of where I was or where to go. In a panic, I called my husband. He spoke reassuringly, calmed me down and stayed with me on the phone till I reached home. Ironically, I was on the street outside my home the whole time where I had the spent the past five years. Later, I remembered having had a few similar episodes but those were so brief that I just tossed them aside. My husband encouraged me to see the doctor, and we found that my iron levels were dangerously low. I knew to take more care of me, but still did not.

Some relief came after a year and a half of our settling here, when my parents each got a Super Visa, which allowed them to travel more freely. However, like everything else, that too came at a cost, not just monetarily in terms of applying for visa extensions, medicals, air tickets, travel insurance and more but at an 'emotional' cost. Being elderly I thank God for their health, yet every time I have to wave goodbye at the airport my heart sinks.

At the back of my mind is, 'What if they needed me and I can't reach them in time. That is the reason why we still haven't applied for Canadian citizenship. I have been trying to sponsor them for the past three years with no success. Being eligible, and still not able to do so, hurts. However, this year is particularly hard. When I sat down with their passports and all necessary details in front of me waiting for the online application to open, in my mind I had no doubt, this time I will get in. I was more than ready for the very, very short window to submit my application.

Prepared, I sat with everything: passport information, digital documents ... I even received a prompt response to my anxious tweet "would the application process open?" It opened. I put in all the necessary information in record time. Four minutes, I was done. I then checked it over. Another four minutes. Confident I had everything correct. I hit submit, at 12:08. That was within eight minutes of the application screen going live. You know those timers that go off when game show contestants don't get the answer in time? That went off in my head as in disbelief I stared at the screen. It had already closed! The application time was over. Suddenly everything seemed dark. I actually felt like all of me had been eaten up by a dark bottomless hole. I kept staring at the computer refreshing it over and over. First it was shock, then disbelief. As it sunk in, I felt anger which quickly turned into grief. Since then I have lost sleep; it's hard to focus. In one word — I feel hopeless.

Some of you must be thinking, what's the big deal? You can apply again next year and that's true, I will! That said, it's another year of uncertainty. When you are unable to perform a task, which you have been doing for years on end, it shatters your confidence.

To me, my parents are pure love: my canvas, my life, my strength and source of my energy. To put it simply, having them by my side makes me happy. Happiness is not a dream; it's effort, belief and conviction. It's doing what you didn't think you could, or pushing more than you ever have. The true education I have gained from this experience is that happiness is a state of mind gained by living in the moment. The truth of our life is in living now – while continuing to push for our purpose.

IGNITE ACTION STEPS

Give yourself the time to acclimatise: Older than the trees, this space belongs to First Nations people, so without their blessings, I was imposing. Two Aboriginal Elders, Laureen (Blu) Waters and Cat Criger welcomed me and my family, which helped me establish ground, find peace and feel at home. Take the example of a sapling that is transplanted. It takes time to adjust to the new soil bed and then bloom. Now think of a fully grown fruit bearing tree, which is uprooted. Whereas children can be compared to saplings, you and I are that fully grown tree. It takes longer to get used to the new environment and take roots.

Practice self-care: Do things that are pleasurable and bring peace of mind. It can be something as simple as a walk in the park or journaling. Coffee and chat with a newfound friend. Exploring activities with family at the local library. Volunteering in the community. Window shopping at the mall or exploring the market stalls for stuff that you have never seen.

Compassion for self and no judgment: "How could I?" is not needed! Every mistake is a lesson learned. Also, every small and big win is a reason for celebration.

Networking: Identify and create your own tribe. Surround yourself with people who have similar values and interests. They will act as your sounding board, hold you in difficult times, validate and applaud your achievements. Good friends are a blessing; all of us need some, if not many.

Change doesn't happen overnight; it's a process. Learn to unlearn and then learn. A full glass can't hold more. Failure at a certain point does not mean you are not enough. It just means the time is not right or there is something to learn; put in the work, or get creative and change direction to rediscover your magic to bedazzle the world. That's what we all have to do. Find our happiness. Find our roots.

Taranum Khan, Ph.D. CCS, Career Strategy & Optimization Consultant I
Author & Speaker. www.etrec.ca

CYNTHIA
V. MORGAN

"Believe in yourself and love every moment! Have faith that
opportunities will come...envision it and take action!"

**My story is designed to empower you to take action when opportunities
present themselves and to trust good things will come. If given a second
or third...or 624th chance, take it! Sometimes you have to experience
being without before you can appreciate when you have it all. Your attitude makes a world of difference in your present day and your outlook
toward the future. Envision the ideal situation and when the opportunity presents itself, take action! Have faith unfortunate events will pass.
Believe your dreams can come true.**

ATTITUDE AND ACTION

The pain was excruciating! It was radiating from the right side of my
abdomen through my entire body. I was afraid of what was causing the
pain as I curled in a fetal position, in the middle of the night, wondering
how I was going to get help. I forced myself to slowly walk, bowed down,
clutching my right side as I went to the bathroom and used the toilet. The
pain was not relieved. I cried and slowly walked over to my parents' room.
I woke my dad. He knew immediately what was wrong! Appendicitis. His
appendix burst when he was going through the U.S. Navy boot camp in San

Diego. Dad carried me down the stairs, placed me in the car and drove me to Balboa Naval Hospital in San Diego. I was 13 years old in 1984 and I was going to have major surgery.

The eight-hour surgery to remove my burst appendix, took a toll on me and especially my mom. She felt so sorry for me and all the medical issues that kept coming up. She stayed by my side during the almost three weeks it took for me to finally be well enough to be released from the hospital. During the early part of my recovery period, complications developed with my entire digestive system. I was hydrated through an IV. I was 'fed' from a bottle with yellow liquid that looked like urine, pumped through a tube that entered into my body through a vein in my chest. If you can imagine, whenever I had to use the bathroom, I had to unplug the power for the IV machine, then unplug the power for the food" machine, and oh, by the way, I also had a nasogastric tube placed through my nose, past my throat and down into my stomach, which helped drain gastric contents into a bag—a bag that I had to also cart along to the bathroom at the end of the long hallway of beds.

It's like the hospital wards you see in old war movies, where beds were spaced every six feet or so and only curtains on rails divided each patient's area for visual privacy when your doctor comes to discuss your health issues. Mainly the curtains remained wide open for all to see, especially when nurses made their rounds. I felt exposed. Ugly, with bed-head and tubes going into and out of my body, and an abdominal incision gaping open, packed with gauze that needed to be changed frequently to allow the pus to drain. All of this prevented me from bathing almost the entire time I was in recovery. I felt so sorry for myself. I didn't feel like I was getting any better.

Every day, mom tried her best to comfort me during the short visiting hours. I was bored as there was very limited entertainment, television was at the end of the hallway, too far to view. I didn't have a Walkman to play the radio or cassette tapes; my family couldn't afford one. I had no real distractions from feeling so gross with everything sticking into and out of me.

When I became an adult, my mom told me how she cried every night after returning home because she had to witness how much suffering I went through, and there was nothing she could do about it. She also helped fill in some of my memory gaps.

It turned out this experience in the hospital actually made me much stronger. I would pick up the Guidepost magazines scattered around the hospital and they became a balm to soothe my soul. I read the miraculous stories of healing, comfort, and kindness from people around the world. It was a spiritual remedy that changed my attitude and improved my outlook. I felt like all I had to do was influence my mind and I could start healing myself. I began praying more, telling God that if I ever got out of the hospital I would take advantage of every opportunity and not take life for granted ever again. I developed my faith that the Universe would look out for me.

In junior high school before my appendectomy, I applied myself but thought that I wasn't as smart as the other kids. I earned average grades, like mostly B's and C's. There was one girl in my class who earned straight A's and I wanted to be just like her. After my surgery, I started at a new junior-senior high school, and I became just like that girl. I earned and maintained a 4.0+ grade point average, unlike my dismal, just passing 2.5 GPA the year before. My promise to myself also paid off in sports. Even though I was shy, I joined the field hockey and badminton teams. There I felt the camaraderie of others and enjoyed being part of a team. I graduated high school and earned the honor to give a speech at graduation as one of the top two valedictorians. I was very nervous about speaking in front of all of my classmates and their families, but with my English teacher's review, it gave me the confidence to do it, trusting my speech about our generation's future was going to lead to cheers. Go Morse Tigers!

I applied and was accepted to the U.S. Naval Academy. I wanted to follow in my dad's footsteps by joining the Navy, to travel the world, meet people from different cultures and backgrounds, and get outside of my comfort zone. Life at the academy was all about chow calls, Professional Report presentations, demanding physical fitness exercises and tests. One had to have the ability to memorize naval information quickly and respond to questions while in a stressful environment that included yelling. It was challenging to my introverted self. I was different from my dad because he loved to tell sea stories over and over to me, my siblings, and all of his buddies. I was always the shy one in class, last to volunteer to do my presentations or raise my hand to participate or answer questions. He was a Navy Chief, and he told me that Chiefs were the backbone of the Navy. He would have to teach officers how to become leaders, and I was determined not to be one of those officers who would not listen to their Chief.

Each command I was assigned to helped me to grow outside of my comfort zone. Every next level of command challenged me with greater and greater responsibilities, leading more people, and being in charge of my personnel. I had to consider the overall command's performance, each individual's performance and advancements, their health and fitness, and sometimes their very lives. My career field as a meteorologist and oceanographer meant that I had to stand up in front of my superiors, peers and subordinates, and give speeches about the weather and its impacts to operations. The weather 'brief', or presentation, was always given at the beginning of any operational brief, because weather could potentially impact all kinds of Naval, Marine Corps, and Air Force operations (aircraft, ships, submarines, landing crafts, communications) —and if the weather was bad, it was like I was on the firing line, exposed to criticism, doubt, and blame. Also, it set the tone for the rest of the brief. All weather persons are just the messengers—we get shot down whenever the message was bad. I would sometimes joke, "I'm just the messenger. If you want to change the weather, go talk to the Chaplain."

For me, personally, I do not take credit for the weather, good or bad. I studied the weather models, trusted my instincts, and had faith that operations would continue as scheduled, or that my superiors would take my advice and delay operations until weather was more favorable. My mission was to have no lives lost and no major operational mishaps due to weather, and my mission was thankfully accomplished.

Around the midpoint of my career after my tour aboard a ship, I felt it was time to start a family. I was stationed on shore duty and my husband and I tried to get pregnant for three years. We were finally given the green light to go through the military's in vitro fertilization (IVF) program at the Walter Reed Army Medical Center in Washington, D.C. It turned out that as a result of my acute appendicitis, my fallopian tubes had adhesions and scar tissue, which prevented us from conceiving.

We went through the initial exam process and a setback delayed us from starting the romantic process of getting pregnant. I found out that I had fibroids in my uterus and one large fibroid positioned in the uterine lining that had to be removed. Finally, we were cleared to start IVF. I was 38 years old when we got pregnant. We were lucky for our first try — as each couple goes through IVF, we had to sign an acknowledgement that there was a chance that we would go through the entire process, pay our fee, and it would result in no pregnancy or no baby born due to a miscarriage.

My husband and I were both on active duty Navy orders. Our commands were flexible enough in allowing my husband and me time off from work to do what we needed to do for IVF on our own dime. We paid a set price for all of our medications as well as the embryologist contractors.

We had a beautiful, tiny baby girl, named Sydney, born prematurely since I had developed preeclampsia a month before she was due. She was perfect, her lungs worked fine so she did not have to go to the NICU. My dad did not get to meet her as he had passed away a year before she was born.

My command required me to go on frequent mini-deployments away from family several times during that first year. My mom moved in to help us when Sydney came home. My mom provided us with the flexibility that no day care could. Thank God for Moms, right?!

While my husband and I were still on shore duty orders, we decided to try to have another baby so Sydney would have a close sibling, and before I turned 40. We tried IVF several more times, but we were unsuccessful. It was heartbreaking each time I got the news that the embryos did not implant. Somehow, I already knew because I would not see the telltale sign of implantation bleeding that happened a couple of days after embryo transfer. I would dread the feeling of the abdominal cramps, indicating that my menstrual period was on its way, taking with it the two or three embryos we had just transferred. The HCG blood tests would confirm the loss, killing all hope. The waiting was always crushing; the blood test results were all I could ever think about. We were not given any explanations by the doctors as to why the embryos did not take each time. After grieving for a bit, I'd focus back on my Naval career.

In order for me to be more competitive for promotion, I took orders to Bahrain in the Middle East for one year, unaccompanied by my family in late 2011. In March of that year, Bahrain was part of the anti-government protests and uprisings of the Arab Spring. It made sense to me to leave my family in the U.S. while I deployed overseas and sacrificed my family life for my career. To leave my then three-year-old daughter and only see her on Skype once a week due to the large time difference and work/school/sleep schedules made me cry each time I had to say goodbye to her. Some days she would just run by the screen, saying "hi" and "bye," and I would not have a chance to connect with her, grow with her, be with her.

Luckily my tour in Bahrain was uneventful; however, my next assignment at the Pentagon would take its toll on me. With the early morning commutes, late evening returns and the vigorous schedule of briefs, emails, travel, and conference calls, I spent maybe an hour or less with my daughter before her bedtime. She preferred her daddy whenever she got hurt or needed a story of something that happened that day. She wanted him to read her a bedtime story. Her daddy was always there for her. It was that grief of not being her 'person' that changed my love for my Navy career. It was no longer bringing me any fun and excitement. Instead, it was robbing me of the motherhood experience I so deeply desired. Soon, I would have to choose between my career or my desire for being there for my family and maybe having another baby.

In no time at all, the promotion offer came. Sydney was only five and a half years old. I could become captain in the U.S. Navy or I could be a stay-at-home mom and create that mother-daughter connection I so craved. I'd worked so hard for this. If I turned it down, I would be disappointing my peers and my superiors who had invested their time and effort to help me become the future leader for our sailors. But I knew in my heart, taking the promotion, would not align truly to my mothering soul. I turned it down because being a Captain in the U.S. Navy required further sacrifice in family life. Being geographically separated from my husband and daughter and spending longer hours at work did not align to my vision for motherhood. The additional worry about my family might lead me to distraction in key moments where decision making is critical. Therefore, I submitted my retirement papers for June 1, 2015.

In 2015-2016, we pursued our dream to become pregnant again because I wanted to have the full experience of motherhood from the very beginning without military obligations, plus we still wanted Sydney to have a sibling. We went through a civilian IVF Shared Risk program in Washington, D.C. which guaranteed up to six IVF rounds and a baby born, or your money back. My husband had deployed to Afghanistan for the Navy Reserves in the fall of 2015, so we had to make sure viable cryogenically frozen samples of his sperm were stored before he left, or else our dreams of another baby would be on hold until after he returned.

My faith in another baby sustained me, and we were willing to do anything to have our dream come true again. It took us eight years of hoping and dreaming, five IVF sessions with a grand total of about 624 shots and several medications. We managed to get pregnant! Precious Violet was worth the wait (and every one of the 624 half-inch to 1.5 inch 'long' needles).

My heart swells with love whenever I hug and kiss my daughters. I feel so connected with each of them because I breastfed both of them, Sydney for a few months and Violet for more than 24 months. I am able to be present with Sydney when I volunteer at her school for events like play rehearsals, parent assistant for the school newspaper, and especially as homeroom parent. Infants and toddlers are so innocent and dependent on their parents, that makes those special times fleeting since they grow up so quickly. I am forever grateful for every single opportunity to be there for my children, caring for them and sharing with them the ways to become kind and loving people. I help them to remember what it means to be human, knowing that each person is valuable and deserving of love and kindness.

By making the leap of faith when I retired from my successful career in the U.S. Navy to start my new chapter as a full-time mom, was the best decision I have ever made. Each moment with my children resonates with power to see them constantly learning from my husband and me. It is my goal to inspire them and you to do whatever it takes by having a positive attitude, envisioning your goals, making necessary course corrections, and always taking action. You'll get there. I believe in each of you.

IGNITE ACTION STEPS

While I was recovering in the hospital and reading the stories in the GuidePost magazines, I envisioned myself getting better and better each day. I saw myself without the IV, without the feeding and nasogastric tubes, looking healthy and walking out of the hospital. It gave me the strength to keep going each day. And while I was stuck at my Pentagon job, I focused on the finish line, my retirement, and I looked forward to starting my dream of motherhood all over again.

What worked for me, may work for you. Surround yourself with positivity, people who support you, and keep dreaming about your ideal situation. I am amazed each time my vision comes true, but deep down I know that I am responsible for what happens to me. I have adopted and practice the mantra 'believing is seeing!'

To keep me on track, I take slow deep breaths, especially before stressful situations, like speaking in front of people. I envision the best outcome while I am breathing in for five counts, holding my breath for five counts and then exhaling for five counts. I do this five times in a row, twice a day.

When I look back, I realize that most situations were never as bad as I had feared initially. Do what works, what feels good for you and trust that good things will come. Every person's path is never a straight line to the top. It is in the journey that we grow and fulfill our perfect destiny; however long or short it is. Enjoy the process and love every moment because it has made you who you are. Be positive in your attitude and take action!

Cynthia V. Morgan, President, Love Prosperity 93, LLC, WildFit Coach.
loveprosperity93.com

CAROL BENSON

"Do you ever wonder if people know the real you?
Express yourself often as a powerful reflection for who you
choose to show and be."

I share my story for those of you who have hidden your true nature away to fit into a mold of expectations. May you be inspired to unleash vulnerable, creative and real parts of you. All the parts yearning to be expressed in how you contribute through work and in the rest of your life. That voice inside you cheering you toward your true authentic self! To live a life filled with joy, celebration and meaning.

ALLERGIC TO YOUR WORK?

Aversions surface in strange ways.

It was my first month in clinic as a communication disorders graduate student. I was tightly wound, stress hormones on drip, while reviewing a pediatrician's notes on a three-year old's language development. But being a perfectionist type, I thought I was ready. And then, it happened.

My voice went on a break. No really, it did! Abandoned me in the cold Detroit winter like it went to Ft. Lauderdale during spring break! How was I going to do the session? My hoarse and crackly voice sounded a mix between a heavy smoker and an exhausted opera singer on tour.

Then, an urgent note to meet my advisor. Immediately. Was I in trouble? An emergency? A loud inner monologue attempted to pull me off course into the 'I'm not enough' zone. Ever been there?

Fearfully knocking on the kind but precise, Dr. Frank's door, "Come in!" I hesitated then entered an organized office. Dr. Frank indicated a stiff leather chair to sit in. "There's a sensitive case. Teaching staff agrees you're the best one for it. We've reassigned your next session." He paused, "By the way, you comfortable with voice assessments?"

What?!!! Oh no! I've never done one before! Only studied the protocol! I had prepared for a child evaluation! Now a voice one? Fear escalated inside me.

Hoarse voice primed, inhaling deeply, I said, "Thanks for this opportunity. Pretty sure I know how." His jaw dropped. He didn't even try to hide his surprise.

"What's going on, Carol?" I had a reputation to maintain as a top student. "I'm okay. I definitely want to do this. Any details?"

He hesitated, "Sure it won't strain your vocal cords?" I nodded. Skeptical, he added "She's transgender. Wants her voice more feminine."

Suddenly my manufactured confidence melted. Unsure if I could I pull it off.

Masking my truth, I said, "Thanks, helpful knowing that. Uh, observation room open?" Dr. Frank nodded. I felt the pressure to perform knowing the mirrored room would be 'standing room only'.

Statuesque, Eve, was dressed impeccably in jacket and pants, scarf very French-like with manicured fingernails. An epitome of a well-dressed femme. Even her fragrance was divine. I felt an urge to stand on tiptoes to appear taller than I am.

I observed she already embodied ranges of feminine quality and pitch. Straining my hoarse voice, "I'm curious, what's a more feminine voice to you, Eve?"

"I want to sound sexy. Like Marilyn Monroe did."

To this day, Eve's comment hits on societal expectations for women at work and in life. How often do women: Defer from their calling and soul's purpose to act a role? Hide behind an archetype or identity to fit in? Or try to please others?

Eve wasn't a voice therapy candidate. I helped her explore feminine vocal characteristics, nonverbal traits, to come to the realization using a breathy voice long-term could damage her vocal cords.

"When I first changed, I thought people would laugh at how I sound. Didn't think I was doing it right." Beaming, Eve added, "I'm more confident as a woman now. Thank you."

Anxious to witness reactions for my performance, I opened the observation room door. It was standing room only. Peers and teachers gave me a standing ovation! Yet, I questioned if I knew what I was doing. Do you ever wonder if people know the real you? Did I know the real me?

I had become masterful at acting. Cloaking away parts of me I believed didn't fit into the mold of this profession. Looking like a success to everyone else but me. As if I was acting in a play.

Sheltering my laser-fast creative spark from others. Spending decades acting parts in this career track. Unfulfilled and exhausted the end of most days. Working clever ruses to fit in. In my career identity and personal life, as a daughter and wife. Was some higher power with a wicked sense of humor messing with my authentic self?

In hindsight, I failed to honor myself. Rewinding back to my early role as 'Daddy's girl', I was still invested in pleasing him. I adored my dad. He was bright, creative, and loved corny jokes. There were, however, times I felt discarded by him. When I was an early teen, I remember Dad at the kitchen table with my younger brother explaining how to read financial stock pages in the Wall Street Journal. I asked if I could learn too. He said, "You and your sister don't need to worry about that." He waved me out of the room. In that instant, I started feeling invisible in my family.

Nonetheless, I felt more like my dad than my mom. I wanted to walk in his footsteps. Driven, he left a 'sure thing job' in the marketing department of a big auto company in Detroit, Michigan during the industry's heyday.

With three little kids at home plus a mortgage and my mom's financial savvy behind him, my dad risked security to launch his own advertising agency. His dream turned into a success story. Even winning several Clio awards (aka the Academy Awards of the advertising industry). I yearned to pursue my creative calling like he did. Ironically, women were still limited to expected roles. I was already dreaming big and I couldn't see how I would be happy playing small. I wanted to become a successful entrepreneur like my dad.

What I didn't anticipate was how I caved in on myself. One month before my sophomore year of undergraduate school, my dad asked what I planned for my major. I boldly shared, 'marketing and journalism'. He said, "No. Not paying for that pipe dream." What I heard was: 'entrepreneurship isn't for women'.

My mom added, "Writing's a good hobby, honey." My dreams and desires abruptly dismissed. Growing up I saw her stand behind my dad. Sad to reflect now, knowing she was brilliant and wanted to be an attorney. Her dream unrealized.

I felt crushed. Shunning my soul's calling, I permitted my parents to squash my dreams. No excuses but I lacked confidence then to say to my parents, "No problem. I'll figure out the financial part on my own." Wanting to avoid conflict and have their approval, I gave up significant parts of myself.

Urging me toward secure careers like medicine or nursing, they retreated when I pushed back, saying, "No!" to several school acceptances! Their judging scowls spoke volumes.

To prove I wasn't a total loser, I completed the Master's degree; even passed qualifying boards as a Speech and Language Pathologist (SLP). You already know I felt like a fraud. Talk about 'imposter syndrome' rearing its head. Still, my creative spirit called to me, taking evening and weekend courses and writing on my own.

Curiously, during the years I practiced as an SLP, I'd get sick being around dripping little noses. A poor immune system? Or allergic to the work? I knew there was a connection. But I didn't understand it yet.

Silently kicking and screaming, I had agreed to a career life sentence; believing a creative career wasn't financially viable. What I know now is: I bought into a hidden message - women shouldn't become entrepreneurs. That I would fail. In my family, financial security counted most. I also learned my opinion and needs didn't matter. My brother was encouraged to do whatever he wanted. My sister wanted to be an artist, but she also caved into getting a degree in medical technology as a 'fall-back' career.

I began not letting others see the authentic me beneath the surface. On the outside, I acted the successful and skillful professional. Inside, I hid my spirited, creative ball of playful energy. Yet, a select few noticed.

In college, one of my brother's friends perceived, "Carol, it's like you landed in your family from another planet." I laughed then, painfully realizing truth in his comment. There were many times I felt like the 'black sheep''" knowing I didn't fit into the mold they expected of me.

More like my dad, I was extroverted, social, loved to sing, dance and tell stories. My mom didn't have patience for that. She wanted me more focused about schoolwork like my brother or quieter like my sister. In high school, it terrified her when I had a serious boyfriend. I expressed my creativity and sexuality in ways she repressed. Suspicious by nature, whatever I said or did, she judged as wrong. Even as recently as a few years ago. My sister called me after the three of us had lunch together and said, "Mom is so mean to you." I reminded her it was the norm.

Even acting the role of designated, responsible professional, I think my mother feared I might let my playful self out of the box. She needn't have worried; my younger self was plugged into the 'I'm not good enough' and 'people pleasing' melody.

Recognizing my parents loved and wanted the best for me, knowing they didn't have skills in how to trust, honor or value my choices. Their fears got in the way. Yes, I had resentments. It's taken a lot of personal growth to forgive, have compassion and understand they handled it the best they could.

Still, my personal vision wouldn't evaporate. It stuck around until I decided not to play small. Stop. Playing. Small. Seeking happiness as my north star and wanting to contribute in a greater way to others' happiness. My purposeful path continued to elude me. Whenever 'hoarse voice' showed up, it nudged me to pay attention. As if my vocal cords were my private truth barometer! Although I knew I needed to be braver, I was a slow learner in the 'how' part.

Not yet able to bail the profession I clung to for financial security, even if it wasn't serving me. I endured the undercurrent of trying to fit in; against my natural flow of doing what I loved. My pursuit of being happy and whole, continued to elude me.

Until one day, walking my dog on a glorious sunshiny day, flowers in bloom. Tears streaming down my face, pulling back the veil to expose a truth I had avoided. I felt alone in my unfulfilled life. The realization I was living 'NOT CAROL'S' life was replaced by determination. I was done living an inauthentic life and not the one I craved. Not certain how to proceed until a week later. I opened up my kitchen cabinet, a glass fell out on the bridge of my nose. I was bleeding. I must have needed one more whack. That night I turned to my 'practice husband', "You're not happy, and I'm not happy. Why are we prolonging this?"

Life Reviewed:

First, allowing my parents to control my life and career path. Then in about ten seconds of insanity, caving in to say "Yes" to my 'practice husband's' marriage proposal; knowing we weren't true partners. It was a time when all my girlfriends had found 'the one' and started having babies. I settled for only a portion of what I ached for in a partner. That seemed to be a theme in my life. Settling.

Then along came my two sons, who I adore and love. They've been my greatest teachers. From them, the courage to not shy away from my authentic nature any longer.

After fifteen years of sleepwalking, shamed and scared, I chose uncertainty. To become 'Real Carol'. 'Practice husband' and I lovingly released each other. Our kids came along with me. Inner resilience and love for my sons motivated me to debut living 'Real Carol's' life and not someone else's expectations of me.

Definitely not for the faint of heart. 'Not Carol's' voice was so loud and forceful, I had to work at reclaiming 'Real Carol'. I reached out for support. Surprisingly, the perfect 'teacher/coach/mentor' has always shown up exactly when I needed them most. Grateful for all of the wise support I've had!

Deciding to claim, 'Real Carol' has been a game-changer. I finally learned to honor, nourish and love myself as enough. That's also when one of my screenplays began a three-year journey toward a paid writing job. I'm not an overnight sensation!!! I knew something had shifted when my dad asked me to print, or stop in and read to him, my published articles. The last chance I had to read to him was when he was near the end of his life. My heart healed, hearing him express pride in me and my creative work.

When Paul, my 'real' husband showed up, I wasn't looking or wanting a relationship. My life felt full. But he fit right in, with the capacity to step into an instant family: a wife, two boys, a dog, a cat, and the ex. Well-matched in how we each champion growth; not trying to change to please one other, we share both personal and professional lives.

No longer can I say "Yes" when my soul means "No way!" In my business, "It Doesn't Feel Like Work," I serve others by being in flow with my creative spirit. Living a 'Not Carol's' life, provided a full spectrum view of times I agreed to other's expectations of me. I now stand behind my authentic self. Farewell to doing life 'Not Carol's' way! I rarely get sick; it's been well over a decade since I've lost my voice. Being aligned in my true authentic nature, there's no need to be allergic to my work. How are you saying "Yes!" to all parts of your authentic self? The doorway is open and inviting you in.

IGNITE ACTION STEPS

When I was re-discovering myself, some tools helped me become more authentic, confident; appreciating all parts of my life and deepening self-love. Here are a few things you can do to reclaim anything in the way of having a thriving, happy life full of ease:

• Ask yourself, "Am I doing what I truly believe in and what I'm really passionate about?"

• When have you hidden your true self away in order to play it safe in your career and life? Spend some time to reflect and write your thoughts down.

• Then, make a list of your natural talents. This can feel uncomfortable as I know without a doubt there are some surprises for you to welcome into your perspective in how you view yourself.

• The next part is definitely both uncomfortable and freeing. Make a list of all the areas you believe you're 'Not enough'. The next part is to review each item and ask, "Is this truth or fiction?"

I'm rooting for you to ignite authenticity in all parts of your life so, "It Doesn't Feel Like Work!"

Carol Benson, Speaker, Author, Mindvalley Master Certified & Intuition Trainer. It Doesn't Feel Like Work. itdoesntfeellikework.com

JOANNA MERCADO PETERS

"YOU have magic inside of you… You just need to learn to pay attention and let your magic shine"

I am sharing my story with the purpose to ignite a spark of hope in your heart even when all appears lost. I'm hoping my decisions to always move forward and pay attention paves a path for you. These two acts will connect the dots even when at the beginning we do not completely understand the whys and the hows. You'll see and in your heart you will understand.

FINDING MYSELF IN A NEW WORLD

In some of my dark moments, people always tell me, "Everything happens for a reason," "You will understand the WHY later." "Nothing is a coincidence." and "There is a purpose to everything." To be honest with you, I used to hate listening to those phrases. Especially when I was in the middle of one of my own meltdown crises. When in my opinion and perception, the world was close to an end and sometimes I even felt the world was already over.

Hopefully you know what I mean. You are in the middle of the worst storm since the beginning of time. When the only thing you want to do, is scream, cry, and yell – and that wise, calm friend or family member tries to calm you down, to make you feel better – and shares how the bigger picture will make sense one day... I probably pictured in my mind a few times how to push them down into a deep waterfall. I know it sounds terrible, but I used to hate hearing that. Let's be honest. When you are in the middle of your storm and you lack the tools or knowledge to handle it, the last thing you want to hear is someone else telling you that everything will be ok. I mean, 'HOW DO THEY KNOW??!!!'

Now that I've showed you how dramatic and attached to my outcomes I can be, I'm going to share how I experienced a sequence of events proving how those nice, calm and irritating statements can turn out to be true. I'll start giving you some context.

I worked in a Fortune 50 company right out of college in my home country of Colombia. I was third generation of my family working in that company and very proud of the fact I was employed and advancing in the same company where my Dad worked all his life. I progressed in the company from one promotion to another. Very soon, I moved from being on a student placement as a requirement of finishing my career degree, to be a leader in charge of the quality of our final product. Also, I was responsible to help and support the development and daily activities of almost 200 people.

My life was going as I expected; soon I was taking a role where I was able to travel around the world coaching and teaching teams about continuous improvement and quality on how to develop sustainable processes. One day I got this once in a lifetime opportunity: they called and asked me if I could help with the startup of a brand-new plant in China. That is the dream job for any engineer in the world, as you are able to develop the systems and process right from scratch and also help create the right culture, training and teamwork.

I already knew I had to move outside Colombia, if I wanted to keep growing in my career. The factory here was small and the organizational structure pretty lean. I saw the China trip as an opportunity to show my potential, and get the company to transfer me to another country, where I could start my life in another place and keep learning and growing.

I went to China in June of 2011 and I loved every minute of my time there. A few weeks before I had to return to Colombia, one of the managers in China told me his boss wanted to interview me for a regional job in the Asia Pacific region. This could be my ticket to the next step in my career. I was so excited and honoured.

The interview went well. A few weeks later I returned to Colombia with so many lessons learned and memories I will treasure for my entire life. After a couple of weeks of not hearing anything at all, I started doing some follow ups. One thing I learned early in my career, is the importance of networking, developing good connections and making friends along the way. The Asia team was really excited about me joining them except, my current manager had to approve and release me to proceed on this journey.

Well, unfortunately, my manager did not practice good succession planning and did not have anyone to replace me. He told them I could not go to Asia. Asia fought to have me, but my manager held too much power over this transfer. This went on for months. By the time it was resolved, the Asia Pacific region went into a hiring freeze. They were not able to take me anymore.

I cried until I thought there couldn't possibly be more tears and more kept coming; I just could not believe how my boss could just block me in that way, how he could just ruin my future and my dreams. I was sooooo bitter about it; it was hard even to look at him as I lost all respect for him as a leader. Only thing I was able to think was: 'How dare he ruin my career and stop me from a once in a lifetime opportunity?'

Remember all those wise friends? I couldn't hear them. I felt in my mind, my career was over, the sky was falling. I was so full of anger and resentment. Then I read "Radical Forgiveness" about full ownership how to create your own reality by Colin Tipping. I decided to take action. I updated my resume and started applying for other jobs in other companies. As I kept on applying, I started feeling confident something better will occur. To be honest with you I just wanted to run away from that boss, that place and never look back. It was just too painful. Every time, every day I was there, it was a reminder of my beautiful China opportunity and how it vanished in front of me.

Then in June of 2012, only three months after this event 'ruined my life', derailed my career, and stole my opportunity something magical happened. I received an email for a conference call that week with someone in my company's headquarters in the U.S. The invite did not have a lot of information, just 'Opportunity in U.S.'

I accepted the invite and two days later I was talking with the regional manager in charge of North and South America. He asked would I be interested in an opportunity to work as a regional engineer for the North America team. I still remember my heart beating so fast, my hands started sweating and my eyes watering. I tried to not jump and cut him off to tell him my bags were already packed. I was ready. I actually did tell him those very thoughts when five minutes later he asked my thoughts. They figured out a way I could come to the U.S., without needing the blessing of my current boss.

I said, "YES, YES, YES," and five months later, after I was able to complete all the paperwork and visa requirements, I was on a plane on my way to Akron, Ohio. Unlike in China, where food was taken care of for me, I started this new life by myself, only bringing my clothes and a few small, furniture items I had in my bedroom at my mother's house, where I had lived all my life. I had to learn how to live alone and take care of myself. The change was big – huge, in fact. I exchanged a life of living with my mom and siblings and having someone to help us at home every day – to living all by myself. I had to learn the basics like washing my clothes, (I had at least one batch of whites that become Unicorn pink) how to balance housekeeping, work duties and how to cook.

That was the hardest thing - learning how to cook for myself. I felt alone, leaving family and friends behind. Even months after, my circle of friends was very small, so cooking for ONLY ONE, was a painful reminder of family times. I was afraid to admit to my family and friends how hard it was, and how I was actually not prepared for all the pressures I was living. I kept it to myself, smiling to the outside world and struggling to keep all the balls in the air in the inside.

It was so much easier to eat out every night or to buy 'yummy' and 'easy' food to snack on at home. I found comfort and escape in take-out and 'treats'. I concentrated so totally on being successful in my new life, my new job, my career, I just told myself my pants didn't close because of all the layers of tights I would put on in order to stay warm. Then the spring came and without layers, the pants were still not closing!

I still remember the day I weighed myself and jumped off the scale in shock; I gained 20 pounds in a few months without even noticing or at least admitting consciously what was going on. I went to a dark place in the following months. Depression took over. I felt bad about myself and how I looked in the mirror, in pictures and even in the reflection of storefront-glass in the mall.

At the same time, I did not know what to do about it. I felt so bad that I stopped taking pictures of myself or allowing my boyfriend (now wonderful and magical husband) to take pictures of me. That was a big deal for me, because I am Queen of the Selfies. It was just too painful to see pictures of myself and confront the reality, so I kept hiding, avoiding the facts and the truth. Hiding didn't allow me to escape 'feeling bad' about how I looked in the mirror. I stopped looking at myself naked. It was too painful.

I knew I was blessed. I knew I had everything I wished for, but I still felt horrible with myself and my image, I felt I had no right to feel like that about my body, I consciously knew I was not obese. When I had the courage to talk about it, people looked at me with crazy-eyes, that said, 'you are not fat, PLEASE!!!' I decided to stop talking about it. The conflict became even worse, more hiding, more denying and still feeling bad about my image. I didn't have a 'real' reason to feel that sad and depressed.

I hit my lowest point, the day after my wedding, April 24th 2016. I was with my all best friends from Colombia, Australia and Bolivia to be with me on my special day). It was not yet noon, when I got a facebook post from my photographer, sharing the preview pictures of my wedding. I planned the whole thing, putting time and love into every single detail. Eager to see, I started scrolling down the pictures looking at decorations, some makeup and hair shots... Then I saw a picture of me from the back. The zipper of my open-back dream-dress, barely closed.

It hurt so badly. I felt betrayed by my friends. None of them said anything. I remember my guilt and shame. Not wanting to make a scene, I pulled myself together and kept scrolling down, but now I just concentrated on the details. The breaking point occurred when one of my best friends' mom called and while in speaker mode, she said, "What a beautiful wedding... Joa is getting chubby." I went to the bathroom and cried, wondering if I might ever stop.

That day I decided:

Enough was enough. I was not going to live like that anymore.

I will not look at any of my wedding pictures.

As soon as everybody was on their way back home, I decided it was time to take ACTION! I started searching for exercises I would enjoy. Zumba appealed to me; I also remember how much joy, peace and love yoga gave to me, so I signed up in a Gym first-time ever, that offered both Zumba and Yoga.

I started slowly, instead of attempting workouts seven days per week I started with three days per week: Those days I would leave to work with my gym bag already packed. I knew if I went back home after work, the chances to get out again were almost zero. After work I spent 1 hour and 45 minutes doing Zumba and Yoga. As my body started to get stronger, so did my self-esteem. I started feeling motivated and looked to find new ways to do exercise with my husband. Hiking and exploring, was spending time with my sweetheart and at the same time, moving and exercising. It was a perfect combination. Exercise changed from something boring and mandatory – to something I really enjoyed. I felt great after each class, each one a small victory and my sweating body was a signal of accomplishment. I COULD DO IT!

I learned that a pound of muscle and a pound of fat are very different in volume and I can feel okay with a few more pounds than my non-fit self. I learned that goal + desire = success. I feel sexier and comfortable with my body again, I am in the best shape of my life. It has been three years since my wedding and the journey is slow but steady. Regarding my wedding pictures, I'm still working on it. I'm not yet ready to see them, but I'm closer and closer. I'm sure I will look at them in the perfect moment, when my internal healing matches up with my external beliefs.

The key point here is our society, wired so many 'shoulds' in our brains that we end up doubting ourselves and what we are feeling. We end up comparing ourselves with everybody else, and judging how we feel against society's expectations. We as warrior females need to STOP this nonsense, tune back into our hearts, listen to our inner voice, pay attention and respect our own wisdom and intuition more than any 'should' of society.

I am telling you my story to invite you to TAKE ACTION. Be it your job, career, promotion, future, desire, wishes or weight, find inside of your heart what makes you smile and work to get your spark back. I invite you to give yourself permission to explore and to feel. To kick the guilt out of your heart and understand it is OK to feel however you are feeling right now. I am sharing my story to inspire you to believe that there is not a right or wrong approach to anything. How you start is perfect for you. I encourage you to try 1, 10, 100, 1,000 times and then one more time, to explore and try new things until you find the magical recipe that works FOR YOU, because YOU deserve TO HAVE IT.

About those dots... Here I am now, after seven years and looking backwards, I can connect ALL THE DOTS. I can see how that moment, at that time, my transfer being refused was the worst moment in my life, yet was exactly what I needed to be able to be where I am now. I will never know how my life would be now if I took the China job. For example, I never would have met my sweet husband in China. What I do know is my life is MAGICAL, because I made it all mine. This is my invitation for you, my dear sisters and friends, to feel comfortable knowing the dots always connect backwards and it is almost impossible to connect them only looking forward.

Sometimes we all get lost in frustration and ego, wondering why something happened or didn't happen. We waste so much of our energy and magic in storming about missed opportunities when there is always another opportunity or life experience on its way. I am here to tell you that you can use all that energy for a better, more useful action, that moves you forward in igniting your life. As I learned, no matter how much energy I put into fretting, the dots won't connect sooner, only later.

We all have a purpose in life, and all the events in our life align to ensure we live that purpose and conquer obstacles that we came to this lifetime to experience. I want to encourage you to keep trying, keep finding the sweet parts of life, keep finding reasons to smile. Share joy with others, create moments of self-care and self-love, and move forward, even if it is with tiny little baby-steps. My dear sister, I know in the future when you look back, you will also be able to CONNECT YOUR DOTS. That experience, situation or moment, that hurts or aches right now, will make all the sense in the world! So don't waste your precious time or energy trying to connect the dots forward. Do take ACTION forward today and IGNITE your life – in the best way you can right now.

IGNITE ACTION STEPS

1. Meditate, or remember of at least one past situation, however small, that felt bad or disappointing in the moment it occurred, and it turned out to be a good thing in the future. Journal about it; just open a notebook and start writing.

2. Start finding stories that happened to you in the past, and after you finish each story, start thinking what things, people, memories and experiences you would not have now, if that one thing never occurred. As soon as you find a positive connection with each past memory, circle it and write: 'I CONNECTED THE DOTS BACKWARDS FINALLY!'

3. Make a commitment with yourself to be present in the NOW, I know it is not as easy as sounds, but it only requires for you to be committed to doing it TODAY, just NOW. Go and write in your bathroom mirror: 'I am here, RIGHT NOW!' Training our brain to stop wandering to the past or the future, is probably one of the best gifts we can give to ourselves and our families. Remember, we have the most control over our present.

Joanna Mercado Peters, Founder & CEO of Namasarte LLC
www.joannamercado.com

ANNIE LEBRUN

"If you have been waiting for a sign, this is it!"

My intention for us is to break the silence about menopause. To share how it is a normal transition in life rather than a verdict; a liberation rather than a burden. I want my story to help end the isolation and social taboo women feel, and instead promote the body's connection, understanding and acceptance for everyone.

TICK TOCK MY BIOLOGICAL CLOCK

It was 8:15 am... My hand froze in place, holding my mobile phone five centimetres away from my ear. My jaw dropped open. My eyes dazed, as my mind felt confused and my eyelids rapidly blinked. This phone call was a life moment that stopped all of my thoughts and responses. I was speechless!

When I rung up the phone all I could hear was the clock on the wall going tick tock, tick tock just like Gwen Stefani's song, What You Waiting For? Or was that just the sound that started ringing loudly in my head?

Over the last eight years, I have resigned myself to travelling between two continents; between my homeland, Canada and my new home in Germany. I was visiting and caring for my mom and step-dad while maintaining my relationship with my husband. Yes, I was utterly exhausted, riding an emotional roller-coaster destined to crash!

As an only child, I felt guilty for living so far away. My mom, now 73, has survived breast cancer and surgery on both knees while caring for her husband who was suffering from dementia. Feeling responsible for my parents' health and compelled to make myself available during bouts of ill health, a ritual developed: I'd quit my job in Germany, find one in Montreal. Quitting! Finding! Quitting! Finding! My husband was our financial pillar, and being with each of them kept me going back and forth from one continent to another.

Fearing the worst for my parent's health, I followed my heart; I wanted to be near, to see, feel and touch my Canadian family. Sleepless nights haunted my psyche. Awake and powerless to be in two places at once, I wondered, how could I go on? Or if I could somehow remove the Atlantic Ocean which kept us all apart? Precious time was leaking out of my own reserves...

Marcus, my husband, had two children. I did dream that we would live in my homeland together one day. But I had no wish to separate a father from his two teenagers. I knew what it was like to be raised by a lonely, single parent. I would not pressure him or ask him to leave everything behind, but that didn't stop me from hoping he might.

After nearly ten years of travelling back and forth, my wish of living in Canada was further postponed. Tick. Tock. Tick. Tock. My cherished younger Canadian cousins, whom I considered as my nieces, were now taller than me. Grown-up girls with a light trace of childhood left on their cheeks. Everything reminded me that I was missing out. Tick! Tock! The Atlantic felt so immense.

In 2007, I met this wonderful loving being, Marcus, in the Dominican Republic. We had two precious days. It was love-at-first-sight. After a one-year long-distance relationship, I made the jump. The synchronicity, the clarity, I just knew, my life was linked to his. My heart and soul confirmed to pack my bags and accomplish my destiny, my mission. It spoke so profoundly within me, I knew I couldn't ignore it. I didn't know what to fully expect. Yet, at 34 years old, I followed my intuition, this exquisite burning feeling to answer yes to life; to have complete F-A-I-T-H.

Visiting Europe was still on my bucket list. I joined Marcus, in his hometown in Germany.

Initially, my first plan was to stay in Germany for a year and then, return to Montreal, Canada, the land of my birth with my future husband. That's what I told my mom. My first plan didn't happen, and life turned into Plan B. Then it became Plan C, D, E, ... Z. all the way to Plan 'Mission Impossible'.

But when? Feeling powerless, I just couldn't find a suitable answer and life had always a better one than mine. When the bills are paid, when I've saved enough, when I have enough holidays, once I find a better job. It felt like a Slinky was escaping out of my hands, distracting me continuously from the NOW.

Life had played its cards, and I thought I had a winning hand. Yes, good cards with good intentions, but they could not beat a full house. All my life's chips were bet. I felt my life wasn't in my hands.

Without control over time and things, it seemed I had to bear down and wait powerlessly until everything settled and I could progressively achieve, and attain my goals. They seemed to be bumped further away, like dominoes... into the future... out of reach.

My personality type likes to be organized and to know what's coming next. Paradoxically, it wasn't like that; the last ten years have been just pure reaction instead of action. It felt like I was wearing one hat after the other one. Sometimes many hats at the same time, besides my own.

Adapting, finding solutions, trying to fit in the German-box, absorbing new culture and language, becoming a stepmom, a full-time step-parent, having financial issues and parents with health issues. Tick. Tock. Parents and family members were leaving for heaven. TIME reminded, carving its ticks on my forehead.

It seemed my NOW was consuming itself by extinguishing one burning fire after the other. An adrenaline cocktail was keeping me in an Amygdala state; just living with anxiety and fearing the future, waking me up each night at 2 am. What do I do when mama... what do I do if mama dies before step-daddy?

As 2017 started, the worries were pulling me out of my sleep. What about my retirement financial security? How long do I have to work physically like this? Will my hands last as long as I work as a bodyworker? Can I handle another 25 years? Should I find an extra income? How will my head stay above water? When? If? How?

Tick. Tock! Even though I was following my heart, I felt more and more empty, exhausted and more than slightly disillusioned. 3:00 am: The hamster in my mind was still running in its wheel. Every night – stress! I hated it.

It was 8:16, Monday morning, still waiting on the phone, for the results of my blood samples. I was expecting an anaemia diagnosis. My Doctor, Mrs. Guttmann announced banally - Das ist es!

That's it? I am in Menopause !?! At 43 ?!?

Speechless! Only screams and cries could translate the rage bulking inside of my throat and how shocked and confused I felt. Words would have been meaningless.

Life put a label on my forehead saying, out of order???!!! That's it? I

280/ wait

will never be a mommy!!! Tick! Tock! The clock finally struck its gong.

I barricaded myself in, constructing a cocoon on my sofa with all the blankets. I needed to swallow this pill. I could only do it with a load of Schnapps! Zum Wohl! ('To your health!')

Over the next few months, in my self-made carapace, I searched for the meaning of life. What was I still good for?

On the internet I found:

Menopause noun   men·o·pause | \ 'me-nə-,póz Definition: 1: The final cessation of the monthly courses of women. From medical Latin menopausis, from Greek men "month" + pausis "a cessation, a pause," from pauein "to cause to cease,".   2: Cessation of menstruation from other than natural causes

Still a rebellious teenager in my heart, I wanted to answer back to life with my middle finger!!!

I started listening to this longing call, the one waking me up night after night. I wanted my voice back. Over the years, the frustration of losing my identity plagued me. Who was I? What would, or who would be my baby now?

How was I going to embrace this? What would be MY baby-steps?

For many women, their inner clock ticks for children. Like them, I felt the urgency of conceiving and giving birth to something meaningful and giving back to life, to the world. So what now? - Asked my insomniac calls every night. I didn't know the answer.

What I read in many books and internet forums: If you don't know the HOW, start by taking action! - About embracing my identity and fulfilling all my longing dreams!?!

Ok! Here's one: I wanted to touch the world! Utopia! I was naturally born optimistic.

I listened further until another response emerged and it was brilliant:
ME- NO-PAUSE

I simply permuted the syllables. Enthusiastic, I loved the idea! I would be busy creating, learning and conceiving ME. No more pressing 'pause' on ME!

After consulting and working with coaches, I realized what was waking me up at night. It wasn't Freddy Nightmare, nor my panicking hamster. I grasped the bouncing pictures and took a closer look at them. I had the power to change their shapes. Each time I would be awakened and feel an emotional charge, I mentally pictured a stuffed animal. A pink elephant I named Elfi to be more precise.

Elfi was there to be cuddled. Thanks to him, I embraced my fears, shames and doubts with love. Instead of trying to push back those emotional states, I'd hug them and be grateful for them. Elfi would highlight what should be my priorities rather than being a victimized, sleep-deprived woman. Elfi, accompanied with hot flashes, was a part of me tracking down and acknowledging my insecurities, fears and dissatisfactions.

Wow, isn't it great that my own body was showing me the inner reflection of 'my-self'? Elfi was my positive trigger. He helped me to identify emotions and reflected my wishes by lifting up my cloudy glasses. As he was dancing in the dark, tapping my shoulder, he reminded me, everything is a matter of life's perspective. Affectionately, Elfi sang Bruce Springsteen's lyrics from Dancing in the Dark - You can't start a fire without a spark.

My body wasn't shaking me nor torturing me. My body was kindly asking me to look more toward the woman within, reminding me to find my balance, my homeostasis. I just had to listen more carefully. Feeling anxiety meant I was disconnected from myself, from my body and my purpose.

Inside my internal cocoon, I started to move, to press and tear open the envelope. My wings needed more space, and it was time to come out. As I searched the way out, I scratched with my fingers, my nails. I knew there was a world outside of this. Despite my fears, my desire to meet this new world was stronger. The space I was in didn't match my identity anymore.

The Now rushed me to conceive, after 24 months of pre-post menopause, newly defined as Me-No-More-Pause, I gave birth! To MY-SELF! A new Me. Spreading MY wings. Wings ready to fly over any ocean.

In this past year, I launched my first online business. I wanted to help people to get physically unstuck and reconnect with themselves as I did. I couldn't find a better way than movements. Mindful ones. A commitment of the cultivation of self-awareness and compassion. A synergy between mind, body, and spirit.

As I emerged from this chrysalis stage - Me-No-Pause, the new me, ticked ready for a new experience - embracing my whole being. Inexperienced, I dove into the business world, discovering all my possibilities and abilities. Embracing the ones I haven't met and never imagined or dreamed of. It didn't matter if I would fail or win because I was creating a new path, mine. Me and freedom.

The biggest challenge has been to open my mouth. I tried doing everything by myself. It was very overwhelming, and I barely went anywhere. But then, my desire to take a chance on life again was stronger. I put my fears aside as I asked for help.

Accepting to move by baby-steps may test my patience and my courage. I watch my clients struggle with their physical restrictions every day. I know awareness is the key way to change postural habits and bodily movement patterns. I just needed to apply this philosophy to my own business.

We may think we learned to walk and stand tall as toddlers. Life shows us though, at any age, physically, mentally, and emotionally we continuously have to relearn to walk and stand for better health and to become bolder and taller at any age. Tick! Tock! Each second is delicious and tick your present.

IGNITE ACTION STEPS

Lesson 1 - A new beginning! Your body is so intelligent and tells you to go back to you. If you need a nap, take it. Go back to your cocoon. There are billions and billions of cells evolving together, and their union is YOU. Each cell communicates its truth every second. Listen to them they know your truth. To re-establish the communication just MOVE. Walk. Dance. Stretch. Roll your feet with tennis balls or other body parts. It helps you to reconnect with your body and activate your felt sensors. Your focus will automatically switch toward the inside.

Lesson 2 - Timing, not a pause! This cessation shows how we women need to take back our lives. After so many years of giving and caring, our embodied symptoms demand gentleness and care. It might be time to switch our focus towards us. Write down your wishes and dreams daily. Keep your list on your night table and read it before going to sleep.

Lesson 3 - Listen to your body and your heart ♥. What brings you a spark of Joy? Take the time to listen to your body. Focus on what's positive. As we explore different life experiences, we often know what we don't want instead of what we want. Let your inner voice and desires beam to the outside, (and those hot flashes can fade away in the heat of our new desires.)

Waking up at night might not be menopausal hot-flashes. Your body is gently asking you to fulfill what you are burning for. Days and nights, remember you're HOT, Babe! Charisma and positive vibes combined are the sexiest outfits. They suit you perfectly. Beam them.

Lesson 4 - The outburst of emotions. Oxytocin, the love or cuddle hormone, reduces aggressivity and adjusts our level of stress. As it decreases during menopause, we feel less empathy, interfering with control of our feelings. Massage relieves stress; book an appointment. Let your fears fuel you to go cuddle your partner, children, family members and/or your pets. Hospital nurseries often need volunteer cuddlers for babies. Visit seniors' care facilities as there is always someone in need of a visit and smiling face.

Acknowledging your emotions in the moment, this allows you to release unsolved stories. When I wake up in the middle of the night, feeling anxious and watching my little hamster running, I am kind to myself. When the body biologically recognizes an emotion, it wants to release it. We build more stress when we try to repress.

Good stress has a positive impact on you; it makes your heart pump faster, irrigating all your tissues and organs, especially your brain. Embrace the Now because it suits you. There is beauty at every age.

Lesson 5 - It's not the end. You cannot stop the years but you can choose how you age. It's just a matter of consistent work on us. Ageing is just a matter of perspective. Leave the limited social beliefs behind when they do not serve you. Brain fog might be an excellent tool to reconnect yourself and stop the multi-tasking. You can create your own reality with what is most important. Clarify your values, your goals and what you still want out of life. Still confused or don't know where to start? Open your mouth. Talk, share how you feel. If you need, ask for help to find out what is still in your bucket list. Life coaching or any personal development courses could be beneficial. Most important: communication instead of isolation. Because, tick, tock, it is never too late!

Annie Lebrun, Founder at Body-Matrix Specialist.
www.bodymatrixspecialist.com

RUSTI L LEHAY

"It's up to me to believe in me.
I'm the only one with the power of me."

In my hope to solidly occupy the present, stop the regrets, and accept the flow there is in these moments, I also trust my story to shine a light for others. If you have yet to step into your own wisdom and power and just be the light you were meant to be... the time is now.

IT'S TIME TO BE ME!

In a small-minded farming town in middle Alberta, Canada, 44 years ago, the vice-principal and principal called me into the library for a meeting. I had my science courses picked out and submitted. I planned my subjects needed to be accepted by Palmer College in Iowa, United States, to become a chiropractor. I don't know if they met all the students to discuss our "career" tracks. Science was going to be my ticket out of Warburg, where the population sign of 450 hadn't been painted or changed all during my school years. It remained that same dingy sign during the 25 years after, whenever I drove through to visit my mother.

I pulled out the tall stool and sat down, oblivious to their somber looks. "We've looked at your course choices. They aren't suitable for you. We strongly suggest you take the secretarial classes." Derailed before I even climbed on my freedom train.

If they said anything else, I don't remember. I do know I read between the lines: I was too dumb to graduate if I took chemistry, math and biology combined. So, another three years in that town, in that school; but now, without a dream to help make the bullying and ostracism bearable.

I took the science courses, anyway. Mr. K taught chemistry and didn't even try to help. I think it especially irked him that I could add numbers in my head quicker than he could enter them in his calculator. They didn't have today's fancy-schmancy scientific, handheld, soft-touch devices in 1975. I passed Chemistry 10 with only 14 percent above failing, Chemistry 20 with just an 'extra' 8 percent; and I flunked Chemistry 30 in grade 12. Accordingly, I applied for correspondence. The only problem was I needed two signatures, my mother's and one of theirs. Finding a tutor would be necessary. They refused, insisting it would be wasting my time and my mother's money. More programming of the "You're too dumb" variety. How would I graduate now?

After going to the same school for 11-1/2 years, I pleaded, begged, and whined for my mother to let me, her youngest, go to another small town that had a quarter of my town's population in Grade 12, alone. I could live with my sister. She had already mothered me once, being almost 10 when I was born. I was more her baby than our mother's.

At that high school, Mrs. Marshall helped me raise my failing marks up to 67%. I did it. Graduated high school out of sheer stubbornness and didn't go to Palmer College anyway. No career for me. Mr. K's message was running the operating system of my brain at some fight or flight sub-level. I can't count the amount of times I ran from opportunities of success. Whenever I made a decision about something, I rarely proceeded without calling friends who had expertise. I lived in perpetual self-doubt, always looking outside myself for the authority. Sadly, I didn't learn to trust my own inner knowledge until I was past 50. I now insist on making decisions without phoning one friend.

What to do with a high school diploma? I wasn't good at much. I knew I wasn't university material, so I chose a community college. I distinctly remember my only criteria in choosing a course direction was how could I help people worse off than me. I earned a Rehabilitation Practitioner diploma, to work with the physically and/or mentally challenged. Instead of seeing myself as smarter, or even smart enough, I was helping those who were worse off. It was a saintly way of living out the "too dumb" recording in my brain.

After graduating, I did nothing traditional. No 9 to 5 for me! I did part-time shift work in an orphanage and waitressed. The tips told me I was good, so I always waitressed. I became a foster parent (to help), and when my son was born, I needed work where I could take him with me. Not really wanting work, I dropped resumes off everywhere, just to prove to his father and an employment counsellor I was trying. No way I was putting my son in daycare. The only way I could ensure his safety from the harms of my childhood was to be his only caregiver; and never, ever close my eyes or turn my back on his world.

I hustled into a laundromat/dry cleaner a few blocks from home and politely asked if I could leave my resume. Poised to walk away, a tall, elegant woman nodded yes. Handing one to her, I'd already headed for the door when she stopped me and asked, "Can you sew?"

Flipping my right palm up and down in the "so-so" motion, pun intended, she asked, "Do you want to work for me?"

"Can I bring my son to work with me?"

"Yes. Do you have a car?"

"Yes." So began a seven year "career" as seamstress. I seam-ripped broken jean zippers and installed functional ones as good as new. I learned how to repair by dismantling stitch-by-stitch and then reassembling. People paid ridiculous amounts of money to patch their favorite sweaters, replace coat and sleeping bag zippers, repair purses and even old blankets. Maybe I can make a living from sewing. My sister drew a needle and thread for my business card, making the thread swirl into the final 's' on Rusti's Repairs and Alterations. I sewed see-through pockets to hold the cards and posted them on local bulletin boards. I started that business with an old manual treadle sewing machine that only sewed straight forward, nothing fancy. By the time I gathered contracts for three dance companies, picked up piece work from three other dry cleaners, and sewed custom dresses for larger women, I needed to leave my son's father.

First priority was to find my own place to live. My Rehabilitation Diploma came in handy as I landed a non-traditional job that luckily came with a residence. I had my own apartment in a daily-living training facility, in addition to a wage for being home every night 9 PM to 8 AM to be on site for the tenants who required night time supervision. Day staff trained basic life skills. Every night I had to listen to a baby monitor for one of the occupants who sometimes took off outside our apartment. With his pyjamas flapping he'd stop traffic, shaking his fist at any midnight cars, yelling "Aunt Harold, you eat shit out of a can! Uncle Madge, you're uglier than a cat's ass!"

His rantings and the image of him shaking his fist at cars has never left my brain, though his name is long gone. Regardless of the craziness, the salary and 'free rent' allowed me to pursue what was most important – revisiting education. That position lasted 4-1/2 years, one of my longest gigs, likely because it was sweet being paid for mostly sleeping.

I returned to college as a mature student. My good friend from college, Theresa, would whisper in my left ear, "You are smart," then cup her hand over it and reach around and whisper in my right ear, "You are smart." She quickly put her hand over that ear, looked me in the eyes, gently shook my head and asked if I heard her; hoping the trapped message might stick this time. I was 30 and going to a college offering university courses! I fretted, "What if I can't manage?" I waitressed the supper hour, again for employers who let my son hang out in the staff kitchen. Then, I would go home, tuck my son in, do homework, wake up to send him to school, and off to my own classes. I loved all my classes, even biology. Philosophy was a bit of a brain twist, but the dreamy professor was hot. I enjoyed history, but the creative writing classes lit my pen on fire blazing across my journal pages.

Then I had the worst waitressing night of my life. The bar was hopping. I slipped on grease beside the kitchen trash barrel, up to my armpit, the inside tender flesh crashing down on the rim as I fell on my knees beside it. I spilled three plates of food and spilled beer all down my chest into my waitress belt. Patrons paid with a $100 dollar bill, leaving a great tip. I gave it away as change to a patron paying with a $20 in a dark corner of the lounge. They left without finishing their drinks. I understood later, when counting the beer-soaked money in my belt I found only small bills. Not a shining career waitress shift.

The next day I was wailing, nose sputtering, gasping for air with heaving breath. Incoherently talking through sobs to Marlene Brouwer, the college counsellor, I asked "Now what … am I going … to do? I'm stupid! …At least I could wait tables for a living. I've met career waitresses. They're so competent, they never spill beer, go home sticky or smelling like a brewery. They don't lose their tips or fall into garbage cans. I'm… not… good… at… anything! What…do… I…do… now?"

When I finally ran out of words and was breathing somewhat steadily again, Marlene asked what my grades were like. I shrugged, not sure what her point was. She asked if I had any 4s, which were just above failing on their 9-point grading system. I vehemently shook my head, feeling insulted. Any 5s? Again, a head shake. My breathing slowed as she asked, "Any 6s?" "Only one, but I'm not really enamored with the prof," I replied. As she progresses up the scale, I whisper: "A few 7s." My brain catches up. I nod slowly in awe. I am earning 8s in some classes. There is a thought creeping into my consciousness. Her final question, wordless, waits for me. "I do have 9s! You mean I am smart?" She didn't say a thing, just sat back and made me do the work installing this new idea: I. Might. Actually. Be. Smart.

My mind was racing now. What would happen if I did the work, really did it, like in advance? Not just opening the books the night before and plunking random bits from various resources to dump into one essay draft, forcing transitions to work. What if I actually read the course material, instead of skimming the bolded parts just before an exam? What if I completed all the reading and studied ahead of time?

With that new knowledge in my mind, I held study groups, watching my brainy classmates grasp the material and then help the rest of us. I made the Dean's List. I transferred to an actual university. I did a year's exchange at New Mexico State University, the best year ever, where I began a double major in Women's Studies and English, earning a spot on the Dean's List again. I returned for my final year, graduating with distinction on the Dean's List in my own home city.

You might think I was ready for success then, right? I betrayed myself again by taking whatever crossed my path, working for a dysfunctional organization with youth at risk. The property had six group homes. I railed against their rules, arguing for better ways to teach them things like portion control. They saw me as troublemaker for saying they were setting the kids up for eating disorders.

When that job forced me out, I sat down to take stock. What was I going to do with my one glorious life? I had no idea. I came upon another intersection, but instead of turning down my path, I turned away from me one more time, squandering my talents in temp work. Saved, my first creative writing professor urged me to join the Stroll of Poets. Once a year, immersed in a sphere of words and writers, I held my breath between the annual festivals. The Universe felt my joy with words and/or maybe grew tired of waiting for me to wake up, and I landed that first freelance writing article in my lap. Random bits of the word-business followed, sneaking in the edges of my life. Then I was asked to teach a writing course. I loved it and they loved me, though I felt like an imposter at first.

For 33 years I let my grade nine teachers infect my operating system. I rebelled against outside authority yet sought outside approval. I was stuck in the "I'll show you!" attitude, with too little time asking myself what I really wanted to do, or who I really was.

I have since realized my rebellion towards those teachers equipped me with an "I can do this" attitude, although I spent too many years viewing their words from a place of victimhood. I used to think it was a sign of my entrepreneurial spirit to never have had a traditional J.O.B. (Just Over Broke). It's not that. I see I've let their pronouncement go deeper than the initial trauma I conquered with Marlene Brouwer. I'm responsible for not examining the hidden beliefs I took in: "I'm not good enough for a career. I'm not worth a vocation with meaning." I know now, with my adult mind, we all have power and are free to choose to make other people's lives better one kind act at a time. I didn't need to be a chiropractor to be a good or skilled person.

The big message? I waited far too long to take charge and update my operating system. Nobody can tell me what I am and what I am not, but me. I spent years telling myself I am less than what I am, based on one incident of my youth. I realize the roots of my one driving force, and now veer towards people who strive to better themselves. If my Rehabilitation Diploma taught me any one fact I still carry, it is this: Whether you are labelled trainable to Mensa-level smart, there are always ways to evolve, grow, and become a better human. Some of us need a bit more help learning how to drive a stick shift, navigate buses, or learn how to breathe gratitude in and out.

It was challenging to release my inward-directed anger. I wasted years believing their small-minded thinking when my brain is relatively the same size. My 'justifiable anger' detoured me, further squandering my passion for words. I've written since I was 13, filling shelves with journals. I delayed until my 50s to really know soul-deep I AM a born wordsmith-doula and midwife-of-writing, both for my own and others. I've been teaching for almost 10 years now, loved by my students and the writers I coach. Deciding to love myself and believe in my talents puts me out there for those with trapped, stuttering, or escaping words and stories to find me. I occasionally need to remind myself that regretting the years gone by or cringing from the aged face in the mirror is also misplaced energy. It's a daily choice to grasp the chances, the moments right now, in front of me.

The world needs each "me" and "you" to step up, be vital, own our passions, and ignite our dreams, becoming the best 'me' we each can be. It is our time to be fully ourselves. Sometimes I renew my commitment to myself hourly, less and less I wait for outside approval. It's a good day when I just know my talents and gifts are mine to share. I am the only me to offer to the world. Join me on the journey.

IGNITE ACTION STEPS

*Make a choice, a commitment to continue evolving, ever striving to become the best version of you. Remember to strike your own balance on that fine line to never settle for less. Strive for more. Really embrace this present moment, from breath to breath. You are enough right now, in this moment. Remember: Intellect is not an exam score. It is about who we choose to be and how we live out our choices.

*About breath: If you catch yourself holding your breath when stressed or too much is on your plate, create a habit or cue that reminds you. Deep breathing is not autonomic. We need to learn how to do it for ourselves. Try a breathing app on your phone. Mine makes a specific sound with a cheery little message, 'This is your breathe reminder.' I now have taught myself to take at least one full deep breath 90 percent of the time my phone trills, beeps, or rings. I'm especially obedient to the breathing reminders.

*Like me, you have likely heard many gurus say that the first hour of the day is the power hour. For over a year, I've resisted taking my phone to bed. Try a different kind of alarm clock or set it out on a shelf somewhere outside your room. When I first restarted this habit, successfully ignoring my phone, my morning writing was like wading through chest high water; nothing really there but resistance. Six days in, I found my rhythm again. What do you wish for your power hour? Write, stretch, take a walk, make a scrumptious breakfast, write an old-fashioned letter on paper to connect with someone dear. Claim your power hour for three weeks and evaluate how you feel.

*I use fun dry-erase colors, writing different statements in the square shower tiles. I've never thought the shower was a place to linger after soaping and rinsing your bits. Now I stand still, make myself breathe in and out, reciting my statements: "I am enough. I am gratitude. I am peace. I am a freedom magnet. I am love. Money is an energy flowing out and in." Most importantly, "I'm the only one to be me."

There is no one else on the planet better suited to be you. Journal about who you are or who you want to be. Remember, it's never too late to be who you are meant to be. I'm living proof of that.

Rusti L Lehay, Empathic Word Doula / Inspirational Speaker. Word Quest.
www.rustilehay.ca

Books and Resources Meaningful to the Ignite Your Life for Women Authors

Alex Jarvis: Man's Search for Meaning by Victor Frankl.
Andrea Reindl: How Women Rise: Break the 12 Habits Holding You Back by Marshall Goldsmith.
Angela Legh: Reality Unveiled: The Hidden Keys of Existence That Will Transform Your... Mind to Matter: The Astonishing Science of How Your Brain Creates Material Reality by Zia Masri.
Astuti Martosudirdjo: The Biology of Belief: Unleashing the Power of Consciousness, Matter & Miracles by Bruce Lipton.
Cynthia Morgan: Communion with God by Neale Donald Walsch.
Joanna Mercado Peters: Radical Forgiveness by Colin Tipping.
Katarina Amadora: The Four Agreements by Don Miguel Ruiz.
Marnie Tarzia: Science of Well Being and Flourishing referred to as Positive Psychology by Dr. Martin Sielgman.
Suzanne Hall: www.robertholden.com/quiz/self-acceptance-test/
Trish Mrakawa: Code of the Extraordinary Mind by Vishen Lakhiani
Virginia L Lehay: White Bears and Other Unwanted Thoughts: Suppression, Obsession, and the Psychology of Mental Control by Daniel M Wegner, Genogram in Family Assessment by Monica McGoldrick & Randy Gerson.
Vivien Hunt by Autobiography in Five Short Chapters www.doorway-to-self-esteem.com/autobiography-in-five-short-chapters.html

If you ever feel the desire to share your story.. .please reach out to us. We'd love to hear your IGNITE transformation. We would be happy to help you unveil your story and IGNITE others around the world! www.igniteyou.life/apply or support@igniteyou.life

Upcoming Books in THE IGNITE SERIES

please apply at www.igniteyou.life/apply